The* SPOKEN WORD ReVOLUTioN Redux

edited by **mark eleveld**

* sourcebooks mediaFusion

An Imprint of Sourcebooks Inc.®
Naperville, Illinois

HELEN M. PLUM MEMORIAL LIBRARY
LOMBARD, ILLINOIS

811.08
SPO

Published by Sourcebooks MediaFusion, an imprint of Sourcebooks, Inc.
P.O. Box 4410, Naperville, Illinois 60567-4410
(630) 961-3900
Fax: (630) 961-2168
www.sourcebooks.com

Library of Congress Cataloging-in-Publication Data

The spoken word revolution redux / [edited by] Mark Eleveld.
295 p. cm. : ill   246 : Redux
   Includes bibliographical references and index.
   ISBN-13: 978-1-4022-0869-0
   ISBN-10: 1-4022-0869-3
   1. American poetry—21st century. 2. Performance poetry. 3. Hip-hop—Poetry. 4. Oral interpretation of poetry. 1. Eleveld, Mark.

PS617.S67 2007
811'.608—dc22

2007004306

Printed and bound in the United States of America.
LB 10 9 8 7 6 5 4 3 2 1

To Michelle Mega,

"You are beautiful and it is the least interesting thing about you."

To Finnegan and Ava,

"We must not cease from exploration and at the end of all our exploring will be to arrive where we began and to know the place for the first time." T. S. Eliot

Table of Contents

Prologue: My journey

My name is Mark Eleveld. I am a high school English teacher, and I am the editor of the *The Spoken Word Revolution*. I backed my way into doing that first book. I was a call-in radio guest, asking questions of a publisher and also a soon-to-be Illinois Poet Laureate. My two aces: I had been reading poetry for a long time, and I am a good friend of poet Marc Smith. In 1991, I took Marc's class at Lewis University. I was interested and edgy enough to find myself at shows and dinners and parties filled with poets. Poets who I did not know but would soon read and see perform. Poets who mentioned other poets who I would then read and see perform. A bohemia always at arms length but one which bled over into my daily life—now of wife, kids and classes. (I've had two children since the first book.) The original did well enough that I was allowed to do another: here it is, *The Spoken Word Revolution Redux*, again with a CD.

When I began this second book my goal was to make the most eclectic poetry book ever made. I wanted to put poets who would never be in the same room together under the same cover and on the same CD. I will let others decide if that mission has been fulfilled. I can tell you that it has been a seemingly endless ride of interconnections. I would look for one poet and turn up ten others by mistake. And in this book I wasn't limited to poets. This book also includes songwriters, actors, performers, and others. It was built from letters at the dinner table, poets on the couches, my kids next to me thumbing through books. Students listening to cuts. Friends shaking their heads. Editors pulling out their hair.

In this book I want to invite the reader into the world of the spoken word as Marc Smith and all the cast of characters invited me. Join the *The Spoken Word Revolution Redux* and become part of the slam family, or the poetic community, or the hip-hop poetic or the new bohemia. Call it what you will. But let me help you out. And let narrators Marc Smith and Kevin Coval help you enjoy the enclosed audio CD.

So let's get started, and since I bleed Chi-town, Green Mill poetic blood, let's go there first, with Marc Smith's poem "Nobody's Here."

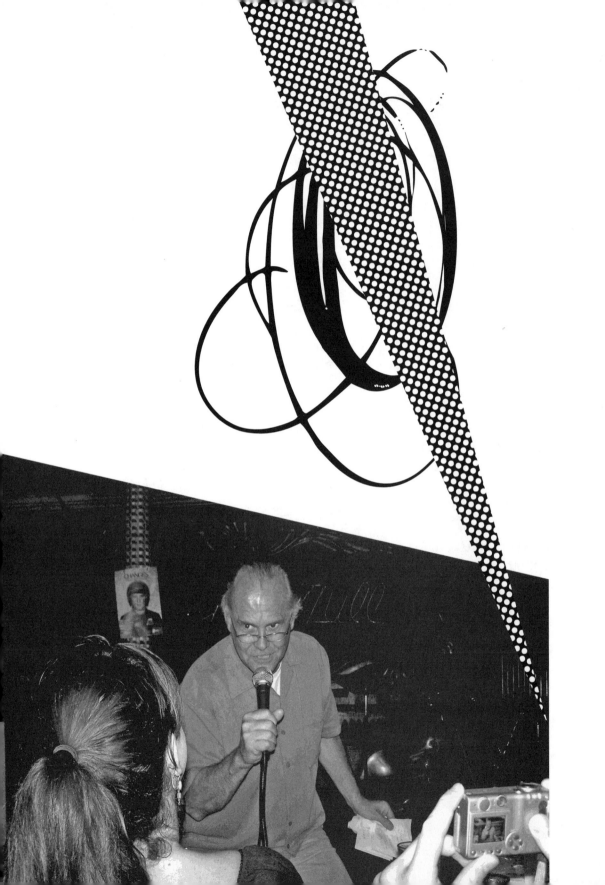

* Nobody's Here

Marc Smith

Poetry Slam Founder, 1986,
first National Poetry Slam Team Champion 1990

TRACK 1
Portions featured
in Montage

Nobody's here.
All the could be's in another place.
All the pulsing neon
Bleeding on the city's shoulders
Pointing glass tube fingers somewhere,
But not here.

Hit the jukebox Donnie! Put some dollars in its
    throat.
Hang our hooked hopes up
For one more smoky hour
Of "I want you" conversation,
Dreams runnin' down the *Old Style* bottles
Like tears down somebody's cheek.

Quarters in the jukebox Donnie!
Tell all the passed over dreamers who wanna
    know
That somewhere, some starlight Daddy
Hops atop the telephone lines
Above this gray and obscure city
Poppin' his fingers
And makin' a moon.

Makin' a comet's tail
Spin out of a stone axe grinding
Off a wheel, shootin' sparks
Into the dead black sky

Ridin' a train of lights
On rails that scream
Midnight ... two ... and four a.m.

Tellin' us all to go back,
Go back to somewhere
Even if we don't know
Where that is.

Hit the jukebox Donnie!
Let all the songs play out.
Ring the last call bell Tommy!
Turn the lights up.
Shake the loveless hearts alive again Lois.
Send them off home
To sleep another night, alone.

'Cause nobody's here. Nobody's here.
Nothing here.

Poetry as a Basic Human Need

*

Ted Kooser

U.S. Poet Laureate 2004-2006,
Pulitzer Prize in Poetry, 2005

… huge numbers of people, are following poetry today, poems of every kind, because of the energy overflowing from performance poetry, and that's a good thing for all of us …

During my two terms as U.S. Poet Laureate, I must have been asked a hundred times what I thought of spoken word poetry, how I really felt about rap, slam, cowboy poetry, and hip-hop, which for my purposes here I'll lump together under "performance poetry." "Is it *really* poetry?" someone would ask from the back of the auditorium, someone who, I sensed, was hoping that I would answer, with the authority of my elevated post, that, no, it was *not* poetry, definitely NOT!

Within a few weeks of my appointment, I learned that the people who asked that question really did want a no. They were uncomfortable with performance poetry in its many forms, were on the defensive because the poetry they'd studied in school was different. After all, the poetry of their schoolrooms were words on a page; it wasn't very, well … entertaining. It was a job. On my travels around the country, no one who advocated for performance poetry ever raised that question, possibly because many of those who enjoy and participate in spoken word poetry don't worry about that.

Of course, it's also quite possible that nobody in any of my audiences follows performance poetry. After all, why come hear some geezer in a gravy-spotted necktie and eyeglasses stand at a podium and drool over his book in an unenthusiastic monotone, when in a noisy tavern just down the street there is an open mike and a lot of performers drawing a crowd? With beer and pickled sausages, too!

If you squint when you look at our world, you'll see that every one of the thousands of occupations we are engaged in is an extension (or braiding together) of original occupations: food, clothing, shelter, sex, and spirituality. Some of today's occupations may seem quite far removed from basic human requirements, but if you look deeply within them you'll see their roots in the original set of occupations. The door-to-door Avon saleswoman is not too far removed from a fellow who ventured into the woods to pry up the rocks. The auto mechanic, too, has a part in hunting and gathering … every job addresses, in some way, a set of human needs.

We may be at our happiest when we're employed in one of the original occupations. That may be why someone who shuffles contracts in a law office and lives in a high-rise apartment complex has a small rooftop garden. That may be why some men like to relax by knitting, why some woman love to cook. And, of course, like our ancestors, we do love stories and storytellers. We sit in front of the flickering fires of television sets in the darkening night and let stories absorb us. We tell jokes, swap anecdotes, make up lies about our adventures, and sing in the shower.

The luckiest among us are those people who make their living cooking or digging in the ground or tending children or telling stories. They are those whose work most directly addresses basic human needs. Among us, of course, are the occupations closely related to the work of the artist-priest—the novelists, painters, composers, and poets whose work is just a step removed from the tasks of the original storyteller. That one step, it seems, is the abstraction of written language. Together, type and paper are, of course, an abstraction of the spoken word, and they stand one step removed from the direct telling of an experience. The original artist-priest sang her stories and poems; today's traditional writer sits at his computer and taps out what might otherwise be sung.

Who among us could be happier than the person standing before a group of people eager to listen? That's the foundation of performance poetry; that pleasure in speaking to and entertaining one's close community. "Is it art?" asks the voice from the back of the auditorium. "Not much of it is," comes my answer, "but some small part of it may be."

Performance poetry is less revolutionary than–dare I say it?–reactionary. It is a reaction to old geezers like me, dowdy at their podiums, believing that they are a part of Literature with a capital L, a part of something that will endure for hundreds of years. Often boring the hell out of their audiences, too, reading poems that only a select few appreciate. Performance poetry is a turning away from the dull, a turning back toward the excitement our ancestors felt as they sat close to the fire and listened to their shaman tell stories.

But lots of people find it troubling, this performance poetry thing. Why? Well, because they had to put in so much time in school learning what poetry was. They are fully invested in the idea that poetry is a peculiar rectangle of words arranged on a page that poses a kind of riddle that one must solve, or die. They think that only teachers know the secrets of poetry, and that the rest of us have to be tutored. Many of us who had that awful public-school experience of poetry are now invested in those teachers' ideas of what poetry is and was. We are unsettled by any kind of poetry that we can understand without a teacher's assistance, and especially disturbed by a poetry that is genuinely entertaining. After all, who ever told us in middle school that poetry could be fun? Heaven forbid! Poetry was like plane geometry or chemistry. You studied it because you had to pass the course.

Performance poetry can be a good thing. It can serve our centuries-old need for song and story. It can "delight and instruct" us, using the Romantics' terms. I am all for it. I am for many and all kinds of poetry. What it may not be able to do, and I say this stuffily from my podium, is endure, in the way that some poetry set in type has endured for centuries. Performance poetry can be ephemeral—like the mayfly, which lives and dies in one day and whose taxonomic name is, in fact, *ephemerida*. Our experience of performance poetry is mostly of the moment. The poet is present to perform his or her poem, and the performance aspect is essential. The performance poem depends to a great part on the quality of the performance. It lives and dies in a day.

Thus the writing (the words and their arrangement) still has to be good, friends, really good, excellent, if it's to endure, because endurance requires that a poem, or a story, or any work of art, holds up when the artist is no longer with us. We "literary" poets, some of whom look down upon performance poetry, need to keep that in mind, too. If a poem depends too much on the skill with which the author delivers it, well, how will it hold up in a hundred years? Will it still have the ability to touch us, to persuade us? As Jerry Lee Lewis says, "Who's gonna play this old piano after the Killer's gone?"

But we all know, don't we, that for anything to last it has to be well made. That goes for refrigerators and it goes for poetry. And perhaps it's not important that a poem employed in a performance have any life after the poet is gone. Perhaps performance poetry should be looked at less as "Literature" and more like dance. If, and only if, it's important to somebody, a audio recording can make a performance endure, at least a little while. And, of course, some poetry used in performance is good enough to endure once the performer has gone on to the great slam in the sky.

What is really important about what in this book is called a "revolution" is the terrific energy and momentum this movement has engendered over the past few years. The American colonials had that kind of energy and enthusiasm for their revolution in 1776. Half a country on board. It's fun, you know, and nothing's really wrong with that. More people, huge numbers of people, are following poetry today, poems of every kind, because of the energy overflowing from performance poetry, and that's a good thing for all of us, however you shake it. The really good writing will endure, I believe with all my heart, and the rest of it will be gone with the wind.

slammers and laureates

part 1

Selecting A Reader

Ted Kooser

U.S. Poet Laureate 2004-2006, Pulitzer Prize in Poetry, 2005

TRACK 3

First, I would have her be beautiful,
and walking carefully up on my poetry
at the loneliest moment of an afternoon,
her hair still damp at the neck
from washing it. She should be wearing
a raincoat, an old one, dirty
from not having money enough for the cleaners.
She will take out her glasses, and there
in the bookstore, she will thumb
over my poems, then put the book back
up on its shelf. She will say to herself,
"For that kind of money, I can get
my raincoat cleaned." And she will.

*

galumpf deez nuts . . . .
galumpf deez shoulders, spines, eyes and collarbones of mine

Anis Mojgani

National Poetry Slam Individual Champion, 2005 & 2006

in my underwear i write poetry

two headed poetry

three legged poetry

poetry with ten spigots and no training wheels

there are gold flames airbrushed on my bot-
tom and i have bare feet

i have BEAR feet

hhAAHGGGGHHH   FEET

i walk with big sticks in my ear

speak up

i am filling twigs with sentences and filing my
nails with memories

my love shaves diamonds

scientists speculate over it

i come from the moon

neil and buzz and the third guy walked on my
tummy

i giggled

and a spoonful of cherub tasted like cherries
and wallabies

i write two headed poetry

i write two underweared poems

i take off both underwears

my poems dance around the candelabra naked
in the livingroom

i write wrists and rubberbands on the backs of
bathtubs

press my lips to the shower's belly button

and breathe

the goat man is in the woods dancing!

the golden nugget!

the chupacabra

the book man!

there is a cloud splintering like a kneecap

buy me pants

buy me pants mother

buy me a hat

there are moths in my shoulders

i am shaking

i am full of love

i was full of love

i carved out pear shaped slices of it

and fed a million tired ankles

God sat on my shoulder like a cricket

i swatted a bee like a father's advice

and asked for it again

tell me where i can go when every bridge has
wheels running alongside its bottom

but i write poems with no training wheels

i write my skull

like it was a color i was picking up and exam-
ining inside my hands for the first time

at the corner of central park east and 63rd
street

i clutch a football like a small child

stand two inches in front of a yellow wall and
    scream:
"GO DEEP!"
fling the pigskin at the bricks and as my child-
    hood bounces back at me
try to snatch it back up
GO DEEE E E P .
    !!
    !!!!!

I AM THE 3 HEADED GALUMPF!
A BLUE GIRAFFE!

A water fountain on the Mooon!!

Catch me carbon!
Catch me galumpf!
Catch me galumpf catcher, catch me
Lord
hold me
like a bowl
like how the clouds
hold the moon
holding the rooftops of this city
holding me and mine and mine memories:

in my veins

there is a lonely mermaid murmuring all
day
long

she sing ee sings singzzs such
beauuuti-ful songs

her throat

is a girl i once knew
her nose
is made of silver
her backbone is a plum

her backbone a plum

*

Anne Frank Huis

Andrew Motion

UK Poet Laureate, 1999-Present

Even now, after twice her lifetime of grief
And anger in the very place, whoever comes
To climb these narrow stairs, discovers how
The bookcase slides aside, then walks through
Shadow into sunlit rooms, can never help

But break her secrecy again. Just listening
Is a kind of guilt: the Westerkirk repeats
Itself outside, as if all time worked round
Towards her fear, and made each stroke
Die down on guarded streets. Imagine it –

Three years of whispering and loneliness
And plotting, day by day, the Allied line
In Europe with a yellow chalk. What hope
She had for ordinary love and interest
Survives her here, displayed above the bed

As pictures of her family; some actors;
Fashions chosen by Patricia Elizabeth.
And those who stoop to see them find
Not only patience missing its reward,
But one enduring wish for chance

Like my own: to leave as simply
As I do, and walk at ease
Up dusty tree-lined avenues, or watch
A silent barge come clear of bridges
Settling their reflections in the blue canal.

*

*the Raised Voice of Poetry

James Fenton

Professor of Poetry at Oxford University

Poetry begins in those situations when the voice has to be raised: the hawker has to make himself heard above the market hubbub, the knife grinder has to call the cook out into the street, the storyteller has to address a whole village, the bard must command the admiration of the court. And even today, in the prolonged aftermath of modernism, in places where "open form" or free verse is the orthodoxy, you will find a memory of that raising of the voice in the phrase "heightened speech." Poetry is language to which a special emphasis has been given, whether by paring it down and arranging it pleasingly on the page, in lines whose length may be baffling to all but the poet, or by the traditional means, which include raising the voice in order to be heard above the crowd; raising the voice in order to demonstrate its beauty and power; chanting the words; reciting the words rhythmically; punctuating the units of speech (what will become the lines of the poem) with rhymes; setting the words to tunes; setting the words to tunes and singing them in unison, as in a drinking song.

Some decades ago, it was considered bad form, in the world of poetry readings, to do anything that smacked of performance. That poets had once performed their works, chanting them in a manner that approached the bardic, was very much held against them. It was showing off. It was inauthentic. It went out with Yeats and Dylan Thomas.

One night I found myself reading at a technical college, next door to a rugby club dinner. There was nothing for it but to raise the voice, to raise it as loud as I dared. Competing with a drinking song, I turned what I had imagined to be a meditative poem into a full-volume declaration of identity: this is who I am, I seemed to be saying; here I stand, I can be no other! Somewhat—but only somewhat—to my horror, the poem appeared to go down very well. I was no stranger to showing off, but I would never normally have shown off in that particular way. One read, or one recited, in the way W. H. Auden recited his poems: the proper style was self-deflation.

Since then, I have visited countries in which very few of our assumptions about poetry are shared. I remember a Cambodian picking up my copy of Larkin's anthology of English poetry and chanting a few pages to himself, uncomprehendingly—because there was to him no other way of rendering a line of verse than by chanting out loud. In Borneo, I was lucky enough to hear a contest of improvised song, which went on through the night. In the Philippines, I knew an illiterate man who had the gift for extempore verse in the traditional Tagalog form, and I paid attention to the way he raised his voice to an appropriate pitch for eloquence.

Some of my educated Filipino friends were aspiring poets, but their aspirations were all directed towards the United States. They had no desire to learn from the bardic tradition that continued in the barrios. Their ideal would have been to write something that would get them invited to Iowa, where they would study creative writing. My friends thought of themselves as nationalists, but they did not seem to connect their nationalism with their native poetic traditions. Of course they knew about these traditions, but they probably felt that they could not compete on that ground. Whereas my uneducated—indeed, illiterate—friend, to whom the word Iowa meant nothing, had a living part in his own tradition because it was oral, not literary.

Around the same time, I came into close contact with some aspiring American poets—not far from Iowa—and noted in them a familiar negative attitude toward poetic tradition. They felt, in some degree, antipathetic to any poetry not contemporary, and they seemed to recognize contemporary poetry only through a set of negative definitions: it did not rhyme; it did not use meter; it was not interested in form other than what was called "open form," which was understood to be, when it came down to it, no form at all. "Heightened speech" was the mantra these poets used, when cornered, to distinguish poetry from prose, but their heightening could not include specifically poetic words, or archaisms, or the special tricks of grammar poets have used in the past.

Most striking to me was the fact that these American poets had a range of tastes in music, and therefore in lyrics, that bore no relation at all to their taste in poetry. It was as if a separate part of their brain dealt with these matters; and, what is more, in that separate part of the brain things were really much clearer than in the poetic part. In the musical part of their brains they knew very well what they liked and wanted to hear, and wanted to imitate if they, for instance, were to pick up a guitar and play a tune, or even compose a song. Whereas in the poetic part, their judgments were defensive and somewhat nervous. There was clarity on one side, confusion on the other.

It occurred to me that these poets would be happier if they broke down the barriers in their own brains, if they accepted that the person who was studying creative writing with the aim of producing poetry was the same person who had a car full of country and western tapes, or whatever music delighted them. The person who tolerated bad lines in a song lyric was the same person who would tolerate no rhymes at all in a poem. The taste that delighted in the rhythms of rap belonged to the same owner as the taste that had banished meter from poetry.

There was another notable thing about these aspiring poets when seen in action in front of an audience. It was quite clear that they would have liked to perform for the pleasure of the audience, but were hampered by the fact that what they were reading out had been written for the page. They knew this, with one part of the brain, for they asserted, under pressure of questioning, that modern poetry, properly understood, was written for the eye rather than the ear. Whatever "heightening" it involved, or whatever they did to increase its specific gravity, aural considerations did not enter. But when they stood up in front of an audience, often they would seek to provide some kind of extra interest by making up for what was lacking in the text. And, often, one hears successful and respected poets doing the same! They read to the audience in a manner that is designed to convey what the poem looks like on the page, since, truth to tell, the poem was written to look well, not to sound well.

But these poets also would be happier, it occurred to me, if they—without going so far as to change their basic poetic practice—did themselves a favor and wrote something, a single poem even, that they could perform. So that, after the agony of standing in front of an audience reading words that were specifically designed not to be read out loud, they could, before leaving the podium, cheer everyone up with something worth hearing. Now you might ask how it came about that these poets ever even considered mounting the podium, since the precepts of their art militated against it. The answer is that they had probably never really thought through the consequences of their poetic practice, which, as I said, was to proceed by a series of negative definitions: no rhyme, no meter, *et cetera*. Sometimes, however, I think that poets make no connection between what they do when writing and what happens at a reading.

This may seem implausible, but I shall never forget a confrontation between an African and an American poet at an international poetry festival. The African poet had brought along musical instruments. He sang and accompanied himself, extemporizing on themes that he, in between times, would explain to the audience. The American was one of those poets who "wrote for the page," and over dinner one night he decided to tell the African poet how inconsiderate his performance had been. You don't realize, he said, how difficult you make it for the person who reads after you, when you sing songs and play instruments. The accusation was that the African poet got the audience into a mood that prejudiced them against the type of poetry the American had to offer—which, he implied, was *mainstream* poetry (at least as far as the festival was concerned).

The African replied in terms that surprised me at first. You American poets, he said, and you European poets, you think that because you are poets you are very important, whereas I am an African, and I don't think I am important at all. When I go into a village and begin to tell a story, the first thing the audience will do is interrupt me. They will ask questions about the story I am telling, and if I do not work hard, they will take over the story and tell it among themselves. I have to work to get the story back from them.

What had struck me as overweening in the American poet—his view that, because his poetry had only limited appeal, other poets should rein in their own performances so as not to show him up—was, to the African, only part of the story. We all assumed that, because we were poets, the audience would listen to us in appreciative silence. A hush would fall when we approached the rostrum, and when we sat down there would be applause. But to the African these seemed arrogant assumptions. To him, every scrap of attention and appreciation had to be worked for.

In the long run, however polite the audiences have been to our faces, the African poet is right: every scrap of attention and appreciation has to be fought for. A text may be written for the page, or the written words may be no more than a notation for a performance, but even the most docile of audiences will feel, in the end, that we have overdrawn on its goodwill if we do not ensure we deserve the attention we demand. What the African poet knew within seconds of standing up, we will assuredly learn in due course.

We will learn whether we deserve to be heard.

* THICK

Sonya Renee

National Poetry Slam Individual Champion, 2004

TRACK 7
(excerpt)

I continue to be amazed
How my curvy hips and heavy breasts manage
    to make men
See nothing less than sex
In their interaction with me
Whether summer dress cute or business suit
Their eyes be watching God in my thighs
Despite my intellectual bearings
Men be only hearing moans and sighs
In our conversations about secret societies
    and presidential lies
But I know why

It's cause I'm THICK
Like molasses
Pouring slow out of that bottle
Onto your mind, saturating you with poetic
    time
And with every word I coat your brain
Yet you're still only able to watch the way
I pour from that bottle

I am THICK
Like your Aunt Sarah's pound cake
Sweet, sweet, lip smacking sweet
Filled with sooo many enticing ingredients that
You never bother to ask about
Given that you only want to eat
SLOW DOWN BABY
Check the recipe

You might be allergic to the eggs, vanilla, flour
Charisma, abstract eccentricity, power
And I don't want you to get sick

Cause I am THICK
Like eight year old black girl hair be
You want to put lye to me
Put dye to me
Slap on a just for me
Unwillingly I yell
"Stop trying to change my natural state!"
I am so THICK
In jeans it's like I was born the color of denim
But if you stared as intently at my thoughts
As you do at my thighs
Maybe one day you might
Be able to get in them
But I doubt it

You fail to realize that
I'm not just hourglass THICK
Lots of class THICK
Not to be sarcastic but I died
Was resurrected last week
So as a poet, I am past sick
And you need to know this

The *American College Dictionary* states that
    THICK means
"Numerous, abundant, plentiful"

Having a lot of whatever's around
It also states that THICK means dense, deep,
 profound
And in an average interaction
It is certain that I am bound to be described as
 THICK
While that description might fit like these
 jeans on my behind
It is well beyond time you realize THICK also
 describes my mind

See these hips you watch are curvy wide as
 God knew
I would need to birth enigmatic knowledge like
How she can be both Father and Son at the
 same time
Seated at his own right hand side
These heavy breasts would someday feed
 worlds wisdom
Hold secrets they confide nestled at my chest
The softness of my thighs flesh would
Give my wounded warrior
A quiet knights rest
So my God made them THICK
He laced my words with wind so each utterance
Might sail swiftly into spirits and manifest
 through pens
My sins will be a road map to the promised land
So it is essential insight that you comprehend
That while your thinking may be thin

I am THICK
Like reading the Bible from beginning to end
Like the thirty poems I'll write that may never
 score tens
Like the wilderness that landscapes the roads
 where I've been
Like that burning Phoenix
I will rise again
Cause I am THICK
So whether you watch the way
I sway or I pray
Or lay these words that I spit
Recognize the Divine has blessed you
To receive a slice of it
Cut THICK
As an extra added gift
A glass of cute to wash it all down with
So the next time
You find it hard to draw the line
Between my mind and my behind
Recollect these words and realize
My Creator made me multiply defined
As ....THICK!!!!

*

Brightly Colored Boats Upturned on the Banks of the Charles

Billy Collins

U.S. Poet Laureate, 2001-2003

TRACK 10

What is there to say about them
that has not been said in the title?
I saw them near dawn from a glassy room
on the other side of that river,
which flowed from some hidden spring
to the sea; but that is getting away from
the brightly colored boats upturned
on the banks of the Charles,
the sleek racing sculls of a college crew team.

They were beautiful in the clear early light—
red, yellow, blue and green—
is all I wanted to say about them,
although for the rest of the day
I pictured a lighter version of myself
calling time through a little megaphone,
first to the months of the year,
then to the twelve apostles, all grimacing
as they leaned and pulled on the long wooden oars.

*

Labeling Keys

Taylor Mali

TRACK 9

Four-time National Poetry Slam Team Champion, 1996, 1997, 2000, 2002

the spoken word revolution redux * 13

Though not a secretive man,
my father understood combination locks and
   keys.
He was a Yale man, had a love affair with brass
and a key rack as organized as the writing
on the label of each key was neat.

It's the same angel that made him label and date
Butcher-paper-wrapped leftovers in the
   refrigerator
with Christmas-present creases and hospital
   corners
and a 2 by 2 inch yellow post-it note listing
   contents, date,
and possible suggestions for future use:
"Turkey scraps. Eleven-twenty-three.
Perhaps a yummy treat for the D-O-G?"
secured with (count 'em) two rubber bands,
one for snugness, the other for
symmetry.

But there's an art to labeling keys;
the one you keep to your neighbor's house
   across the street
cannot say on it:
NEIGHBOR'S HOUSE: ACROSS THE STREET
(IN MAINE FOR ALL OF MAY).
So SILVER CABINET, GUN RACK,
SPARE SET OF KEYS TO SAAB IN GARAGE –
these are labels you will not see at our house.

Instead, my father wrote in his own argot,
in a cryptographic language of oblique reference;
the key to the burglar alarm was THE SIREN"S
   SONG
the gun rack, THE INFERNAL RACKET,
the neighbor's house across the street was now
the FARM IN KANSAS.
VICTOR was the Volvo, HENRY, the Honda,
   GABRIELLA,
the Saabatini.
A security of the mind, no doubt,
and not so much precluding burglary
as offering a challenge to the industrious burglar.
as well as evincing from my brother and me
much in the way of loving parody,
such as the key to the side door,
which we labeled, *NOT* THE KEY TO THE SIDE
   DOOR.
DESTITUTE NEIGHBOR'S SQUALID HOVEL
   FAR, FAR AWAY.
BOATHOUSE IN DJIBOUTI.

Among the neatly labeled keys
(some to cars we no longer have, like
   POTEMKIN and GERALD, the Ford)
is a brass ring of assorted expatriates
called KEYS TO SHANGRI-LA.
Little metal orphans, they have all lost their
   locks; or rather,
their locks have all lost them,

misplaced them all in the same place,
on the same ring, which is a sadness no bolt cutter can cure.

Even the key that says simply HARTFORD –
somewhere there's a door, a box,
a closet full of secrets locked –
and the only thing I know about it is
that it is probably *not* in Hartford. .
I keep them all, jingling and jangling,
turning the tumblers of the past.
Who knows when I might not be in Hartford again
and have a need for such a key?
Who here knows nothing of magic that escapes
every time a key that should unlock a door
does?

*

Open Letter to Neil Armstrong

Mike McGee

National Poetry Slam Individual Champion, 2003

10...9...8...7...6...

Dear Neil Armstrong,

I write this to you as she sleeps down the hall
I need answers that I think only you might
    have

When you were a boy and space was simple
    science fiction
When flying was merely a daydream between
    periods of history and physics
When gifts of moon dust to the one you loved
    could only be wrapped in your imagination
Before the world knew your name
Before it was a destination, what was the
    moon like from your backyard?
Your arm; strong, warm and wrapped under
    her hair
Both of you gazing up from the back porch,
    summers before your distant journey

But upon landing, when the Earth rose over
    the Sea of Tranquility, did you look for her?
What was it like to see our planet and know
    that everything you could be, all you could
    ever love
And long for was just floating before you?

Did you write her name in the dirt, when the
    cameras weren't looking
Surrounding both of your initials with a heart for
    alien life to study a million years from now
What is it like to love something so distant?
What words did you use to bring the moon
    back to her, and what did you promise in
    the moon's
Ear about the girl back home?
Can you teach me to fall from the sky?

I ask you all of this not because I doubt your
    feet/feat
I just want to know what it's like to go somewhere
    no man had ever been
Just to find that she wasn't there
To realize your moonwalk could never compare
    to the steps that lead to her
I now know the flight home means more

Every July I think of you
I imagine the summer of '69
How lonely she must've felt while you were
    gone
You never went back to the moon and
I believe that's because it doesn't take rockets
    to get you where you belong
I see that in this woman down the hall and
    sometimes she seems so much further

But I'm ready for the steps I must take to get
    to her

I've seen many skies and the moon always
    looks the same
So I gotta say, the rock you landed on has got
    nothing
On the rock she's landed on
You walked around, took samples and left
She's built a fire, cleaned up the place, and I
    hope she decides to stay
On this one, we can breathe

Mr. Armstrong, I don't have much
Many times have I been upside-downtrodden
But with these empty hands comes a heart
    that is full more often than the moon
She's becoming my world, pulling me into
    orbit and
I know I may never find life outside of hers

I wanna give her everything I don't have yet
So, for her, I would go to the moon and back
But not *without* her
We'd claim the moon for each other with flags
    made from sheets down the hall
And I'd risk it all to kiss her under the light of
    Earth

The brightness of home
But I can do all of that and more
Right here, wherever she is
And when we gaze up, with my arm around her
I will not promise her gifts of moon dust or
    flights of fancy
Instead, I will gladly give her all the Earth she
    wants
In return for all the Earth she is
The sound of her heartbeat and laughter
And all the time it takes to learn to fall from
    the sky
Down the hall and
Right into love
I'd do it everyday
If I could just to land next to her

5...4...3...2...

ONE small step for a man
But she's one giant leap for my kind

*

*Tract

Kevin Stein

Illinois Poet Laureate, 2003-Present

This poem's subject is the cantaloupe tilting
its burnished head in the garden's black dirt.
Its sensuous tumescence. Its musky scent.
This poem does not give a gnat's whit about
tomatoes the learned once called "love apples."
This poem's subject is the ripening cantaloupe.
This poem does not rely on catalog, nor does
it switch topics unrelentingly. This poem
esteems the cantaloupe, from Italian *Cantalupo*,
papal village near Rome where the good pontiff
prayed hard for the seed to take hold. This poem
eyes the cantaloupe's spritz of dew first glisten
then vanish, its veined skin blush as sun comes on.
This poem has no particular interest in the watermelon
whose belly plunks *not yet* beneath a hand's tap.
This poem's subject is the ripening cantaloupe,
its fringed leaf and tendril corkscrewed around
the sweet pepper stalk as if around a little finger.
This poem bears no ill toward Cortland apples
hard as cats' hearts, nor the pears just assuming
their young breast shape, but this poem's subject
is the cantaloupe ripening in black dirt – a moment
so near its stem has begun to unbutton. This poem
won't employ simile to imply the process is like
a woman's ripening, when mind rushes its juices
through her body's flushed fruit. This poem
is not meditative. Reader, do not ponder what
it means to ripen, wane, and die. This poem's
subject is the cantaloupe ripening in black dirt.

*

the spoken word revolution redux *

Mayda Del Valle

National Poetry Slam Individual Champion, 2001

i remember
someone once said
to me,
"Ugh
Puerto Ricans and Dominicans sound
sooo uneducated when they speak Spanish
cutting off all those letters
it's so lazy
at least even the poorest most uneducated
    Mexican
can speak to you in 'proper' Spanish."

and i had nothing to reply
anger ate the words out my mouth
and i swallowed back the acidic comeback
    which consisted of something like:
"Pue vete p'al carajo cabron!"
but
ur
verses i subvert
my comebacks come quicker now
mouth opens wide with retorts
in defense of the inflections in my accent
in defense of the articulations of my cultural
    enunciations
in other words
i'm defending sounding like a dam Puerto
    Rican

and i got words
doing Mary Lou Retton flips off my tongue

slurring syllables
warring accents
authenticity goes to shit
Spanglish slips off my lips
and i'm speaking in tongues

ain't gonna get grammatics correct
i'm overcome by urban street tinged tongue
    tactics
this   city slicker demeanor ain't acted
    out
i'm taking out
all traces of proper English
this   vocal pattern is just now bein' enacted
independent of margins that hold my syllables
in check
i'm declaring a state of language revolution

all the words in our vocabulary have declared
    a universal strike
saying that we've been practicing unfair talk-
    ing laws and not paying them for their
hard labor
threatening to leave our civilization speechless

all accent marks are attending an emphasis
    convention at Webster's place the vowels
    are demanding to be worth at least $2000
    on the *Wheel of Fortune*
Shakespeare's sonnets are making record
    deals with Puffy to be sung in rap form

dictionaries are on Prozac suffering from an
    acute identity crisis
saying "We can no longer provide all the
    meanings for words in your lives –
we now want to tell stories."
and
thesaurus's are translating into
ebon-glish-espan-chino-con-zulu-jammin'-
    german-parlez-yo-frances-con-portuges-
    con-patois-mon-creole-combining-creating
sounds that is music to my ears
y pue' pentejo a mi no me importa si tu cree
    que mi espanol is not as good as yours!

i'm crossing borders
abriendo puertas
tongue waggin'
clickin' off the roof of my mouth
rolling ere's
comiendo ese's
yo tengo el toque de tito's
timbalero
kimbara kimbara kimba kim bam bam
kimbara kimbara kimba kim bam bam
writhing on my lips
i'm riding waves of
language deconstruction

wear ur hardhats
little chicken heads
coz the alphabet is falling from the sky!!!

i'm daring to deliver dialects not commercially
    created
and destroy ur nit-wit imbecilic notions of
    what language i should speak

ain't gonna get grammatics correct
i never suffer
from a lack of lovely
luscious
lingual
lullaby-like
syllables flowing off these lips

don't give a dam if it's grammatically correct
don't give a shit if you think it's incorrect
i never lack the abilit-i to come correct

so get hip to this style papiiiii...

'cause i dare you to write a 15 page analytical
    essay due by Tuesday at four in my mailbox
on any subject of ur choosing that moves the
    crowd like
WOA

and read it on a mic

and read it in ur uptight
educated sounding proper tongue

'cause
i'll still be here
with these tongue tactics
never getting gramatics correct
and still making these folks go

like WOA.

*

Old Man Leaves Party

Mark Strand

U.S. Poet Laureate, 1990-91, Pulitzer Prize in Poetry, 1999

It was clear when I left the party
That though I was over eighty I still had
A beautiful body. The moon shown down as it will
On moments of deep introspection. The wind held its breath.
And look, somebody left a mirror leaning against a tree.
Making sure that I was alone, I took off my shirt.
The flowers of bear grass nodded their moon washed heads.
I took off my pants and the magpies circled the red woods.
Down in the valley the creaking river was flowing once more.
How strange that I should stand in the wilds alone with my body.
I know what you are thinking. I was like you once. But now
With so much before me, so many emerald trees, and
Weed whitened fields, mountains and lakes, how could I not
Be only myself, this dream of flesh, from moment to moment?

*

The Great Poet Returns

Mark Strand

When the light poured down through a hole in the clouds,
We knew the great poet was going to show. And he did.
A limousine with all white tires and stained-glass windows
Dropped him off. And then, with a clear and soundless fluency,
He strode into the hall. There was a hush. His wings were big.
The cut of his suit, the width of his tie, were out of date.
When he spoke, the air seemed whitened by imagined cries.
The worm of desire bore into the heart of everyone there.
There were tears in their eyes. The great one was better than ever.
"No need to rush," he said at the close of the read, "the end
Of the world is only the end of the world as you know it."
How like him, everyone thought. Then he was gone,
And the world was a blank. It was cold and the air was still.
Tell me, you people out there, what is poetry anyway?
    Can anyone die without even a little?

*

Mandate

Roger Bonair-Agard

National Poetry Slam Individual Champion, 1999

(After Patrick Rosal)

To laugh at weaker boys (or at least the less sharp-tongued)
to kick ball till the moon rose
or something vital bled – we lived
To wait like predator
for the first note of a slow jam
to grind ourselves into the wall
with a pretty girl between us
and make sure our boys were watching
We were tropical suave post-colonial oil money niggahs
and we had to do well – in all things
in Latin
in the First Queen's Royal College Scout band
in talking shit
and especially in football
so we practiced memorizing where
our defenders were
so we could look the other way
as we went past them
cuz it was only cool
if you made it seem effortless
we were sophisticates like that
looking for immortality in the tales of others
and most of our friends were still alive
To buy two sno-cones from George
    whose rickety cart parked outside
     the school each day
To have the cones stacked with extra syrup and condensed milk
To gather around the cart

because George always had sensible shit to say
To follow that with the hottest spiciest
    doubles from the doubles-man behind the cafeteria
    who built two multi-level homes
    off the profits from our purchases
To laugh at that irony
To pick on the faggot boys
  because we wanted our fathers to think we were men
To join the new dance-craze revolution
To stop traffic on Frederick Street
    just to see Doc, Scientist and Froggie
    spin on vinyl, pop-lock, head-stand
    electric-boogie, dead-man
To sit on the steps
  of the downtown shopping plaza
  and stare at the beauty of our women
To believe at sixteen
    that they were *our* women
To welcome satellite TV and music videos
    like it was God
    because who can see the future anyway
    it was 1984
and we were busy looking good
mimicking everything we saw
to go watch Gip play better than the rest of us
to see him collect the ball on the outside
of his left foot count the on-rushing defender's footsteps
and slide the ball deftly through his legs
while looking the other way
  effortless like that
Our bodies hadn't begun to betray us yet
Kirk and Gregory and Rudy and Peter were still alive
Dave still had his legs
and the worst thing wasn't not doing well
only seeming   like you were trying too hard

*

the Revolution will be *

Guy Le Charles Gonzalez

(Originally published in POETRY IN AMERICA, Poets & Writers Magazine, Special Issue, April 1999)

> *the Academics have much to*
> *fear*
> *and they will not die*
> *without a dirty fight.*
> —Charles Bukowski

Faced with the surging popularity of spoken-word and the poetry slam, the Academy of American Poets, long known for its gala reading series, was forced in 1995 to reevaluate its approach to their mission of creating a wider audience for contemporary poetry. "[We] certainly could no longer claim to be an innovator in this regard," says William Wadsworth, executive director of the Academy. "Looking at how much emphasis was being put on the performance aspect of poetry, I came to feel that it was the Academy's proper role, as an institution, to do whatever it could to reinforce the book of poems."

After a year of planning, the Academy launched National Poetry Month in April of 1996. The event rolled into bookstores, all aglow with its mission to "foster an appreciation" for poetry among the masses. During its fourth year, buoyed by a media blitz, National Poetry Month claims over ninety sponsoring organizations and promotional tie-ins that include everything from the distribution of 40,000 books of poetry by Volkswagen to this special issue of *Poets & Writers Magazine*.

A noble mission, no doubt, but there are many that look on with a smirk and wonder, What took them so long to realize the need for something new?

Fifteen years ago at the Get Me High Lounge in Chicago, Marc Smith, construction worker by day, poet by night, decided he'd had enough of the status quo. He'd grown tired of the stale politeness of the academic poetry reading, where the poet was placed on a pedestal and had no obligations to his audience other than to show up and read poems. His solution: Empower the audience—take poetry down from the tower and not only make it available to the so-called masses, but make it answer to them. Thus was born the poetry slam, a grassroots vehicle for fostering an appreciation for poetry year-round. In the years since, despite often harsh criticism from the academic world, poetry slams have sprung up in nearly every major city and several smaller ones, both here and abroad.

This revolution against the establishment is not unique in the history of poetry. "When Ezra Pound and T. S. Eliot came along," says Wadsworth, "there were a lot of poets who thought the world had gone to hell. The values changed. A new generation came along and really changed things. That's always the case. I'm sure there were poets who were upset when people started writing in English instead of in Latin."

Since the advent of slams, the spoken-word movement has offended the sensibilities of the establishment on several fronts, not the least of which has been its insistent democratization of the art form. In the slam, anyone can get on stage to read a poem—and the standards of quality rest entirely on the subjective appreciation of randomly chosen members of the audience, who rate poems, Olympic scoring-style, from 0 to 10. Academia's seal of approval is neither required nor sought.

"Back in Chicago," remembers Patricia Smith, four-time National Poetry Slam Champion, as well as an award-winning journalist, "there were pundits in the academic world that said [slam] would never last and it would be the death of poetry. [It] began to get a lot of attention, audience, and press without being 'sanctioned.' No one was able to 'discover' slam. It birthed itself. It grew despite no grant money, no kissing ass, not worried about being published…"

Charles Bukowski, arguably one of the most influential anti-academic writers of our century and an honorary "slam" poet, wrote in 1990:

to disrupt this sanctuary
is to them like
the Rape of the Holy Mother.
besides that, it would also
cost them
their wives
their automobiles
their girlfriends
their University
jobs.

The irony was that many of these "slam" poets were no different than those that saw them as barbarians at the gate. They, too, were the disenfranchised, seeking an opportunity for their voices to be heard.

Brenda Moossy, an MFA student at the University of Arkansas and a successful slam poet and organizer in the Ozarks, always incorporates her work in slams into her classes. "[It] gives permission for people to think outside the box, allows for creative leaps and jumps…lets them see that everyday language and experience are very valuable and, in fact, at the core of what poetry is about."

"Poetry itself is revolutionary," says Bob Holman, who went from directing the readings at the St. Mark's Poetry Project in the late '70s in Manhattan to creating the slam scene at New York City's Nuyorican Poets Café in the early '90s. Holman says, "To write a poem, even to read a poem, to take on all that language can give you is to become an activist. To get the poem to people in this world, you have to utilize the mechanisms that this world provides. I love teaching poetry and performance. I [get] a lot of theoreticians who want to experience experience."

Of course, none of this is surprising to those who realize that, long before Gutenberg ever gave thought to moveable type, poetry had flourished for centuries as an oral art, and, perhaps most interestingly, as a competitive one.

"In the history of poetry," says Wadsworth, "a lot of classical or ancient traditions included the same principle, competition between poets; it was judged in one way or another but it was very much like a competitive sport. Slam has roots that go all the way back in the oral tradition."

And yet, one of the major criticisms of slam is its competitive aspect. Many in academia decry the thought of poems dueling on stage for the approval of an uncredentialed audience. *SlamNation*, the award-winning documentary of the 1996 National Poetry Slam by ESPN producer Paul Devlin, sparked controversy with its tagline: the "Sport of Spoken Word."

The father of the slam, Marc Smith, views such objections as hypocrisy of the highest order. "Poetry in [academia] is competing all the time," Smith says. "You compete for [the] editor's approval, for admission, and it's a closed competition. [There is] more competition in MFA's, more serious, more cutthroat than there ever could be in the slam world. Most slammers realize [slam is] just a format, a mock-competition, a drama that makes an audience focus its attention."

Walt Whitman once said, "To have great poets, there must be great audiences." And the audience is growing. In 1990, the first National Poetry Slam was held in San Francisco, a one-night event as part of the now-defunct International Poetry Festival. Two teams of poets, from San Francisco and Chicago (with Paul Beatty, an MFA student from Brooklyn College, representing New York), sparred verbally before a crowd of over three hundred people, the festival's biggest turnout. The ninth annual National Poetry Slam in Austin, Texas, featured forty-five teams of four poets each, from the US and Canada, participating in four nights of nonstop poetry, which culminated in a finale witnessed by a standing-room-only audience of over thirteen hundred people.

"Like it or not," says Wadsworth, "this is what's going to bring this art form into the twenty-first century. I think it's the creation of a new genre, the creation of a new music. How it evolves will be very interesting."

Bukowski put it this way:

we have come from the alleys
and the bars and the
jails
we don't care how they
write the poem
but we insist that there are
other voices
other ways of creating
other ways of living the
life
and we intend to be

heard and heard and
heard
in this battle against the
Centuries of the Inbred
Dead
let it be known that
we have arrived and
intend to
stay.

"Every revolution becomes an institution. Though it's being adopted in academia, the main movement is still very radical. It's still fresh and evolving. The mission isn't anywhere near completed," Smith said.

Note: Includes excerpts from Charles Bukowski's "the Rape of the Holy Mother," *Septuagenarian Stew: Stories & Poems* (Black Sparrow Press, 1990).

* Bagram, Afghanistan, 2002

Marvin Bell

Iowa Poet Laureate, 2000-2005

The interrogation celebrated spikes and cuffs,
the inky blue that invades a blackened eye,
the eyeball that bulges like a radish,
that incarnadine only blood can create.
They asked the young taxi driver questions
he could not answer, and they beat his legs
until he could no longer kneel on their command.
They chained him by the wrists to the ceiling.
They may have admired the human form then,
stretched out, for the soldiers were also athletes
trained to shout in unison and be buddies.
By the time his legs had stiffened, a blood clot
was already tracing a vein into his heart.
They said he was dead when they cut him down,
but he was dead the day they arrested him.
Are they feeding the prisoners gravel now?
To make them skillful orators as they confess?
Here stands Demosthenes in the military court,
unable to form the words "my country." What
shall we do, we who are at war but are asked
to pretend we are not? Do we need another
naive apologist to crown us with clichés
that would turn the grass brown above a grave?
They called the carcass Mr. Dilawar. They
believed he was innocent. Their orders were
to step on the necks of the prisoners, to
break their will, to make them say something
in a sleep-deprived delirium of fractures,
rising to the occasion, or, like Mr. Dilawar,
leaving his few possessions and his body.

*

*Oya

Regie O'Hare Gibson

National Poetry Slam Individual Champion, 1998

> *Lighteningweb walking a graveyard*
> *windsepulcher where storms are born.*

She drinks the Eden hour
heavies wind into murder
lightening suckles her ossified bosom.
She signs the sky a ragged syntax.
Incants water song from marrow.
She the storm uncoupling blood
disemboweling us across her scythe
of black salt.

Cats 'round here say she one of the few folks left in the 'hood who came up from the South— say
she from Mississippi, or Georgia, or something like that. Say she used to be a preacher woman— a
real fire and brimstone bride of Jesus— say she had *the touch*. They say, one Sunday night at this
used to be church, she used to pastor at, she was doing some healing, & rebuking & casting out
demons & that's when something got in her. No— No! some *thing* got in to her.

That's when her left eye went blood
& she just walked right out the church
& never came back— never spoke
another word to nobody.
Just about everybody
who remembers that day
is gone now
& the few left won't even tell
nobody her name.
It's like they all made some pact

with each other to not speak
about her, except to warn
the young bloods to stay
as far
from her
as possible.
Well, when she come down the street
mumbling to herself & pushing that
shopping cart with them old bottles,
dolls heads and all them rats all up in it,
every body just get out her way. Me?
I get all the way to the other side of the street.

Cuz' man they say if she even look at you
with that blood eye of hers it means
                                        somethin's coming for you by the end of the week.
        I mean, cats that ain't got no respect for they mama
don't even look cross-eyed in her direction.

                                                        Go ahead,
laugh if you wanna
                                        but all I know is that there was this   one cat,
    T-Bone— this thug brother
from the projects, right?
Tried to show his ass in front of his boys

by runnin' down the street
after she pass by and screamin'
that he don't give no fuck
'bout some old dry bitch
with no teeth, no hair, one eye,
& a shopping cart full of rats
and other peoples shit.
                                                        Well, next day,

    we saw this crippled rat walking

down the street toward the jets, right?
So we followed it to see where
it was goin'.

Man, you know that thing dragged itself
all the way to T-Bone & his mama
and them building, jumped

step by step up 9 floors
walked down they hallway
& died right in front of they crib?

Coincidence?

                                        My ass!

Next day we saw T-bone, & told him
that he need to go & apologize
to that old lady. We told him
how that rat was a bad sign
that she had put somethin' on him.

                    He just laughed & said:
                    "Man, fuck what ya'll talkin'
                    'bout I don't believe in all that
            Ol' spook & demon shit."

                        Well, two days later T-Bone fell out the window of his
        mom's apartment. Man, you know that brother
was laying in that vacant lot behind
the building for 5 hours before Drey found him—

            and when he did his spine broken,
his jaw was shattered to powder

& his bottom lip looked like something
had been nibbling away at it.

    Now, you would of thought that brother
would have died, right? — & if that had
of been an act of god he would have.

                                                                But, uh-uh

.

Now he crippled
from the neck down,
can't talk at all

                                & doctor say he gonna'

 be like that
the rest of his life.

Every now & then you see his mama rolling
him around in that squeaky wheel chair. Him lookin'
like a cadaver on wheels, drooling on himself
& mumblin' 'bout rats, graves, and mercy.

*

* A Winter Journey

David Allan Evans

South Dakota Poet Laureate, 2002-Present

There I was, where I hadn't
planned to be: in new snow
up to my calves, walking north
toward her house. Many times
I veered to the west or the east,
but some internal compass kept
correcting my direction.
It was very cold, yet the sky
was mostly clear, with a few
streaks of clouds. Sparrows were
chittering in the windbreaks.

It wasn't until I got to the cattails
at the edge of the lake that I
could see her house, about a mile
away on the opposite bank.
I hesitated, not being sure
if the ice would hold.
I remembered as a boy sliding on
bare spots of snow-covered lakes,
swept by the broom of the wind,
but this time there was only snow.
I imagined the big Northerns
looming under my boots,
and thought of the one I caught
through the ice a decade ago—
with a hook embedded near its
glassy eye, and about a foot of
snapped line above the leader.

Naturally, the one that got away
and got caught again was
still in my head by the time I
reached out with my mittened
fist to knock on her door and
heard her lovely, perilous voice
saying, *Come on in.*

*

* messiahs

Da Boogie Man

National Poetry Slam Individual Champion, 1997

messiahs are not found in palaces or cathedrals

they're allergic to silk, don't go well with royalty
or dignitaries, avoid the self-righteous
and are not trained in the etiquette of class and economics

they're a repulsive flavor of discomfort
stinging the tongue of mass approval
carrying truth in sacks draped across shoulders

in their pockets, are loneliness and misunderstanding
the spare lack-of-change offered by hypocritical well wishers
who pass comments beneath the table of hearing
about how saviors need to take a behavior bath
trim non-conformity into obedience
then put on clothes more suitable for social acceptance

but saving the world is manual-love labor
requiring getting blood and spirit under fingernails
digging in the brittle field of human cruelty
irrigating it with compassion, hoping to create
fertile ground for love to grow

the promise land comes with a price
with struggle/with dirt grit and sweat
messiahs must come prepared to work
with attitude/fire
messiahs aren't pretty pictures

they are

    reformed crooks   the poor and unlearned
    used to be killers   buckers of authority
    questioners of   religion and tradition
    the stubborn   who accept nothing less
        than the truth

if jesus was here today he would be called baby j
hang out in tenements and frequent corner dice games:
all the time, warning wayward souls about the odds
of spiritually crapping out

he would disrupt church services and political
forums, asking "why wasn't GOD invited"

he would heal people without insurance,
call hospitals hypocrites. feed the poor,
call grocery stores selfish

he would sing gospel but understand the blues

he would be despised and ridiculed
labeled trouble maker and conspiracy theorist,
unattractive and no one would want
to be like him, homeless and depend on you for food
in response to kindness he would heal your
flesh and save your soul

feeding the homeless might save your soul
past allegiances with lies might make
you the best ally of truth. your imperfections
might make you the perfect messiah

you could be the savior

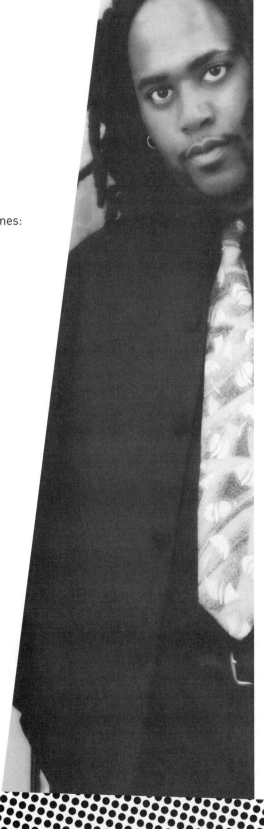

the fate of the world could rest in your hands
no matter how ugly or imperfect you think
            they are

in your hands could be redemption, power, and salvation

nonbelievers will place a crown of thorny doubts around your mind
screaming sarcastic nails into the pulse of your self-confidence to pierce
the side of the voice calling your soul, hoping you will hang, suffer, and
suffocate on their crucifix of ignorance and hate

don't come down /you will live again
don't come down/you will conquer the unconquerable
            don't come down

     stay on that cross
    use it to make yourself perfect
            then
come to your people messiah

    they're waiting on you
            to
    save them

women take the slam

From 1990-1996, all of the National Poetry Slam Individual Champions were women.

When the Burning Begins

Patricia Smith

First ever and four-time National Poetry Slam Individual Champion, 1990, 1991, 1993, 1995

For Otis Douglas Smith, my father

The recipe for hot water cornbread is simple:
Cornmeal, hot water. Mix till sluggish,
then dollop in a sizzling skillet.
When you smell the burning begin, flip it.
When you smell the burning begin again,
dump it onto a plate. You've got to wait
for the burning and get it just right.
Before the bread cools down,
smear it with sweet salted butter
and smash it with your fingers,

crumple it up in a bowl
of collard greens or buttermilk,
forget that I'm telling you it's the first thing
I ever cooked, that my daddy was laughing
and breathing and no bullet in his head
when he taught me.
Mix it till it looks like quicksand, he'd say.
Till it moves like a slow song sounds.
We'd sit there in the kitchen, licking our fingers
and laughing at my mother,
who was probably scrubbing something with bleach,
or watching *Bonanza*,
or thinking how stupid it was to be burning
that nasty old bread in that cast iron skillet.
When I told her that I'd made my first-ever pan
of hot water cornbread, and that my daddy
had branded it glorious, she sniffed and kept
mopping the floor over and over in the same place.
So here's how you do it:
You take out a bowl, like the one
we had with blue flowers and only one crack,
you put the cornmeal in it.
Then you turn on the hot water and you let it run
while you tell the story about the boy
who kissed your cheek after school
or about how you really want to be a reporter
instead of a teacher or nurse like Mama said,
and the water keeps running while Daddy says
You will be a wonderful writer
and you will be famous someday and when
you get famous, if I wrote you a letter and
sent you some money; would you write about me?
and he is laughing and breathing and no bullet
in his head. So you let the water run into this mix
till it moves like mud moves at the bottom of a river,

which is another thing Daddy said, and even though
I'd never even seen a river,
I knew exactly what he meant.
Then you turn the fire way up under the skillet,
and you pour in this mix
that moves like mud moves at the bottom of a river,
like quicksand, like slow song sounds.
That stuff pops something awful when it first hits
that blazing skillet, and sometimes Daddy and I
would dance to those angry pop sounds,
he'd let me rest my feet on top of his
while we waltzed around the kitchen
and my mother huffed and puffed
on the other side of the door. *When you are famous,*
Daddy asks me, will you write about dancing
in the kitchen with your father?
I say everything I write will be about you,
then you will be famous too. And we dip and swirl
and spin, but then he stops.
And sniffs the air.
The thing you have to remember
about hot water cornbread
is to wait for the burning
so you know when to flip it, and then again
so you know when it's crusty and done.
Then eat it the way we did,
with our fingers,
our feet still tingling from dancing.
But remember that sometimes the burning
takes such a long time,
and in that time,
sometimes,
poems are born.

*

* Hell Night

Lisa Buscani

National Poetry Slam Individual Champion, 1992

for Patricia Smith

It is winter in New England:
ice patches roads risky in illicit thought,
old light falls off to strong nostalgia,
Boston freezes in Demeter's Darker hour,
but not where we are.

It is Hell Night at the Ragin' Cajun Cafe,
where each dish
is spiced and peppered to screaming,
earth's burning fried and
sided with searing.
Hot ain't just flavor here,
It is God.

We roll our winter hands like tinder,
anticipating that culinary spark
that lights such exquisite misery:
when our eyes mist like spring windows,
our lips line with succulent scorching, and
our tongues long to loll elsewhere . . .
BRING ON THE PAIN!

As we wait for internal immolation,
 it is announced that any patron
who successfully digests The Flamethrower,
a murderous Habanero casserole
guaranteed to conjure Castaneda visions,
gets a special medal.

Always suckers for wreath and wing,
a little tin victory on the Korean cheap.
We agree and order two portions.

Our first taste is as bland
as Sunday beige
and we curse the chef
and question his lineage.
But the heat tears along our taste buds
to take its throne in our throats
and we stop in mid-conversation
to audition new vowel sounds,
from floor to walls to roof,
an agony as cinematic as *Backdraft*.
By the final forkful,
we are crying like veterans
of a ten-hankie Meryl Streep weeper,
eyes screwed like new cats,
clutching our chests in a Fred Sanford exit.

We beg mercy of the other elements,
douse the hurt with wine and breathing,
and swear on the graves of relatives not yet dead
that we will never do this again.
Holding, cooing,
we wait the pain down to cooling embers.
I pocket my medal and
you order seconds.

I know you are not hungry.
You are far from hungry now,
and hunger was never an excuse
to push you beyond the rules
that protect the rest of us from the exceptional.

I think to switch to crossing guard,
arms splayed stop in a mom's admonishment,
to show you lines you've blurred,
stories needlessly embroidered,
walk you some sensible shoe,
less is more.
Instead I offer the fat of my hands
in a worthless gen X benediction:
whatever, whatever, whatever.

And I see you rising,
beyond goal and challenge and
sad, West Side shadows,
over struggle and breaks and breaking,
to flame.
Flame circling you like a demanding pet,
draping your shoulders like a stole on a show girl,
flame curling thought, and
buckling gift, and
rendering all reward to memory.

I see you in flame.
And I wish you the balm of water.

*

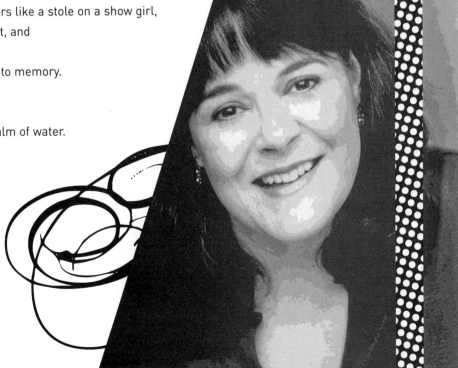

* Funeral Like Nixon's

Gayle Danley

National Poetry Slam Individual Champion, 1994

Brown and shiny casket
Expensive
Draped with the American flag
Poised
Resting in the front yard of my girlhood days
Gleaming brilliantly in the honeysuckle April
    sun

When I die
I want a casket like Richard Nixon's

And when I die
I don't want Ms. Flora from the Wheat Street
Baptist Church Missionary Circle #5
To go stuttering thru my eulogy
Pantyhose
Girdle
Shoes from Payless

Let it be known
Right here and now
I want the Right Reverend Billy Graham
To lie about me

I want him to tell channel 5, 11, CNN and
    World News Tonight
That I, Gayle Danley
Was the world's most honorable Black woman

Billy please don't tell 'em bout the one night
    stand
The shot of bourbon
Tell 'em I was pure
A martyr
A goddess (at the very least)

When I die I want a funeral like Richard Nixon

As a matter of fact
When I die I want my ass enshrined
Right after the 20 gun salute
One (kapow!)
For each one of my sins

Bam bam bam bam bam
For watching Mom and Dad shaking the
    sheets unnoticed
(I want to be inserted into a marble wall
Like a Pope)

Bam bam bam bam bam
For masturbating on the back of the nursery
    school bus
(I want to be on the cover of *Time*)

Bam bam bam bam bam
For that luscious one night stand
(I want mourners there
Oceans of snot drooling from grieving noses)

Bam bam bam bam bam
For playing Doctor with my cousin

I want a funeral like Nixon

No acne no smell
No fuck-ups
Barbara Bush on the front row

No memory
Ass clean
Butt wiped

Let me break this down for you:
You see
I just want to die like a white man

Blameless
Timeless
ageless

*

Read by the Author: Some Notes on Poetry in Performance

Henry Taylor

Pulitzer Prize in Poetry, 1986

I wear neckties, and hear myself called an academic formalist. I taught for thirty-seven years, thirty-two of them at the same university. So it is possibly a little weird that one evening in August of 1996, at an arts and crafts celebration in Brunswick called the Maine Festival, I was on a small, well-lighted stage in a tent, wearing black Teva sandals, a pair of shorts, and a long-sleeved T-shirt with a picture of a rhinoceros head on the front and a rhino footprint on the back, reciting one of the few poems of my own that I know by heart and giving it as much theatrical energy as I could. The shirt's price tag was sticking up from a point at the base of my neck, just under my left ear.

This persona was an uncalculated development. The shirt was a desperate, last-minute purchase made at a nearby festival booth, to which I had rushed as the sun set, the air turned cold, and the Maine Festival Poetry Slam got under way. I didn't know about the price tag—a kind of Minnie Pearl allusion—until the slam was over and I had shaken hands with Russ Sargent, the runner-up, and collected the winner's check for a hundred bucks.

What in the world could have brought an old academic pro to such a pass?

I've been around poetry readings, as presenter and audience member, for almost fifty years. It feels odd to reflect, after such a time, that most such performances are barely tolerable. This realization won't keep me from attending just as many readings as I have in the past; I keep going back, for the traditional reasons. Over these years of vocation, enthusiasm, boredom, and duty, I have earned a few beliefs about poetry readings, which become more deeply confirmed with every new experience. Writing poetry and reading it aloud are separate and distinct skills, and the idea that they ought often to be found in the same person is a slice of the unexamined life, like various superstitions about poetic inspiration. Writing poetry is usually best done in some kind of solitude; even poets who can write in noisy surroundings, drawing energy from the environment, are capable of self-sufficient withdrawal into their own concentration. Performing in front of an audience seems to draw on different kinds of resources.

Many poets, moreover, appear not to have thought much about these matters. By the time they are asked to give readings, they have heard dozens or hundreds—most of which have not struck the audience dumb with awe at the magnitude of the task.

People who attend poetry readings with any regularity do so for reasons other than the purity of oral performance. They hope to add something to their experience of poetry and the poet's work. A moderately effective reading leaves echoes in the inner ear, and future silent encounters with a poet's work revive in the reader's mind the poet's actual voice. Occasionally, a strict critic might deplore a poet's facial mannerisms or body language; yet for the reader of this poet's work, these habits or tics might deepen the experience of personal encounter with the poetry. Or, as often happens, they will constitute a barrier between the audience and the poetry, so that all that remains in memory is a set of mannerisms—no poems, or even many words.

My own thoughts—or feelings, anyway—about these matters began forming many years ago, when I was in grade school and was encouraged to memorize poetry for recitation before my classmates. In the early grades this requirement devolved on me because my teachers admired my father's way of reciting poems. In the seventh grade, I attended a small private school where every day began with an assembly during which two or three students recited poems. As there were just over twenty of us in the school, our turns came up often. I discovered that I had the capacity to memorize longish pieces, and enjoyed showing off with "The Cremation of Sam McGee" or "The Highwayman."

I think it's significant that I had no suspicion in those days that I would ever write poems of my own. As young as I was, and as distracted as I often was by thoughts of public humiliation if I should forget a line or make an inappropriate sound, I was still developing a sense of the performer's responsibility, and that development was not complicated by the feelings that attend authorship of the piece one is performing. Here was an audience, and its expectations of being entertained were fair enough. Here was the text, with qualities that could be heard and qualities that couldn't. I didn't worry about the latter.

In high school, I took up acting, and I continued playing around in theater throughout my student career. At that time and place it was easy to slip into what I now believe to be a misconception of the poetry performer's task. A skilled actor can achieve things with voice and movement that most writers have not practiced. However, an actor also may hone and refine a specific interpretation of a poem until it is no more than a brief script for a very distinctive and specific character's monologue. Such a performance often conceals the very qualities of ambiguity and faint resonance that make a poem what it is.

This duality—the poem as script versus the poem as a versatile and variously layered complex of verbal cues to emotional response—is one of the things that has caused members of English departments to be condescending toward members of speech departments. Oral interpretation is a form of literary interpretation, but for those students of poetry raised and weaned on the New Criticism, oral interpretation has often seemed primitive and oversimplifying.

The point, for most of the audience, is that the performer is also the author, and it is the author they want to discover. So a reading with performance values that are extraordinarily polished can sometimes seem oddly dehumanized, like those W. D. Snodgrass gave for a few years in the seventies when he was all but consumed by an interest in the discipline of oral interpretation. His delivery was superb, his enunciation that of an energetic radio announcer. The poems sounded like news bulletins, and Snodgrass himself seemed to withdraw behind an invisible shield of perfected diction and occasional surges of overacting.

For a long time I have suspected, without being able to demonstrate it, that various poets read as diffidently as they do in deliberate rejection of modes of performance that seem to them too theatrically polished. Another inhibiting force, as James Dickey pointed out in "Barnstorming for Poetry," was the sheer magnificence of Dylan Thomas's performances, which went beyond interpretation to a kind of singing.[1] Those recordings first began to seduce me when I was in high school; in college I worked hard to perfect a mimicry of his style. I did this merely for the sake of entertaining accuracy; I had no ambition to read my own poems aloud as Thomas read his.

Encouraged by my teacher, George Garrett, I went on from Thomas to the much less spectacular readers on the Caedmon Treasury of Modern Poets. Once in a while at parties occasioned by the presence of a visiting writer, George would prompt me to perform a few lines each of Stevens, Eliot, Empson, Cummings, Spender, and so on. Years later, under similar auspices, the novelist Richard Bausch and I discovered that we could stand at opposite ends of a room and deliver a stereo performance of Thomas's "A Refusal to Mourn the Death, by Fire, of a Child in London." Bausch quickly added a wrinkle it was hard to keep up with: he would shift without warning from Thomas's words to those of some rock-and-roll classic, demonstrating by the way that the intonations of "Fern Hill" will do strange and haunting things to the words of "Blueberry Hill."

Practicing these mimicries taught me that some very distinctive, not to say eccentric, reading styles can have a compelling appropriateness to the work being performed. Standing under the front steps of Mr. Jefferson's Rotunda, in a passageway like a tunnel full of echoes, I recited Auden's "In Memory of W. B. Yeats" in the peculiar mixture of sharpness and flatness that characterized Auden's Caedmon performance, and concluded that I would not prefer hearing it any other way.

Meanwhile, living writers continued to appear where I could see and hear them. As an undergraduate I heard Faulkner, Frost, Eberhart, Spender, Day Lewis, and others in Charlottesville, and one day in the fall of 1962, I went to Washington with another teacher, Fred Bornhauser, and heard readings by R. P. Blackmur, Katherine Garrison Chapin, Babette Deutsch, Langston Hughes, Randall Jarrell, Stanley Kunitz, Ogden Nash, Kenneth Rexroth, Richard Wilbur, and Oscar Williams. By this time I was thoroughly hooked; hearing a reading and thinking about how I had liked it became part of who I am.

Whatever the clarity and force of my opinions about a reading, it is difficult to express them unless they are favorable. Poets have a hard enough time reading unfavorable reviews of their writing; hearing oneself described as a bad reader feels like an even more personal attack. Several years ago I was talking with a poet whom I like very much personally, and whose work has always given me pleasure—except when I hear him read it aloud, in a style so laden with mannerisms that it is almost impossible to keep up with the words. "Why do people read so badly?" he asked me. "I mean, you read well and I read well, but most poets don't." It was enough to make me doubt that I read well, but I kept quiet; we are not such close friends that I could beg to differ with him.

Imagine a journal in which readings are unfavorably reviewed. "Elizabeth Bishop reads as if she has just been awakened from a nap." "Sonia Sanchez seems more interested in yips, moans, and whines than in words." "Many people read without moving their lips; Mark Strand can do it out loud."

Cheap shots; but in a friendlier court we might find these more expensive ones: "Elizabeth Bishop is content to withdraw and let the poem do the work." "Sonia Sanchez makes electrifying use of nonverbal sound in her highly energetic performances." "Mark Strand brings to the delivery of his poems a classical distancing, as if his words were being carved in the air." Let us pass over—as so many poets do—the obvious fact that in oral performance it is impossible for the poem to do all the work.

The poet should not try to make up for that by doing too much of the work. I found myself once in a three-way reading; one of the other poets I will not name here, and one I will name with pleasure: Stanley Plumly read second, and I read third. The other poet put us in a tough spot by opening with a forty-minute reading.

In a decorously controlled fury, Plumly rose from his seat beside mine, went to the podium, and delivered a powerful, beautifully selected reading of about thirteen minutes' duration, and sat down to enthusiastic and well-deserved applause. "Terrific," I said. "Thanks," he said. "It was too long." "Gotcha." So I read for about eleven minutes. Though we were being well paid for this appearance, no one suggested that either Plumly or I had read too briefly; in the circumstances, I don't think we had.

But did anyone ever say anything to the other poet? I didn't; how could I? The only time I ever expressed my feelings about something like that was after one of those multiple-poet programs in which a dozen poets celebrate a thirteenth. The organizers had tried hard to get us all to understand that we should each keep it under five minutes. I am not pursued by such demons as those on the tail of him who went on for twelve minutes—unless it was they who prompted me to tell him afterward that I believed he was not as selfish as he seemed. I didn't like saying it, though I strongly believed it; I don't like remembering that I said it. In the world of mainstream poetry readings, the ethic is to suffer incompetence in silence—unless we are gossiping about absent offenders.

In venues other than universities and libraries, far from any fear of being critiqued, performance poets participate regularly in poetry slams. It is generally recognized that slams started in Chicago before they spread throughout the country and settled here and there, most famously at the Nuyorican Poets Café, celebrated in song, story, and *The United States of Poetry*, which has been both a TV program and a book.

Here, excerpted from the book, is co-editor Bob Holman's characterization of the Slam scene:

> Yes, the Poetry Slam, whose very name sends terror to the civilized. The Poetry Slam, those mock Olympics with judges selected randomly from the audience, judges who dare to score the poem between zero ("a poem that should never have been written") and ten ("a poem causing simultaneous orgasm throughout the audience"). But please use the Dewey Decimal System of Slam Scorification—if there's a tie, we must resort to the Dreaded Sudden-Death Spontaneous Haiku Overtime Round! With tongue in cheek (usually), and competition itself competing with irony and hype, the Slams have brought Whitman's "muscular art" [power] upon the ear of the populace. The Slam is now the most potent grass-roots arts movement in the country, existing in over thirty cities, with an annual National Slam that attracts hundreds of poets...More than anything else, at a time when "poetry readings" connoted a beard chained to a podium, a muffled voice, and an airless ear, Slams allowed a generation to attend a poetry reading without saying they were going to a poetry reading.[2]

Wait a minute, now. Let's get this straight. Are we hearing that poets get up on a stage knowing that when they finish, judges scattered around in the audience will pass numerical judgment?

That's right. Numbers will be called out or held up on cards. A scorekeeper will write them down. Not only that, but some slams set time limits. At the National Slam, for example, three minutes is the time limit for each performance; you accumulate penalty points for going overtime, and these are subtracted from your score after the usual number-massaging—drop the high and the low score, add the others. At the national slam two years in a row, a fine performer named DJ Renegade— a *nom de guerre*, but it's what he goes by—lost on overtime points; it seems that no matter how hard he practices offstage, some chemistry on the stage slows him down those few beats, and he can't hold to three minutes his major piece, a tribute to Miles Davis in which he sometimes sounds like the horn Miles played.

Sounds like the instrument? Vocally imitates a horn?

Yes.

That doesn't sound like poetry to me.

A traditional print poem is made only of words. When read aloud, the words may take on qualities not immediately evident in the print version. But in a performance poem, these added elements are, or can be, as much a part of the poem as the words.

Are performance poems composed differently?

Not the written part, probably. But the performance part is a product of consideration and practice. So when you see on a page the words of a performance poem, you will probably feel that there isn't as much to them as there was when you witnessed the performance. You could say, I guess, that it's analogous to looking at the words of a song without experiencing the music.

And the judges—what do they know?

Whatever they know. They score on the basis of what they like, and probably as the evening goes on they score somewhat in response to what other judges are doing. The audience is usually allowed to attempt to influence the judges; they can boo a score or applaud it. In some venues, they can even be disruptive during the performance; if they're bored by it, they might start snapping their fingers or groaning softly. A room full of people going "Uuuuuuuuuuuuuuunnnnnnnnnnnnnn-nnnhhhhhhhhh" can make you wonder what you're doing there.

What are *you doing there?*

The universe of poetry is large and comprises many worlds. I live mostly in the semi-formalist zone of the print world, but I feel deeply curious about any segment of the poetic experience that has attracted this much attention and looks like this much fun.

How much of what you find there is any good?

Before I answer that, let me ask the same question in another direction. If you subscribe, as I do, to *Poetry* magazine, and read it when it arrives each month, how many of the poems you read in its pages do you want to memorize or read to someone you love?

I see what you mean.

It's a good moment, maybe, to invoke Sturgeon's Law. The science fiction writer Theodore Sturgeon is said to have been asked in public a question to this effect: "Mr. Sturgeon, you are a gifted and accomplished writer. Why do you work in a genre in which ninety percent of what is produced is crap?" Sturgeon is said to have replied, "Ninety percent of everything is crap." But here's a complication. Before you go wishing that only fifty percent of everything were crap, think about how much of the crap is able at the very least to inspire a shred of hope that whoever made it might do better next time, or might have responded with weird appropriateness to a moment you shared but which has now passed. If a poem happens to hit me right, if it works for me just at the moment, I don't give a damn whether it's going to work for somebody else two hundred years from now.

Okay. But are you going over to the slammers? Is this your new life as a poet?

No. I'm not going over there to stay, anyhow. I like visiting there, and I profoundly enjoy the competitive aspect of the thing, because on so many levels it's beside the point. It's a little like shooting pool in a bar: some nights you're hot, some nights you're not. But I can remember a particular day—a twenty-four-hour period—that puts all of this in perspective for me. So: no more questions; I'll just tell the story.

I got into all this in the first place when a bunch of the Nuyorican Café people came to Washington, in the winter of 1996, for about three weeks of schmoozing, performing, workshopping, and so on. Went to lunch with Bob Holman, went to some workshops. Got to talking with Silvana Straw, a performance poet who lives in Washington, and she arranged for me to be the "sacrificial poet" at a slam in April, between a D.C. team and a New York team, at the Black Cat on 14th Street.

The sacrificial poet's job is to perform first, outside the contest, to warm up the judges and the audience. I had not seen any slamming up to that time.

And so my moment came. I took the stage and read a poem, "Landscape With Tractor," from *The Flying Change*. I read it well enough, but the scores were, well, mediocre, three-to-five-ish, I think. So I sat back and watched. Most of the other people didn't read; *they performed from memory*. I felt stupid for not having thought of that; I know many dozens of poems by heart, and some few of them are mine. I promised myself that I would never again stand on a slam stage and read from a page in my hand.

Other moments that evening were a little harder to understand. There's a D.C. poet named Jose Padua who sometimes gives the impression that he's had an unusually large volume of drink. As this particular evening got later, he became less and less coherent, and during one of his sets looked up from his page, called us names, told us to engage in various distasteful practices, and then went back to the poem for a few lines before returning to his attack on the audience. His scores were very high. Now, I don't know how much of Padua's act is real drunkenness and how much of it is shtick, but at its most self-indulgent it has as little to do with poetry as anything I've seen on a slam stage. At other times, he is quietly energetic, almost menacing, and very witty. He is quite capable of powerful performance, and sometimes delivers it.

I witnessed performance skills and moves that evening that I envied and would emulate if I could. For example, the amazing vocal range and control of DJ Renegade enable him to produce electrifying effects with very engaging poetry. It is not his aim to stand on a stage and insult people; and, so far, my experience has not inspired me to do that either. Of course, I can imagine wanting to, and I can even see that there may be times when doing so is the best way of being true to one's art. But such times are more rare than many people think, because it is so hard to know the difference between being true to your art and being true to your childish impulses. Indeed, once in a while they are the same thing.

That night at the Black Cat, though, as I observed the performers and the judges, one thing I learned was that most slam artists really understand the place of competition in their work. The taking turns, the time limits, the judges—all that is part of the setting, but most of the participants know that the results can be unexplainably weird, and that this is part of the point. Bob Holman is fond of saying about slams that the best poet never wins. Of course all the losers can tell themselves that too often.

A year later, in Maine, I could believe that the best poet had won.

It happened that the day after my sacrificial debut I traveled to Arlington, to Marymount College, to hear a reading by Anthony Hecht. To characterize anyone's poems very briefly is usually to do them a grave disservice, but it may not be entirely unfair to say that Hecht's poems are pitched at a level of cultural and technical sophistication that is not widely available among contemporary readers; that they are written almost exclusively in metrical lines, and that these are often rhymed in wonderfully complex and difficult ways, and that, somewhat surprisingly, he is at home with slang as well as with subtle references to the art treasures of Europe.

By all this I mean to say that there aren't many of Hecht's poems that would give much immediate pleasure to a person who had read very little poetry. But a person who has read a lot of poetry, some of it in languages other than English, might come equipped to hear in Hecht's poems a rich contribution to the continuing conversation the present likes to hold with the past, a complex assortment of connections to the shared experiences that make a civilization. It did no harm at all, furthermore, that Hecht had a splendid voice and a firm sense of what is audible and what is not. I sat in that audience at Marymount transported ever more deeply into the kind of verbal experience that reminds me why I am alive, that does more for me than most experiences do. Yes, I was aware that the more I learn about poetry's subtleties, the fewer people there are who will know as much as I do. When I revel in that kind of appreciation, I am not at the same moment complaining that the audience for poetry is too small; at such moments I am not aware of any other members of the audience, nor of Anthony Hecht's many awards and distinctions, but only of the words and what they are doing to me. If among them there is a ballade with a Latin refrain, I count myself lucky to hear it and to be reminded of its forerunners, among which it stands fully as an equal.

I feel lucky, too, that I can move fairly easily between slams and more academic readings. I understand why slammers are bored by most readings, and I also understand why I will not resort to slamming when I give my own more traditional readings. The audience has expectations, and exceeding them beyond a certain point obliterates the poetry. So, every now and then, I may go back to the Black Cat, or somewhere like it, stand in a little circle of blinding light, and blast a poem or two as hard as I can. If I do, I'll get a jolt that will set me up for quite a while.

Notes

1. James Dickey, *Babel to Byzantium: Poets and Poetry Now* (New York, 1973), p. 251.

2. Bob Holman, "Welcome to the United States of Poetry," *The United States of Poetry*, by Joshua Blum, Bob Holman, and Mark Pellington (New York, 1996), pp. 9-10.

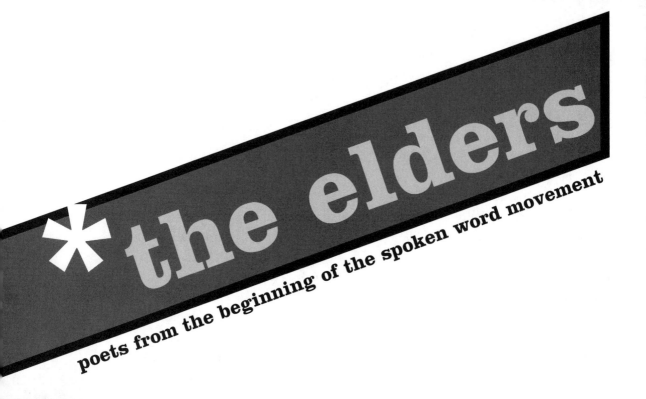

* Night House

Bob Holman

In 1989, Holman helped reopen the Nuyorican Poet's Cafe, where the first New York Poetry Slam began

The wind of 6th Ave kicks in

The lavish kite unscrolls
An ancient tale of love And treachery

It's just one of those Nights

So tired from working
That you can't sleep

And it isn't even funny
As the pen clenches
Your fingers to its end

Life can be like that
One minute
You're running
Around and then

The next you're lying
Still next
To the one
You love

Sure it happens
All the time

Cats asleep
On the sofa, kids
In bunkbeds

Me too
Real soon
Me too

*

*It—the Remedy

Marc Smith

If you need to kiss *it*,
Kiss *it*.
If you need to kick *it*,
Kick *it*.
If you need to scream *it*,
Scream *it*.

But kiss *it*, kick *it*, scream *it*
Now.

If you need to leave *it*,
Leave *it*.
If you need to love *it*,
Love *it*.
If you need to hold *it*,
Hold *it*.

But leave *it*, love *it*, hold *it*
Now.

If you need to squeeze *it*,
Squeeze *it*.
If you need to spill *it*,
Spill *it*.
If you need to tell the world
You've got more to you
Than the world has as of yet
Allowed you to be,

Then
Be *it*, tell *it*, spill *it*,
Squeeze it out of each instantaneous moment.
Make the juice, the jive, the jazz, the jism,
The mysticism that ism you!

Grab at the moon!
And hold the stars hot inside your head.

'Cause now is all there ever was
And all there ever will be.

So kiss *it*, kick *it*, scream *it*
Now!

*

* Maps and Wings

Gary Mex Glazner

National Poetry Slam Founder, 1990

The road looks the same
no matter where you are going.
Some roads take on a magic
from the hum of the wheels
they hold.
Route 66 was my father's road
and his father's road.
Model A with the dust bowl
in the rear view mirror
and California in the headlights.
From being men
to being Oakies.
The vulgarities of newcomers.
A drowsy distant hope.
Plowing and sowing the
stretch of pavement.
A gateway to work and food.
Following the hungry signs.
Route 66 was their plowshare.
They dug into the rank soil.
Held the miles in rusted fingers.
Cracked open its hull using the seeds
for guidance. Maps folded like wings.
A banquet of motion. Summoning us
now with its broken fragments.
Let us piece the road together.
This is the way they went
and we shall follow them
as we are able.

*

Gravitas: In Three Movements

Michael Warr

Founding Executive Director of the Guild Complex

In memory of Fred Fine

I.

In the immortal mind
of this Worldchanger
bottom line was humanity,
      heart.
Breadlines for subsistence
not enough without beauty
riveted into the beams
      of our being
offered to all in reach of his
brilliant, encompassing, light
where would-be Worldchangers
were taught to slay
the golem of cyclical crisis.

II.

Firebird soaring underground.
Entrenched scholar on frontlines.
Bronze-Star soldier, profound.
Mobilizer of each one of us.
Gardener of consciousness.
Scientific shaman. Maven.
Mentor to masses. Agitator.
Code Breaker. Mensch.
Papillon.
      Frail enough to fly.

III.

Freedom Fighter. Father.
Ideamonger.
Immense enough to leave
an imprint on our communal stone.
Today the theory of chaos is true.
The flutter of a butterfly's wing
can equal the force of a hurricane.

*

My Name's Not Rodriguez

Luis J. Rodriguez
Founder of Tía Chucha Press

My name's not Rodriguez.
It is a sigh of climbing feet,
the lather of gold lust,
the slave masters religion
with crippled hands gripping greed's tail.
My name's not Rodriguez.
It's an Indian mother's noiseless cry,
a warrior's saliva on arrow tip, a jaguar's claw,
a woman's enticing contours on volcanic rock.
My real name's the ash of memory from
     burned trees.
It's the three-year-old child wandering in the
     plain
and shot by U.S. Calvary in the Sand Creek
     massacre.
I'm Geronimo's yell into the canyons of the old
     ones.
I'm the Comanche scout; the Raramuri shaman
in soiled bandanna running in the wretched rain.
I'm called Rodriguez and my tears leave rivers
     of salt.
I'm Rodriguez and my skin dries on the bones.
I'm Rodriguez and a diseased laughter enters
     the pores.
I'm Rodriguez and my father's insanity
blocks every passageway,
scorching the walls of every dwelling.
My name's not Rodriguez, it's a fiber in the wind,

it's what oceans have immersed,
it's what's graceful and sublime over the top of
     peaks,
what grows red in desert sands.
It's the crawling life, the watery breaths
     between ledges.
It's taut drum and peyote dance.
It's the brew from fermented heartaches.
Don't call me Rodriguez unless you mean
     peon and sod carrier,
unless you mean slayer of truths and deep-
     sixer of hopes.
Unless you mean forget and then die.
My name is the black-hooded 9mm-wielding
     child in all our alleys.
I'm death row monk. The eight-year-old gum
     seller
in city bars and taco shops.
I'm unlicensed, uninsured, unregulated, and
     unforgiven.
I'm free and therefore hungry.
Call me Rodriguez and bleed in shame.
Call me Rodriguez and forget your own name.
Call me Rodriguez and see if I whisper in your
     ear,
mouth stained with bitter wine.

*

Hammer Heistand (The Police Chief)

Michael Brown

Co-founded Boston Poetry Slam, organized the 1992 National Poetry Slam

In this land of broad hips and weak backs,
recognition comes slowly or not at all.
Even the familiar needs naming, and only
the pastel colors of fuzzy sweaters
distinguish gray-haired women who
all get permed at the same shop.

Too many raisins and not enough sauce,
dry sweet potatoes and slabs of ham
at the church supper where the crowds thin
while the people fatten, the youngest drive,
and this year's story is about
Hammer dying alone in a hunting cabin.

I was the solid, strong guy who kept the peace.
It was an honor the town gave me, a job.
In this land of broad hips and weak backs,
I was the opposite.
The stronger I was, the less I had to be.
My wife leaned on me.
My kids stood protected.
Nobody crossed me,
or went out of their way to please me.

If I had developed my own personality,
I would have studied art.
I think my hands could hold a fine line.
I liked curves and soft things,
but I never had too much pleasure in that.

It's why I died a far away as I could get,
among soft wool, fur, feathers,
the mirage of fire and streamlined wood,
frosted windows, warm food, and
just beyond the porch,
the unpredictable changes of animals.

Private Patrick Gass, the Carpenter, *Makes His Case to Lewis and Clark*

Allan Wolf

An Asheville, North Carolina resident, in 1995 Wolf represented the smallest city to ever win the National Poetry Slam Championship title

Welcome to Fort Kaskaskia, Sirs.
I know that you've had a rough journey thus far,
and I know that you have plenty soldiers to see
so I thank you for taking the time to see me.
Now Captain Bissell claims he can't spare me
but with all due respect I'd like to plead my case.

Do I have any special skills?

Well, I'm a right handy carpenter.
With the proper tools and a few hands
I can clear you a field of trees in a week
and build you a cabin to boot.
Give me a broadax and a hewing dog
and I'll square the logs if you choose.
Give me a froe
and I'll build you a clapboard roof.
Give me a wedge and a maul
and I'll split a hundred rails in a day.
I can saddle notch a log
or make a saddle for your horse.
Or a bed for to lay on or a bench for to sit on.
I know the ins and outs of raising a fort
which I know you'll be needin' up north
and with your permission, sirs, I've an idea or two
to expand the capabilities of your keelboat.
I can row and push a setting pole.

I can shoot a gun and throw a hawk.
I can swim like a fish. I can run like the devil.
I'm strong and I'm fit.
I'm a soldier's soldier, Sirs.
I never shirk and I do my work.
And I do the other feller's too.

What's that? Why do I want to join?

I mainly ... Mainly, I want to see the trees.

*

legacy:
poetic influence

part 2

Robert Creeley: performance Poet

Bob Holman

I'm eighteen, it's 1967, I hear Creeley is reading at Swarthmore, that's where my high school girlfriend is in school, I use the occasion to hitchhike from New York, maybe she'll give up her Barbershop Quartet-singing fiancé, maybe I'll understand what all the Creeley buzz is about.

I'm a Ginsberg fan, Kerouac—these are the guys who made their way to the strangling backwaters of Ohio with a jolt of possibility in raw language. Creeley, I knew I should like him, didn't know why exactly, those little poems, short-liners, neutral language, where's the poem at, the force?

I didn't hook up with the girlfriend, but I did make the reading, and my life changed forever. Creeley sat on stage, hunched over, concentrating, concentrated, like a diamond cutter, he seemed to be writing 'em, not reading 'em. And what came out etched the air with meaning, pulled emotion taut through his quivering voice to my ears of unbelief, believing.

In 2006, we've come to expect certain things from a spoken word poet: charismatic stage presence, poems that rock and roar and are generally near the three-minute Top 40 slam limit so we get that arc, that kapow beginning and entangling mid and snap conclusion, "accessibility." No such thing back then: you took the poem as it gave itself to you, and with Creeley that meant having open ear and mind to walk with poem from its intake expulsion breath sound to its exhale to silence often less than a minute later, myriad twists and twisters later, forty-second journey fragmented time machine, pushing the listener around, every word a change in direction.

Creeley Cyclops, his one eye lighthouse beam, was from a different age. You could feel it, Charles Olson knew it. Those poets at Black Mountain were busy inventing the Open Field which would somehow be outside the academy but inside the form: Black Mountain College, near Asheville, North Carolina, in the 50s, not only would create a whole new direction for poetry—outward, you could say that direction was. Olson called Creeley "The Figure of Outward" in his epic *Maximus Poems*. Or Open, *The Open Field* (Duncan's book), or Projective, as in Olson's paradigm-blasting manifesto, "Projective Verse," required reading for you poet heads out there. Plus the aesthetic seemed to lean on collaboration among the arts—this is where Cage met Cunningham, after all, and where Buckminster Fuller did set designs, so no wonder Creeley himself saw the poem as a "medium" that could work well with others.

Quick, what Hollywood movie was named after a line in a poem? I'm thinking of Creeley's oft-anthologized exploding blink, "drive/ he sd," (*Drive, He Said*) the first feature ever directed by Jack Nicholson, from the poem "I Know a Man" which I first heard at Swarthmore and which continues to give all contemporary US moods/modes in a single poem. Here's the poem ("I Know a Man") in its entirety:

I Know a Man

As I sd to my
friend, because I am
always talking,—John, I

sd, which was not his
name, the darkness sur-
rounds us, what

can we do against
it, or else, shall we &
why not, buy a goddamn big car,

drive, he sd, for
christ's sake, look
out where yr going.

Here in a dozen lines is the whole of US culture in the last half of the twentieth century. Here is the miracle of Creeley reading—you see the page as you hear the words. You don't see characters, actions, pink Cadillac. You see words placed in space, thus they have a time: as music "keeps" time, poetry, from Creeley "makes" time happen.

Maybe the Creeley book that most dented me is *Pieces*, a book-length collection of poems, fragments, "pieces" that was the first new book he published after my conversion. I loved this book, the bright yellow and orange Flower Power cover, its oblique hippiness (you try that)—

　　*

You are all lovely,
hairy, scary
people after all.
　　*

A STEP
Things
come and go.
Then
let them.
*

And like all good psychedelic trips, *Pieces* ends with a simple universal chorus divine,

　　*

What do you do,
what do you say,
what do you think,
what do you know.

The performance wasn't *in* the voice, it *was* the voice, a cracked quaver, a vein of granite laid bare in air.

Working at St. Mark's Poetry Project in the '70s and '80s I got to know Bob. He seemed eternally grateful for one night when I chauffeured him around to dinner and to the reading and the party, getting nice and drunk. So it was terrific to reconnect in the '90s when he participated in *The United States of Poetry*. Most of the set-ups for the poets in *USOP* were masterminded by Mark Pellington, the brilliant director of the series, Josh Blum, producer, Steve Kimmel, art designer, Tom Krueger, cinematographer, the poet, and me, also the poet, and that's how we came to Bob's set.

For Creeley's shot we used the simplest possible conceit. Creeley, in his signature jeans and flannel shirt, looking much younger than seventy, stands in front of a seamless white background. His body is the text, black print on white page. As awkward as can be he stands there, as he frames himself, talking about his high school yearbook, this poem of death as he himself grows older, his friends dead and dying and living and remembering, "Where are they now?" he asks, taking a lurching step behind and out of an actual painting, gilt frame, that most obvious prop metaphor, in and out of focus, Mark Pellington himself doing the jittery camera work. This poem came from a book that included drawings and reproductions of paintings by Francisco Clemente. Creeley loved collaborating with artists; a show of his works at the New York Public Library included Elsa Dorfman, Jim Dine, Alex Katz, Susan Rothenberg, Robert Indiana, Rene Laubies, R. B. Kitaj, Sol LeWitt, Clemente, and others.

In Woodstock, summer '01, I was privileged to hear Creeley read with a jazz band, the same you can hear on the CD, *Have We Told You All We'd Thought To Know*? Here again Creeley embodied Pure Poetry, with performance as simply the mode. I remember learning from Ginsberg, watching him deal with a big band accompanying a squad of poets at the Knitting Factory, taking the time to set a mood, a tempo, give the feel. Nope, not for Creeley. He was never the front man, not even when it was a solo reading! I remember (as Joe Brainard would say) his reading at St. Mark's when Rene Ricard heckled him and Robert turned the event into a family chat.

At the glorious Catskill-lodge-like Woodstock Maverick Theater, Creeley was "just" one of the musicians (David Cast, Steve Swallow, David Torn, Chris Massey), which meant that the band could play ten, fifteen minutes at a stretch, until we all forgot what language was, and then inserting his words with the gentlest power you ever felt, a lyric like a tide that goes out and then the meaning an echo, the tide returning, it's gone, you lost your glasses in the surf, how will you read now? then another spate of sheer abstract sound, Creeley pulls it all together, it's Charlie Parker, the ever improv, the simple bravura, the refrain from the refrain.

Finally, what can we learn about performance from a poet who was the antithesis of performance? Simply that true performance is more than voice and body presenting the poem in an attention-dominating way, true performance is the magic unity of the voice and the poem being one. When presenting the poem aloud, the poet is not performing the poem, maybe that's what an actor does. The poet *is* the poem.

* Creeley's Oral Tradition

Bob Holman

Shit, it's
All oral—

When you
Hear it you

Write it,
When you

Read it, you
Hear it.

*

Creeley's Answering Machine

Bob Holman

Keep it brief—
Can't handle

More than
Thirty seconds.

*

You Got a Song, Man

Martín Espada

For Robert Creeley (1926-2005)

You told me the son of Acton's town nurse
would never cross the border
into Concord, where the Revolution
left great houses standing on Main Street.
Yet we crossed into Concord, walking
through Sleepy Hollow Cemetery
to greet Thoreau, his stone
stamped with the word *Henry*
jutting like a gray thumbnail
down the path from Emerson
and his boulder of granite.
We remembered Henry's night in jail,
refusing tax for the Mexican War,
and I could see you hunched with him,

loaning Henry a cigarette, explaining
the perpetual wink of your eye
lost after the windshield
burst in your boyhood face.
When Emerson arrived
to ask what you and Henry
were doing in there, you would say:
You got a song, man, sing it.
You got a bell, man, ring it.

You hurried off to Henry in his cell
before the trees could bring their flowers
back to Sleepy Hollow.
You sent your last letter months ago
about the poems you could not write,
no words to sing when the president swears

that God breathes the psalms of armies in his ear,
and flags twirl by the millions
to fascinate us like dogs at the dinner table.
You apologized for what you could not say,
as if the words were missing teeth
you searched for with your tongue,
and then a poem flashed across the page,
breaking news of music interrupting news of war:
You got a song, man, sing it.
You got a bell, man, ring it.

Today you died two thousand miles from Sleepy Hollow,
somewhere near the border with Mexico, the territory
Thoreau wandered only in jailhouse sleep.

Your lungs folded their wings in a land of drought
and barbed wire, boxcars swaying intoxicated at 4 AM
and unexplained lights hovering in the desert.
You said: *There's a lot of places out there, friend,*
so you would go, smuggling a suitcase of words
across every border carved by the heel
of mapmakers or conquerors, because
you had an all-night conversation with the world,
hearing the beat of unsung poems in every voice,
visiting the haunted rooms in every face.
Drive, you said, because poets must
bring the news to the next town:
You got a song, man, sing it.
You got a bell, man, ring it.

*

* Apples

Michael Anania

for Robert Creeley

The news—precious little
to hold onto—cuts and burns.
In Buffalo, six taxi drivers,
murdered, their hearts
cut out and carried away.
Lebanese shards. All across
the country victims sprawl.
Terrorists in New York.

In Indiana, just south of the dunes,
Brown cider is put out in Dixie cups,
Along the floor—Jonathans, Red
and Golden Delicious, Winesaps,
frost-skinned Cortlands, Romes—
shelves of amber, home-strained
honey, prize-winning gourds.

At the edge of his new blacktop
parking lot, Anderson, the owner,
tries to explain the two turkeys
in his yard to three Vietnamese
loading apples into a blue Chevrolet.
The tom fans his tail and struts
along the bellying wire fence.
"Look, look," he says, waving.

Winesap as though responding,
topple and roll every which way.
The Vietnamese smile and nod,
pointing at what Anderson
and his turkey have just done—
autumn and gravity, apples
unevenly spinning, feathers
flurried above bright asphalt.

"America," he says, "America,"
as though this were their chance
to see it all at once, part question,
part exclamation, an explanation
insisted upon in the moment,
then lost, his hands at his sides.
They are nodding, *yes, yes*, palms pressed
Together, the scattered apples at rest.

Perhaps, it is always true that each
occasion is its own center, that in
its moment the wobbling Winesap's stem
is the axis to our irregular pasts,
motions that curve inward as they fall
across contending radians, waves
of news and weather invisibly
symmetrical and lost among the leaves.

*

*Short and Clear

Robert Creeley

for Gregory, who said it

Short and clear, dear –
short and clear.

No need for fear.
All's here.

Keep it
short and clear.

You are the messenger,
the message, the way.

Short and clear, dear,
all the way.

A Gathering of memories: Gregory Corso, 1930-2001

Bob Holman
(written in 2001)

"Poetry is seeking the answer
Joy is in knowing there is an answer
Death is knowing the Answer"
　　(from *The Happy Birthday of Death*
　　by Gregory Corso)

For Gregory to die three days before George W. Bush ascends to be forty-third president, where's the logic in that, the poetry? Simply that Corso represents the human born of the soil who is that soil, the cantankerous inevitable, the kicker over of "the ivory applecart of tyrannical values" and W is the human born of tyrant dad and maintains that reptilian vision.

Corso is famous for his invention, "The Poets' Choice": when offered a choice between any two things, always take both of them. In the early '70s, I ran into Gregory at the park on 72nd and Broadway then known as Needle Park. Young poet energy perzapified, I was coming from the Performance Group's production of *Michael McClure's "The Beard"* and was still in its thrall. I accosted him, and on the sidewalk began to enact my favorite scenes, especially the moment where Liz LeCompte explodes from a tiny Jane Harlow to a giant Billy the Kid all in a single gesture. When I turned back for applause, Gregory had disappeared.

At Columbia, Professor Angus MacLeish had been one of the students at Harvard who adopted Corso, published "Vestal Lady of Brattle" or so goes the myth of Gregory on the dorm floors, Gregory with a universal Harvard meal ticket...Raging in the bookstores of Rome or Oklahoma, "I'm Gregory Corso! The poet! I'll sign all the books! and, I'm hungry!"...Introducing Cookie Mueller to me at St. Mark's Marathon, "This is the best poet here, get her on!" and he was right..."I don't know why you hang out with us Beats, we're old," he decried, "if I were young I'd go to the Slam..."

"Marriage," the first poem I memorized..."Bomb," the first concrete poem I ever saw...The alternate titles of "The Happy Birthday of Death," how to get process into text...The Wild Child of Greenwich Village in *Pull My Daisy*...Ginsberg: "He's the best poet of us all..." But comparisons not. When it comes to poets, I take all of them, thanks to the gods' messenger, sweet Gregory Corso.

* Marriage

Gregory Corso

TRACK 23
Read by Ethan Hawke

Should I get married? Should I be good?

Astound the girl next door with my velvet suit and faustus hood?

Don't take her to movies but to cemeteries

tell all about werewolf bathtubs and forked clarinets

then desire her and kiss her and all the preliminaries

and she going just so far and I understanding why

not getting angry saying You must feel! It's beautiful to feel!

Instead take her in my arms lean against an old crooked tombstone

and woo her the entire night the constellations in the sky—

When she introduces me to her parents

back straightened, hair finally combed, strangled by a tie,

should I sit with my knees together on their 3rd degree sofa

and not ask Where's the bathroom?

How else to feel other than I am,

often thinking Flash Gordon soap-

O how terrible it must be for a young man

seated before a family and the family thinking

We never saw him before! He wants our Mary Lou!

After tea and homemade cookies they ask What do you do for a

living?

Should I tell them? Would they like me then?

Say All right get married, we're losing a daughter

but we're gaining a son-

And should I then ask Where's the bathroom?

O God, and the wedding! All her family and her friends

and only a handful of mine all scroungy and bearded

just wait to get at the drinks and food—

And the priest! he looking at me as if I masturbated

asking me Do you take this woman for your lawful wedded wife?

And I trembling what to say say Pie Glue!

I kiss the bride all those corny men slapping me on the back

She's all yours, boy! Ha-ha-ha!

And in their eyes you could see some obscene honeymoon going

on—

Then all that absurd rice and clanky cans and shoes

Niagara Falls! Hordes of us! Husbands! Wives! Flowers!

Chocolates!

All streaming into cozy hotels

All going to do the same thing tonight

The indifferent clerk he knowing what was going to happen

The lobby zombies they knowing what

The whistling elevator man he knowing

The winking bellboy knowing

Everybody knowing! I'd almost be inclined not to do anything!

Stay up all night! Stare that hotel clerk in the eye!

Screaming: I deny honeymoon! I deny honeymoon!

running rampant into those almost climactic suites

yelling Radio belly! Cat shovel!

O I'd live in Niagara forever! in a dark cave beneath the Falls

I'd sit there the Mad Honeymooner

devising ways to break marriages, a scourge of bigamy

a saint of divorce—

But I should get married I should be good

How nice it'd be to come home to her

and sit by the fireplace and she in the kitchen

aproned young and lovely wanting my baby

and so happy about me she burns the roast beef

and comes crying to me and I get up from my big papa chair

saying Christmas teeth! Radiant brains! Apple deaf!

God what a husband I'd make! Yes, I should get married!

So much to do! Like sneaking into Mr Jones' house late at night

and cover his golf clubs with 1920 Norwegian books

Like hanging a picture of Rimbaud on the lawnmower
like pasting Tannu Tuva postage stamps all over the picket fence
like when Mrs Kindhead comes to collect for the Community Chest
grab her and tell her There are unfavorable omens in the sky!
And when the mayor comes to get my vote tell him
When are you going to stop people killing whales!
And when the milkman comes leave him a note in the bottle
Penguin dust, bring me penguin dust, I want penguin dust—

Yes if I should get married and it's Connecticut and snow
and she gives birth to a child and I am sleepless, worn,
up for nights, head bowed against a quiet window, the past behind me,
finding myself in the most common of situations a trembling man
knowledged with responsibility not twig-smear nor Roman coin soup—
O what would that be like!
Surely I'd give it for a nipple a rubber Tacitus
For a rattle a bag of broken Bach records
Tack Della Francesca all over its crib
Sew the Greek alphabet on its bib
And build for its playpen a roofless Parthenon
No, I doubt I'd be that kind of father
Not rural not snow no quiet window
but hot smelly tight New York City
seven flights up, roaches and rats in the walls
a fat Reichian wife screeching over potatoes Get a job!
And five nose running brats in love with Batman
And the neighbors all toothless and dry haired
like those hag masses of the 18th century
all wanting to come in and watch TV
The landlord wants his rent
Grocery store Blue Cross Gas & Electric Knights of Columbus
Impossible to lie back and dream Telephone snow, ghost parking—
No! I should not get married! I should never get married!
But—imagine if I were married to a beautiful sophisticated woman
tall and pale wearing an elegant black dress and long black gloves

holding a cigarette holder in one hand and a highball in the other
and we lived high up in a penthouse with a huge window
from which we could see all of New York and even farther on
                                                    clearer days.
No, can't imagine myself married to that pleasant prison dream—

O but what about love? I forget love
not that I am incapable of love
it's just that I see love as odd as wearing shoes—
I never wanted to marry a girl who was like my mother
And Ingrid Bergman was always impossible
And there's maybe a girl now but she's already married
And I don't like men and—
but there's got to be somebody!
Because what if I'm 60 years old and not married,
all alone in a furnished room with pee stains on my underwear
and everybody else is married! All the universe married but me!

Ah, yet well I know that were a woman possible as I am possible
then marriage would be possible—
Like SHE in her lonely alien gaud waiting her Egyptian lover
so i wait—bereft of 2,000 years and the bath of life.

*

Letter to Jack Kerouac (on the 30th Anniversary of His Death—2001)

Mike Henry

Dear Jack,
I bet you'd be surprised. How
you are a hero now,
when all you wanted was to play football
and love women, burn trenches down highways
with mad sainted brothers
and reveal your own fevered
observations and creations into sinews
of the muscles of pages of long, serpentine
sentences that seemed never ending,
just like this poem. Just like your life.
You started in boots that tramped
happy with hobos and ended
in sandals shuffling
a beat to your Buddhist prayers
as you got fat and drank yourself to death
like a good American,
the stain of your life
still on your hands,
like your father's palms
showed the shadows of ink,
india black, from printing presses.
I want my hands to be
stained like that, Jack. Marked
with the work of my life,
so I can hold them before my face
when I am dying and see it.
It's thirty years now, Jack.

And we know it. Are you surprised?
I want to do as well as you, as humble.
Do you know
there is a Gap commercial about
how you wore tan pants?
I'm sorry about that.

*

* I Will Give You Christmas

Billy Lombardo

This year, I will give you a Christmas. And even
without Santa Claus, it will be like a child's Christmas.
It will be like your first Christmas, before there was
Santa Claus. When there was a lap for you to bounce
on. It was 1964 and there was a Christmas. It belonged
to your brothers, maybe, but it swirled you up in itself
before you even knew it. And then maybe it was gone
for a while. But this year, this year there will be music
and coffee and peace. And when all the presents have
opened and all the ribbons thrown away, it will be
Christmas for you again. I will see to it. And isn't it
funny, my love, how we have had sons who have
waited in bedrooms-their hearts thumping for
seventeen years between them—for Santa, and now that
we have put him away, I finally have a Christmas to
give you. A Christmas that was maybe never mine to
give you until this one. And every year now there will
be a Christmas. And even when Santa returns, as he
must, for we will pull him out again, even then there
will be a Christmas to give you. We will meet in the
kitchen, you and I, to plan his arrival for the sons of
our sons in the peaceful sleep of their Christmas Eves.
Or while they scatter wildly into bedrooms or
basements at the tingle of sleighbells. Or perhaps, for
the daughters of our sons. Perhaps they will be
daughters. We will be ready for them. We will know,
then, how to grow girls. And they will be born on
perfect days, these daughters of our sons. Days of rain
or snow or clouds or sun. They will be the perfect
signs. And when they take their first steps across our

living room floor, we will keep it a secret, you and I, from our sons. And when our sons return to us with their wives from a movie and dinner, we will meet in the kitchen, you and I, to wash and wipe the dishes, and in the living room their daughters will walk for them for the first time and from the kitchen we will feign surprise at their tiny feet padding for purchase on our living room floor.

Yes, perhaps they will be daughters. They will sing in musicals. We will watch them. Which is to say we will watch our sons watch them. These daughters will smile to see us from there. From stages or courts or playlots, they will smile. And their socks will be the perfect color, and all we will do is look at each other and laugh, you and I. And these daughters of our sons, or these sons of our sons, or perhaps just these sons—they will know what it means to have Christmas.

* Keys

Daniel Ferri

On late summer evenings my brother and I would make the sign of the cross
We'd be out playing, and we'd keep playing past dusk and bladder bursting time because even
The time it took to pee would steal some slice of summer

Finally one of us would have to go and he'd try to sneak away
Because maybe if you were first to go it would take less time
Or maybe that was just another round in the game that brothers play

Since I was younger I had shorter legs and a smaller bladder and I'd
Always have to go first
I'd try to sneak off, but my brother would give chase
Catch up by the front door
We'd hit the bathroom door like two-thirds of the three stooges

And that's where we'd make the sign of the cross
Standing over the toilet
Holding our little pickles
Spraying beams of holy water distilled from grape Kool Aid

One evening our father walked in and saw what we were doing so he joined us
He sprayed his big beam across our little beams at an angle
To make our cross Greek Orthodox

That's the first time I'd ever seen my father in all his glory
And I swear to God it looked to me like Zeus had come down from Olympus
And unsheathed his hammer
To spray thunder
And rain wonder
Down on us poor mere mortal boys

He played shortstop on the Navy Base team
I remember one night he caught a grounder and wheeled to throw to first
And I could hear the keys jingling in the pocket of his loose Ralph
Cramden pants

I don't much like baseball
But God I loved that sound
It was like a pocket full of tambourines
Floating up to the lights
Helping the bugs dance

Small men move with their own rhythm
The ease of precision
The grace of a knife

I watched him beat that rhythm into Mr. Sticochizk's chest after those cross-eyed, dim-witted
    Sticochizk boys had beat my brother up one too many times
And I also watched it dawn on Mr. Sticochizk's face that this little man was not only mean enough,
    but he was also just the right height
To reach up,
Grab his vitals,
Rip them off and take them home to feed his pups like a terrier would a stag

In 1962 we were stationed in Norfolk Virginia
One morning we woke up and all the dads were gone
Three days later President Kennedy came on the TV and said
"This is not a blockade of Cuba, it's a quarantine.
And it will stay that way until the Russians take the missiles back."

Then there were pictures of ships on the TV.
Mom pointed to the set and said,
"There, that's where the dads went?"
I remember being afraid that if there was a war we would not be together when we died

But we didn't.
Life was about order then
The great depression was over
The big war was won
The Russians had run away
Mom was home
The kitchen was clean
And boy could that Perry Como sing

That order came apart in 1966 with three boys in puberty
When the news would come on TV Dad's face would go scarlet

He'd rage at the set
He'd bring his anger to the table and finally I'd rise to the bait
We'd stand and bellow at each other like one too many bull elephant seals on the beach
This kitchen.... is not big enough.....for the two of us

My friend Paula gave her daughter a laundry basket for High School graduation
It has her name and a bow on it
She says that when she gets anxious about her daughter going away
She just remembers that the daughter can only leave
If the mother has done her job

Women are running a relay
They don't think so much about the finish line as they do passing on the baton
That takes some pressure off

Us men, we're running sprints
Sticking out our chests,
Trying to be first over the finish line
Then we fall down exhausted, or stand with our hands on our knees
Trying to gasp our spent lives back

When a male bee releases his seed his entire abdomen explodes away
Really

But as far as nature is concerned that's ok,
I mean his job's done.....thanks a lot buddy.....bye
I try to remember that

When we next sit at the table I will let my father rage
Watch him swing his hammer and dream of sparks it once drew
And I will be silent
I will listen
For the sound of keys
Jingling on a summer night

*

So This Guy Walks into the Green Mill Uptown Poetry Slam (Chicago)....

Daniel Ferri

This guy walks into a bar. He gets up to read a poem about his father. He doesn't know that father poems are like love poems, holding a note on pitch or drawing a straight line. These are things best left to the experts; he's no expert. You can tell he's a virgin by the way the paper shakes in his hand, but you can tell that he loves his father by the catch in his voice and the way he looks at us when it's over.

And over just in time. Another ten seconds and the groans would have become audible, father or no father. But he's finished now and he looks up at us. The expression on his face is not about the poem. It's about his love, and our permission for him to tell of it. As we teeter between applauding the teller or turning our backs on the telling, Marc Smith appears right next to the guy, arm around his shoulder, talking about his own father and our fathers too, and when Marc says, "Let's hear it for...?" we applaud. Yes we do. We applaud because we also love, or wish we loved, our fathers that much. Something more important than a poem was at stake.

As I write this, a film that tricks people into humiliating themselves in public is number one at the box office. The maker of that film and the creator of the slam are both experts at getting people to speak. The filmmaker milks the worst from us, then sells our humiliation. Marc Smith teases the best from us, so we share our humanity.

The poetry slam is not about poetry, not any more than poems are about pens. Often what's read at the Green Mill Uptown Poetry Slam has art to it. Sometimes that art is nurtured until the writer is ready to move on; as Patricia Smith, Lisa Buscani, Billy Lombardo, or Regie Gibson have. But often, like that father poem, what's shared on that stage is not artful; but as long and you keep it short we will listen because you might just have something to say. There lies the real power of the slam. The Shinto philosopher Soetsu Yanagi, a founder of the Japanese folk art movement, described the concepts of Self Power and Other Power. Self Power is possessed by those like DaVinci, Mozart, or Shakespeare, whose rare genius is their own way. Other Power is the power of the rest of us. It is the power we gain by learning from the glimmers of genius in those like us. It is the artistic equivalent of collective wisdom or common sense. It is how we weld the best parts of us into a better whole of us.

I believe that Marc Smith has kept that idea alive; that the only license you need to speak is a readiness to listen. That a conversation is like a garden, watered by listening and nourished by respect. Keep it short, don't be too full of yourself, respect the audience and the sun will shine on Sunday nights; right there, at the corner of Broadway and Lawrence.

My Father's Coat

Marc Smith

I'm wearing my father's coat.
He has died. I didn't like him,
But I wear the coat.

I'm wearing the coat of my father,
Who is dead. I didn't like him,
But I wear the coat just the same.

A younger man, stopping me on the street,
Has asked,
"Where did you get a coat like that?"

I answer that it was my father's
Who is now gone, passed away.
The younger man shuts up.

It's not that I'm trying now
to be proud of my father.
I didn't like him.
He was a narrow man.

There was more of everything he should have
    done.
More of what he should have tried to understand.

The coat fit him well.
It fits me now.

I didn't love him,
But I wear the coat.

Most of us show off to one another
Fashions of who we are.
Sometimes buttoned to the neck
Sometimes overpriced.
Sometimes surprising even ourselves
In garments we would have never dreamed of
    wearing.

I wear my father's coat,
And it seems to me
That this is the way that most of us
Make each other's acquaintance—
In coats we have taken
To be our own.

*

*Jonathan

Nick Fox

for my father

You, sweating in a two room
shack shared with your mother.
You, dreaming your way
out of Carolina
poverty with a hope
built of desperation.

You, the boy
who will become
my father, perspiring
before a map of California,
formulating your future
in a place where nobody

has one. Here—Carolina—
Dirt track racer, football blood-
knuckle punch. You are nothing
at worst. Trash on good days. Expected
to shrivel in your fantasies
like dried peppers. There—

California— You will split
your head in the name
of a cause, scream
at 80,000 watts. Your FM stereo
voice building into a new man,
a new life, where you will

suckle the sweet fruit of the new
world while drought fires
burn the mountains of your youth
to crumbs. This is the destiny
that will carry you
through Knoxville, down

from the mountain. Feet burning
Berkeley sidewalks and the sparks
that lit off from your teeth
curling the tips of your mustache
into a smile. This is your life
and you are alone. Not

with regret. Not with the choked
motor of front porch life.
Not with the father known
only by name. Not with
the mother who lost
the day she bore you.

Alone— chewing
highway from Austin to Miami,
back again. Jonathan,
my father,
your arrival was a strangled
miraculous note of grace.

A test of your marrow. A chandelier
swinging aria of a man

who saved himself, who touched
down sprinting in the shoes
of a new life, who in turning
of seasons would lead

two children
through the world
with spines pointed
straight toward God.
You will leap forward
into your third life:

the Patriarch:
and your children will speak

your stories
as myth—your hands
around Olympus, cheeks
grazing the stratosphere.

You are at peace.
You are at home Jonathan,
my father,
in the love of your children
you will never again walk
alone.

✳ The Quicksand Hourglass

Jeffrey McDaniel

I went back to the tree where I carved my initials, and the eighth grade
    desk where I scrawled the word *fuck*,
and the subway wall where I spray painted my tag, and it's all gone.
    You try to leave your mark on this
chalkboard of a world, and they always wash it over, scrub you out,
    say *you ain't gonna be nobody*, and
the Hollywood thing seems so big, but even those stars aren't permanent,
    they grow old and fall apart, despite
their little handprints in the cement outside Mann's Chinese, as if they
    could say *halt* to eternity.

But where are all those people who passed through the subway
    station in my chest, who dropped in

a token? Like those kids I used to hang with on Philly street corners
   when I was thirteen and sporting
a silver rope chain and a tank top that covered half my abdomen,
   and tube socks shooting up my calves
and my first hairs ripping through my genitals, how it was all
   one big explosion down there.

And now I'm thirty-five and can see the life that's ahead of me, and
   the life behind me, can see where
my biceps will turn into mush, where my lungs will unravel like
   a cashmere sweater. And what about
when the person you're out of touch with has your eyes and freckles
   and inflections, sucked from the same
tit as you, got hit with the same hairbrush as you, hopped the same
   fences as you, and that person can't
even leave his room, like he's under some personal house arrest,
   and you know the feelings in his head
are so compressed you're worried his brain might explode like a bottle
   of soda left overnight in the freezer.

And just hearing the word *family* sends a rat running through you
   because the one you came out of
was broken, and you tell yourself it's ok to be the one egg that
   didn't get crushed in the carton.
And you think of all those people that have moved through this heart,
   this Grand Central station in your chest
just big enough for them to reach their hands in and press
   their fingers into the wet cement.

*another two Poets

Jeffrey McDaniel

Matt Cook and Derrick Brown are two wonderful poets from the spoken word realm whose work also has a pulse on the page.

I first encountered Cook at the 1993 National Poetry Slam in San Francisco. The first thing that grabs you about Cook is his voice—like his larynx is a giant crayon, and he's scribbling out his words in thick, muscular strokes, exaggerating vowel sounds and consonants, magnifying the alliteration, the language becoming all chewy in his mouth. It is rumored that Cook once stood on stage and literally read from the phone book, to wild audience approval. And while it's true that his voice will get under an old, dirty carpet in your head and rattle around for months, Cook's writing is strong and smart, too, filled with paradoxes: simultaneously spontaneous and historical, methodical and irrational, a surrealist of the ordinary, delivered in a decidedly American vernacular.

If Cook is Clockwork Orange meets Mark Twain then Brown is Frank Stanford meets Jeff Buckley. Derrick Brown is a romantic. Brown is a poet of feeling. Brown's been trying his hand at many things for the past ten years, being a Derrick of all trades. He's lived on a boat, paddled a gondola, jumped out of airplanes in the army, crooned in an indie rock band, toured relentlessly in the US and Europe, written fiction, monologues, and poems, and moved from Southern California to rural Tennessee. As a performer, Brown uses silence to his advantage. Whereas many spoken word performers turn up the volume, Brown turns it down, perfuming his fishhooks and reeling the listener in with the buttery softness of his voice. Brown honed his performance chops in the world of forensics, but he's blessed with something innate and fearless that can't be taught. It doesn't hurt that he has the deep, handsome voice of a sexy preacher man.

Both of these poets are wonderful.

* The Modernist Bowling Alley

Matt Cook

The forgotten soul who first separated egg whites.
The homeless man wearing the Superman T-shirt.
Their intentions were clearly understood,
Except when they were unintentional and misunderstood.
The gypsy moth is no longer destroying the prized sweaters
With anywhere near his previous curve of frequency.
Shoddy construction is now the more critical threat.
The modernist bowling alley will have the futuristic waiting area
Where you can go and wait patiently for the future.
You will see a clock on the wall that doesn't really look like a clock.
You will distinctly remember having forgotten that before.

*

How the Jellyfish Wishes

Derrick Brown

The farmer's boy was born in a season of drought
and dreamed nightly of a coastline
where it was rumored
that stars were migrating from everywhere
to the west
and were crashing into the sea.

No one knew why.

He awoke with his body in the soft L shape of California
and began to pack.

He was through spending his life between harvesting sweat
and day-gazing upon the scalp of the horizon
for something that felt like home.

He grew up working the soil
and understood that he was just a patch of minerals that rose from the earth
like crops and demanded water.
Crops are based in seasons and transformation.
A life should be no different.

Corn was a maze his family had been lost in
for generations. Some years it was beans.

"Everything changes in this farm but us. Starlight has stopped visiting. I am going West to join it."

He would be the first to seek
the visions of those stars spitting brightly
into the endless onyx of the Pacific.

By dawn, he would not look back.

Orange buckets of light spilled a rusted dusk
across the maple and oaks of Tennessee.

The fields along his route
sizzled with the chamber music of cicadas and bullfrogs.
Possums went squinting at the cackled dawn.
Endless fences poked up like bad teeth in the sunlit mouth of a fallen giant.

He raced away on a lazy train with eighty dollars crumpled and a journal.

Lightning had slammed its brights on outside
as he skimmed earlier entries:

"None of the teachers could explain why
The stars were migrating west.
The word on the street was that some states had fell
into a season of mental drought,
where people stopped moving their beds near windows.
They settled into dreaming of bills, tanning salon gift cards and affordable karate practice.
They stopped wishing.
There was no work for stars here."

When he reached the sea he found headlines in the L.A Times
stating that the stars had come
and the dreams of 'more' in the west were inaudible to the stars.

They felt unwanted and abused.
So the stars slashed onward into the sea,
burning their gases underwater.

They looked like lighthouses being flung into the deep.

And the sea finally had its chance to wish:
How do we know this came to pass?

Have you heard of fish with wings near the Avalon harbor that lift like fat finches?
Have you heard of diatoms wishing for their remains not to be scattered
but to be used in dynamite and toothpaste?
Have you heard of turtles wishing to live longer so they can nap with their children just a few
    hundred more years?
The jellyfish wish their hearts to become luminescent.
The eight armed writers wish to shoot ink at their enemies.
Some fish wishing for only the skin of a rainbow.
Have you heard of the humpbacks wishing for the ability to sing for 10 hours straight to serenade
    their families swimming through the night?
Tiny creatures, tired of their fins, asking to become horses of the sea and they got it.
They all got it
because they asked.
Because they don't know what silly is.

He wishes he could sing. He dives in.

*

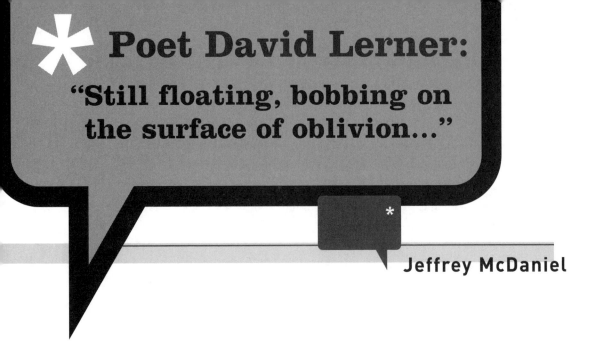

Poet David Lerner:
"Still floating, bobbing on the surface of oblivion…"

Jeffrey McDaniel

"It is said that a saint
only becomes an icon
after many years of polishing."—David Lerner

David Lerner was born in 1951 and died (of a drug overdose) in 1997. In his forty-six years, he published four books, all in a flurry of activity between 1988 and 1992, all with Zeitgeist Press. Lerner was a fixture at the poetry nights at Café Babar in San Francisco (the regulars called themselves The Babarians). The San Francisco (and Berkeley) from which Lerner emerged no longer exists. That San Francisco, with the Mission's fertile edginess, and a plethora of thorny, irreverent reading venues (the Chameleon, the Paradise Lounge) was destroyed (or at least badly damaged) with all the dot.com money that poured in, in the late '90s, altering the city's dynamic energy and making it much harder for scruffy, hand-to-mouth artist-types to survive.

When a poet leaves the earth physically, the phrase "out of sight, out of mind" comes into play. Even the heavily-accolated academic poets (who Lerner despised) with their briefcases filled with olive wreaths and laurels—when they go over the cliff of life, usually their work follows suit, landing with a rarified plop on the slush pile of eternity.

The main reason Lerner's work is alive, still floating, bobbing on the surface of oblivion, is that his poems bring a visceral joy to readers. Lerner doesn't have admirers who stroke their chin and think (in a British accent), "Hmm, quite a simile you came up with there, Davy old chap." Lerner has believers. He appeals to our id, that dark place in the mind where rage and desire blur. His best work stomps a fine line between righteous indignation and spontaneous blasts of humor. His anger at society's injustices, at poetic hypocrisy, is lightened, cut if you will, by his exquisite imagination, his ability to inflict tender, haunting imagery on the reader's brain.

Lerner's poems are often powered by wild, associative leaps. Many poems rely on anaphora (the repetition of a few words at the beginning of a line). The repeating phrase for Lerner functions almost like a canon, that he re-loads and aims in a new direction, firing out blasts of metaphor with great velocity. (Think of the way a star radiates out in multiple directions.) This type of poem also lends itself to (almost demands) a wild imagination, otherwise it will get boring quickly and feel repetitive. (One of writing's paradoxes—how to repeat and not be repetitive.)

Photos of Lerner depict him as a large, furry, almost jolly man—imagine a younger version of Santa Claus who hasn't surrendered the color in his hair yet— but Lerner's poems are anything but big and burly, and definitely not cuddly. His poems are agile and full of kicks. More Kung-Fu than Sumo. As much Travis Bickle as Walt Whitman. Imagine the poetic love child of Etheridge Knight and Robert Desnos. Lerner's a chipped, cross-eyed sapphire in the rough. He's a bearded Mona Lisa sleeping under a bridge.

Perhaps the best compliment I can give Lerner is that for the past four years at Sarah Lawrence College, where I teach, we've put on a show called the Dead Poets Slam, where students memorize, embody, and perform poems by dead poets in a theatrical context. Every year Lerner's poems tear down the house.

* Mein Kampf

David Lerner

> "Gary Snyder lives in the *country*. He
> wakes up in the morning and listens
> to *birds*. We live in the *city*."
> —Kathleen Wood

all I want to do
is make poetry famous

all I want to do is
burn my initials into the sun

all I want to do is
read poetry from the middle of a
burning building
standing in the fast lane of the
Empire State Building

the literary world
sucks dead dog dick

I'd rather be Richard Speck
than Gary Snyder
I'd rather ride a rocket ship to hell
than a Volvo to Bolinas

I'd rather
sell arms to the Martians
than wait sullenly for a
letter from some diseased clown with a
three-piece mind
telling me that I've won a

bullet-proof pair of rose-colored glasses
for my poem "Autumn in the Spring"

I want to be
hated
by everyone who teaches for a living

I want people to hear my poetry and
get headaches
I want people to hear my poetry and
vomit

I want people to hear my poetry and
weep, scream, disappear, start bleeding,
eat their television sets, beat each other to
    death with
swords and
get out and get riotously drunk on
someone else's money

this ain't no party
this ain't no disco
this ain't foolin' a

grab-bag of
clever wordplay and sensitive thoughts and
gracious theories about

how many ambiguities can dance on the head
    of a
machine gun

this ain't no
genteel evening over
cappuccino and bullshit

this ain't no life-affirming
our days have meaning
as we watch the flowers breathe through our
    souls and fall desperately in love

this ain't no letter-press, hand me-down,
wimpy beatnik festival of bitching about
the broken rainbow

it is a carnival of dread

it is a savage sideshow
about to move to the main arena

it is terror and wild beauty
walking hand in hand down a bombed-out
    road
as missiles scream, while a
sky the color of arterial blood
blinks on and off
like the light on Broadway
after the last junkie's dead of AIDS

I come not to bury poetry
but to blow it up
not to dandle it on my knee
like a retarded child with
beautiful eyes
but

throw it off a cliff into
icy seas and

see if the motherfucker can
swim for its life

because love is an excellent thing
surely we need it

but, my friends...

there is so much to hate These Days

that hatred is just love with a chip on its
    shoulder
a chip as big as the Ritz
and heavier than
all the bills I'll never pay

because they're after us

they're selling radioactive charm bracelets
and breakfast cereals that
lower your IQ by 50 points per mouthful
we get politicians who think
starting World War III
would be a good career move
we got beautiful women
with eyes like wet stones
peering out at us from the pages of
glossy magazines
promising that they'll
fuck us till we shoot blood

if we'll just buy one of these beautiful switch-
    blade knives

I've got mine

*

* BLEED, BE

hydi zasteR

come to me childlike death
breakneck dance over
lukewarm porcelain water
toes poking up above
the surface, below
the rusted faucet
at the end of the tub
stubby toes with cornflake skin
small yellow seashell toenails

come like breath-like silence
newborn mini-death

come at me why don't you
rack my bones like lamb
cut me like a side of beef
kick this stool
out from under me

get down here
hang me
get me raw
hook me for slaughter
and slay away
get down here with me
get had, get been
done and over
get begun

at least look at me

blink once for yes, death
like the fluttering
eyelashes of a hundred
haunted dolls

*

Truce

Viggo Mortensen

Sore arm and sunshine on dirt driveway cracks loud and
painful at the shoulder when you pull yourself up the
sandstone archway into a sit and view of scab-knuckled
hands resting in lap, seeming dead but for slow swell of
blue veins and pale hairs rising against the chilled breeze.
Back and knees will not forget to settle old scores every
wishful waking hour from now on.

*

Utopian Chaos

Hank Mortensen

If I were a rabbit and you were a bear
would we still be friends?
If you were here and I were there
would we meet?
If you wrote my name and burned it
would I smell it?
If he were gone would you
love me instead?
Or would you
just be dead?

*

* Why I'm Not a Businessman

Hank Mortensen

TRACK 29

"Going up?" she says.

"No" I say, even though I am.

Something about her just makes me want to say "No."

It's not that I don't like her,

I don't even know her,

she's just "her" to me,

but I say "No" and wait for the next elevator,

which doesn't come.

People come and go,

catching and leaving their elevators,

but mine still doesn't come.

I'm already 20 minutes late

and I'm starting to get worried.

I figure I'm going to need to get some supplies

if I'm going to last much longer.

I go over to the drug store by the entrance,

buy a sandwich and some fluids.

Right as I get back,

I see my elevator

leaving.

I just miss it, realizing I might have to spend the night in the lobby.

However, luckily for me, my elevator comes in a few hours.

By the time I finally make it up

and tell the receptionist about my appointment

and explain my situation,

the elevator, and why I'm so late,

she doesn't seem nearly as understanding

as I was sure she would be.

In fact, she doesn't say anything,

she just turns around in her chair

and stays that way.
"Great" I think,
"At this rate, I'm gonna have to set up camp here for the night."
As I'm collecting cushions and magazines for my shelter,
the lady from the elevator comes out.
"It's a good thing you missed that elevator"
she says, "It took the entire day to get up here
and the weather was horrible."
"That's too bad" I say, "You'd better get going
if you want to get back to the lobby by tomorrow."
"Good point" she says, then leaves.
I get back to work, and realize
it's going to be a long, cold night
if I don't find some way
to make a fire soon.

*

musicians meeting poets
music meeting poetry

* part 3

*8 Fragments of Kurt Cobain

Jim Carroll

1.

genius is not a generous thing
in return it charges more
interest than any amount
of royalties can cover
and it resents fame
with bitter vengeance

pills and powders only placate
it awhile
then it pulls you in a place
where the planet's
poles reverse
where the currents of electricity
shifts

your body becomes a magnet
and pulls to it despair
and rotten teeth,
cheez whiz and guns

whose triggers are shaped
tenderly into a false
lust
in timeless illusion

2.

the guitar claws kept tightening,
I guess, on your
heart stem

the loops of feedback and distortion,
threaded
right thru
Lucifer's wisdom teeth, and never
stopped their
reverbrating
in your mind
and from the stage
all the faces out front seemed
so hungry
with an unbearly wholesome
misunderstanding

from where they sat, you
seemed so far up there
high and lived and diving
and instead you were swamp
crawling
down, deeper
until you tasted the earth's
own blood
and chatted with the buzzing-
eyed insects that
heroin breeds

3.

you should have talked more
with the monkey
he's always willing to negotiate
I'm still paying him off...

the greater the money and fame
the slower the pendulum of
fortune swings

your will could have sped it up...
but you left that on the airplane
because it wouldn't pass customs
and immigration

4.
here's synchronicity for you:

your music's tape was inside
my walkman
when my best friend from
summer camp
called with the news about you
I listened then...
it was all there!
your music cutting deeper and
and deeper valleys
of sound
less and less light
until you hit rock solid

the drill bit broke
and the valley became
a thin crevice, impassable in time,
as time itself stopped

and the walls became vises of
brilliant notes
pressing in...
pressure
that's how diamonds are made

and that's where it sometimes
all collapses
down on you

5.
then I translated your muttered
lyrics
and the phrases were curious:
like "incognito libido"
and "Chalk Skin Bending"

the words kept getting smaller
and smaller
until
separated from their music
each letter spilled out into a
cartridge
which fit only in the barrel of a gun

6.
and you shoved the barrel in as
far as possible
because that's where the pain
came from
that's where the demons were digging

the world outside was blank
its every cause was just continuation
of another unsolved effect

7.
but Kurt...
didn't the thought that you would
never write
another song

another feverish line or riff
make you think twice?
that's what I don't understand
because it's kept me alive, above
any wounds

8.
if only you hadn't swallowed
yourself into a coma
in Rome...
you could have gone to Florence
and looked into the eyes of
Bellini or Rafael's
portraits

perhaps inside them
you could have found a threshold

back to beauty's arms
where it all began

no matter that you felt betrayed
by her
that is always the cost
as Frank said
of a young artist's remorseless
passion

which starts out as a kiss
and follows like a curse

* Tom Waits, I Hate You

Simone Muench

the way your voice snags
my skin when I'm waltzing
through a coffee shop, for the thousand
crows caught in your throat,
how it rains
every time I play "Tom Traubert's Blues."
I hate you for every valentine you never sent.
Call me indigo, azure, cereulean; call me
every shade of blue for being born
two decades after you.

I hate you for every cornfield, filling
station, phone booth I've passed with my feet
on the dash, listening to you pluck
nightingales from a piano; writhing
as if it were my ribcage being played
beneath a moon that is no grapefruit,
but the bottom of a shot glass.

For every bad relationship, every dead pet,
and every car I've wrecked
into light posts trying to tune you out;
for all the lost radios, Walkmans
tossed over bridges—still the sound of you
rising from water like a prayer at midday,

or the ragged song of cicadas
tugging frogs out of watery homes.

For every lounge lizard, raindog, barfly
I've ever met; for every vinyl booth I've been
    pushed
into by a boy with a bad haircut;
for every man I've fucked
according to the angle of his chin
or the color of his coat.

Tom Waits, I hate you.

Well, the night is too dark
for dreaming; the barman bellows out
last call; and you've turned me into a gun-
street girl with a pistol and a grudge
and an alligator belt, a pocket
full of love letters
that have never been sent.

*

* RULEBOOK

Vernon Reid

TRACK 53
(excerpt)

Terrible Needs Unextinguished by the Passage
Of Time
A Sequence Of Events
Reverberant and Indiscriminate

Countless Pundit Heads
Nod, Whisper, and Judge
far removed from the blast and the scream

A swarm gathers at the Tomb of its Queen
Armed And Furious, awaiting instructions
That Never Come

New Games
are played by Rules
No One is informed of

Stakes Higher
Than You Can
Possibly Know

The Outcome and Its Prophecy
Written in an Unread Book
Burnt to Ash a thousand years ago

*

*Interruption in Arc

Phil West

for Jeff Buckley (1966-1997), who also died in
*   Memphis*

Think if Elvis had taken no for an answer
when they hid his hips on Ed Sullivan.
Think if he'd stayed in the Army,
draped in olive, faded.

Think if the delta mouth had swallowed him,
if he'd let the Memphis waters take him thin
and beautiful. You would watch
the rocket shimmer, hint

its upward arc, and then abandon you,
like a lover. You would feel the thinning
of the air as he left, see the black space in sky,
the imprint of a dead star, its farewell note.

To disappear is to disappoint. Even before
you truly arrive, we see you, send the silver car
for you. The Beatles in Hamburg, Hendrix on
the Lower East Side, the caesura.

In death, a slight weight peels from the body,
thought to be the soul. If you sifted Graceland,
through the world he made, you could excavate
what might have left you: the polite Southern boy,

the hair you want to comb with your fingers,
the pitch you want to drink down for its sugar,
taking you the length of Tennessee,
the clarity of voice, the words you believe.

*

Mark Eleveld on Jeff Buckley

Doing press for *The Spoken Word Revolution*, in 2003, a radio DJ asked me the difference between a poem and a song. I still have no answer. Not a good one, except that good poetry and good music, lyrics and music together, often come from the same place. Then I discovered Jeff Buckley's album *Grace* which clouded the issue even more. Every Buckley song seems like a poem. Flash forward to researching poetry audio in Manhattan for the book you're holding, and I end up in the Poets House. They have a room dedicated to the preservation of poetry, in all of its forms; what a lucky find for any self-admitted poetry drooler. The gracious curators set me up with headphones and I sat and listened. And as I was listening, I heard this voice again. This voice that has rung unintentional in my ear for years now. This Jeff Buckley. At the Poets House reading I discovered, Jeff announced *A Letter to Bob Dylan* as his poetry selection for the evening.

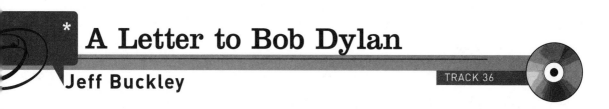

* A Letter to Bob Dylan

Jeff Buckley

TRACK 36

Dear Bob,

I don't know how to start. Last Saturday my man Steve Berkowitz broke it to me that you were told of something I'd said from the stage and that you'd felt insulted. I need for you to listen to me.

I have no way of knowing how my words were translated to you, if their whole meaning and context were intact, but the truth is, is that I was off on a tangent, on a stage, my mind going where it goes, trying to be funny. It wasn't funny at all. And I fucked up. I really fucked up.

And the worst of it isn't that your boys were at the gig to hear it. It doesn't really bother me. It just kills me to know that whatever they told you is what you think I think of you. Not that I love you. Not that I've always listened to you and carried the music with me everywhere I go. Not that I believe in you. And also that your show was great. It was only the supper club crowd that I was cynical about. And that's what I was trying to get at when I said what I said.

And I'm sorry that I'll never get to make another first impression. You were really gracious to me. To even allow me backstage to meet you. I'll never forget you, what you told me as long as I live. You said, *Make a good record, man.*

And I'm very honored to have met you at all.

I'm only sad that I didn't get the chance to tell you before all this intrigue. The intrigue is not the truth. Lots of eyes will read this letter before it gets to you, Bob. Which I accept. Some day you'll know exactly what I mean, man to man.

Always be well,

Jeff Buckley

Now you know who's gonna read this? The president of Sony records, my A&R man, my manager, his two managers, his friend *Ratso*. And this is my personal plea of love to Bob Dylan. And this is what happens when you're not nobody anymore.

*

* A house is not a home

Scott Woods

First a fact,
then a secret.

Black folks love Queen.
Always have, always will.

We could tell from the beat of
"We Will Rock You"
that Freddie Mercury spent plenty of time
beating on high school bleachers
like we did,
though we did it because our school
didn't have a band.

9 out of 10 black people
know the words to "Bohemian Rhapsody",
and no less an authority on blackness
than Public Enemy sampled the
theme to "Flash Gordon".

So black folks love Queen.
Always have, always will.

That's the fact.

Now Freddie?
I'ma let you in on the secret:
We always knew about you.
Didn't matter.
Never has, never will,

but you should know just the same.

We knew that sometimes you
beat those bleachers for
the boys on the football team and for them
    alone.

And somehow
that was okay with us
because we figured you were white,
even though you weren't,
but that's just how white folks do sometimes.
And thinking like that?
Well, that's just how black folks do
sometimes.

But somewhere in the world,
there is someone
who cried harder than anyone else
when Luther Vandross died.

And we don't know his name
but we all know he's out there.
We don't know his name because
Luther knew we were cowards.
We don't know his name
    because we prefer feeling good to
    knowing the truth.

Freddie, we've done this before;

forced our idols to play house
against their will.
And I wish you were here when Luther left us
to teach us that it didn't matter.
"Bohemian Rhapsody" was still
"Bohemian Rhapsody", but somehow
"A House is Not a Home" would have been
    different
if we knew Luther sang it through
shower curtains to a man lying in the next
    room;
somehow, "Superstar" would have been "just
    okay"
if we knew he always saw
a pretty chocolate man wielding a guitar
in his mind when he
sang it with his eyes closed,
which is when he meant it the most.

Now Freddie,
I'm not supposed to be saying this to you.
If there's a bigger crime to black folks than
being gay,
it's waving our dirty laundry around.
But I can assure you that
my washing machine handles heavy loads
and keeps the colors in my clothes just fine.

I'm not saying Luther wasn't scared, too,
but his fear couldn't touch ours.
And if you or I or somebody or ANYbody
would have been able to make him believe that,
then we might have heard a slow jam
that would have strangled
Orpheus's harp

and caused angels to drop out of the sky
by the dozens in search of
the nearest dance floor.

Luther might have knocked the bottom off of
his microphone stands too
and sang the love songs
he was put here to sing.

*

* put off your faces,Death:for day is over

E. E. Cummings

put off your faces,Death:for day is over
(and such a day as must remember he
who watched unhands describe what mimicry,

with angry seasalt and indignant clover
marrying to themselves Life's animals)

but not darkness shall quite outmarch forever
—and i perceive,within transparent walls
how several smoothly gesturing stars are clever
to persuade even silence:therefore wonder

opens a gate;the prisoner dawn embraces

hugely some few most rare perfectly dear
(and worlds whirl beyond worlds:immortal yonder
collidingly absorbs eternal near)

day being come,Love,put on your faces

*

Love, put on your faces (excerpt)

Patricia Barber

TRACK 34
(excerpt)

adapted from Cummings

put off your faces,Death

for day is over

not even darkness

will outmarch you forever

and i perceive

several smoothly gesturing stars

clever to persuade

even silence

wonder opens a gate

the prisoner dawn embraces

some few

most rare

day being come

Love,put on your faces

*

* When I Say My Heart

Jeff Tweedy

I mean
an emergency
worse than a clarinet

or an old man who just won't
stand out of the way

I don't mean a parking lot
but the pretty twisting oil slick

the waving arms
of awful drinking

false teeth

an unpopular child
on a swing set
or the least wanted crayon

sometimes I mean
a foil moon

checkpoint charlie
or a ghost

or sitting duck

*

* Another Great Thing

Jeff Tweedy

the best way
to feel your blood
is to lie

tell bold lies
about books
(even better)
say
you write

listen,
lying won't help at all

unless,
you pick the right people

people who know
how to write and lie

o' and then the blood will pound
discoteque-esque
otherwise
it won't at all

*

Poetry of My Heart

Billy Corgan

Revealing now the poetry of my heart
Think birds in flight and you will start to come close
As forces come from the darkness familiar
To greet you hello again
They pluck those strings and sing those refrains I know so well, and
    hold so close
Now follow these birds faithfully, keeping those faces in mind
Over rivers and dales and soft greens until we come to the edge of
    the vast ocean
The biggest sea you may imagine and more
Lift your head and let those birds soar with this sweet music

Fast we fly over the waters
Faster and faster until we blur, and our words blur, and memories
    of lost things blur too
The sun catches you flying
Imagine this from the perception of the sun
Those birds and you moving the speed of light over the blue
Well, if you were the sun, you'd laugh too!
Finally, after such a momentous journey
You slow upon a deserted island, lush with life
And on its barren shore you find a worn sea chest
Polished smooth by years of coarse handling
Open that chest and you could find inside
A single valentine and the poetry of my heart
Dragging that sea chest around the bend
Through sand into a jungle dense with flower and shade
We take the forgotten trail up the hillside
Up towards the laughing sun
Catching its wisdom as it's given

Past the ghost whisper and relics of another past
Climbing to the very top
Because time will not stand still for us
But it will pretend every once in a while
And up here, forgotten, is just you, me
One, sea chest holding a single valentine and the poetry of our
     hearts

A single bulb lights this room
It's dark in here all the time
If the ceiling had only captured my dreams and nightmares alike,
    what stories it could show
She is here, the one
The one I love desire, device, rescue, all to my heart's own sorrow
I'm lost in this room, but this is the place the valentines are written
The site of my greatest thought and saddest song
There are no birds here to take flight
No oceans to fly over, no islands to reach
No sun to catch me crying
This is the gift of oblivion and opaque dance

Revealing now the poetry of my own heart
Its sorrow and the nameless wish I called bliss once
Stripped of its title and junked for show
The bulbs swing, the kids sing
The rooster crows and I seek sleep
Somewhere past the scars and empty cars and endless bars filled
    with reminders
I want to climb from this hole
And dash myself upon the rocks below
But still it requires intent
And intent requires desires
And desire registers in this body as need
Do you need me?
So push me over, my sea chest and me
The birds will follow me down

Retrace the steps, up to the ceiling

Back through the bulb, into the electric wires

And out of Manhattan

Coming out another side

To a kid, a dream

A scrawled valentine with an x and o if truth be told

Revealing now the poetry of my heart

Rage and the canopies it paints

And the drawings it frames

And its real cage, me

*

* # Sonny's Lettah

Linton Kwesi Johnson

TRACK 42

From Brixton Prison, Jebb Avenue London
    S.W. 2 Inglan
Dear mama
good day
I hope that when these few lines reach you
    they may
find you in the best of health
I doun know how to tell ya dis
for I did mek a solemn promise
to tek care a lickle Jim
an try mi bes fi look out fi him

mama, I really did try mi bes
but none a di less
sorry fi tell ya seh, poor lickle Jim get arres

it was de miggle a di rush hour
hevrybody jus a hustle and a bustle
to go home fi dem evenin shower
mi an Jim stan up waitin pon a bus
not causin no fuss

when all of a sudden a police van pull up
out jump tree policemen
de whole a dem carryin baton
dem walk straight up to me and Jim
one a dem hold on to Jim
seh dem tekin him in
Jim tell him fi leggo a him
for him nah do nutt'n
and 'im nah t'ief, not even a but'n

Jim start to wriggle
de police start to giggle

mama, mek I tell you wa dem do to Jim?
mek I tell you wa dem do to 'im?

Dem thump him him in him belly and it turn to jelly
Dem lick 'im pon 'im back and 'im rib get pop
Dem thump him pon him head but it tough like lead
Dem kick 'im in 'im seed and it started to bleed

Mama, I jus couldn't stan up deh, nah do nuttin'

So mi jook one in him eye and him started fi cry
me thump him pon him mout and him started fi shout
me kick him pon him shin so him started fi spin
me hit him pon him chin an him drop pon a bin
- an crash, an dead

More policman come dung
dem beat me to the grung
dem charge Jim fi sus (*for looking suspicious)
dem charge mi fi murdah

mama, doan fret
doan get depress an downhearted
be of good courage
till I hear from you
I remain
Your son,
Sonny

*

slam poetry

part 4

Answering Carol: an open letter from the Margin

Jack McCarthy

Sometimes my wife, Carol, will call my attention to a newspaper paragraph about a famous poet who has died in another country. She'll read me a sentence about people weeping in the *tavernas* and reciting the poet's work from memory. And she'll ask me why this never happens in the United States.

For most of the twentieth century, the term "American Poetry" came increasingly to refer to a branch of literature that Dana Gioia describes as "typographic," to the exclusion of the auditory. The last twenty years, on the other hand, have seen a resurgence of the oral from several directions. Gioia cites cowboy poetry, slam poetry, rap, and hip-hop as disparate elements in a grass-roots movement subsumed under the more general term "spoken word."

> Genuinely new artistic developments...tend to move dialectically from the margins of established culture rather than smoothly from the central consensus.
>
> —Dana Gioia, *"Disappearing Ink,"*
> *The Hudson Review*, Spring 2003

The first time anyone ever interviewed me about poetry, I said "American Poetry is like some ritzy academic town, like maybe Hanover, New Hampshire—the kind of town where if you work there, you can't afford to live there. The spoken word movement is like a carnival that sets up shop on the outskirts of that town. The poetry slam is like the freak show in that carnival, where people pay to stare at mutants. *But evolution happens by mutation.*" Talking about slams in the *Hudson*

Review article, Gioia says, "The poems are typically performed in competition and judged by the audience or a representative jury—an arrangement that both Sophocles and Pindar would find quite natural..."

In 2004, *The Worcester Review* invited me to write an article about the difference between writing for the page and writing for a poetry slam. I had occasion to send a pre-publication version of that article to Donald Hall, and he wrote back to disagree with virtually every assertion I had made. That was the beginning of a delightful and fascinating correspondence.

Last year, while reading a column by Don in *American Poetry Review,* I came to this passage:

> I have a slammer friend with whom I write long letters of combat. He writes me an argument which he thinks will be a winner. He bets me that I cannot find a poem printed in *Poetry* or *The New Yorker* which, read aloud at a slam, will win first prize. I could not agree with him more. To me, the notion of the argument reveals its poverty. What the hell do I care, considering a poem's virtue, about the votes of a bunch of cheerful self-chosen enthusiasts in a bar?

And therein lies the answer to Carol's question. There is no weeping in American taverns when a poet dies because, for nearly a century, the American Poetry Establishment has not *cared* about the opinion of the "people in the taverns." (I leave it for scholars to discuss exactly when the divorce decree became final; as a jumping-off place for their discussion, however, I might suggest the moment, after publication of "The Waste Land," when William Carlos Williams wrote in his journal, "The idiot! He has given poetry back to the Academy.")

American poems are not recited in taverns because, for the better part of a century, the poems of the American Poetry Establishment ("APE") have not been *written* to be recited. How many of their own poems have they bothered to memorize? And why should they if a poem's only meaningful existence is on the page?

In the face of such dogma, I find it interesting that Donald Hall's new book includes a CD, and that in his first utterance as Laureate-elect he talked about getting more poetry on the radio. In the paragraph in the *APR* column, before he mentions his "slammer friend," Don writes,

> I've been to the Nuyorican and other castles of slam, and I have laughed and applauded—but I was never responding to poems. I heard no line

breaks; I heard only thrust and energy. I heard no vowel and consonant play, only drive and good timing and jokes or outrage. In print the work remains inert. Nothing in the marks on the page, those jagged lines on the right, carries the vigor performance supplies.

I think Don's judgment offers very serious grounds for appeal. First, even in the "castles of slam," competition is first come, first served. As at any open mike, you might hear something brilliant, but on any given night some of the poets might be trying out stuff they wrote that same morning. (Patricia Smith once beat me with poems she had written at the bar during the open mike.)

You can't expect the Super Bowl of Poetry at a slam or open mike; what you'll witness is usually more like an exhibition game in the sweltering heat of the dog days of August—half the players will be cut before the season starts. There doesn't exist any one forum where all poets bring their best work at the same time. Judging spoken word as a whole on the basis of one or two visits to these events is like pronouncing the death of page poetry on the basis of a collection of first drafts from random workshops.

What I most object to in Don's indictment is one word in the clause, "I was never responding to *poems*." Clearly, that judgment rests on the perception that what is apprehended in performance is something *other* than a "poem," that a "poem" is a typographic entity that exists on the page *and nowhere else*, and that in being read or recited for an audience, it is transmuted into an entity of some different kind (once you add vermouth to the gin, it isn't gin any more).

In that perception, it seems to me that Donald Hall has spoken not for the whole American Poetry Community, but only for the typographic segment of it, the APE, whose poems are never recited in the taverns because they were never made to be recited anywhere at all. I would exhort our new Poet Laureate to speak for the *whole* of American poetry, which includes a burgeoning spoken word community, and not just for the APE.

And when, in any event, did the APE accord itself the right to dismiss all other choices as something other than poetry? When did standup poets lose the right to prepare a text *as script for a performance*, and call that *performance* "poetry"? And lastly, what new name shall we give to the scrap heap to which millennia of oral tradition have been relegated?

APE, this essay is not a declaration of war on you. This is a petition asking you to consider expanding the limits of your definition of poetry to include work that values thrust and energy, good timing, jokes, outrage, and vigor—even over line breaks and vowel and consonant play. Dear old APE, do you really believe that works that reflect those choices are disqualified from the category "poetry"? Do you believe that future generations will endorse their disqualification?

We just want to join the party. We're willing to sit below the salt for a while, but we think we should have a place at the table.

My vision of the future of American poetry is already coming to pass. Spoken word poets, dear APE, are coming to the colleges where you teach, routinely being paid by your Student Affairs Committees fifteen to twenty-five hundred dollars for a one-hour show, and departing the same night for the next college on their tour. (I tell you this because you may not be aware of it; usually, nobody from the English faculty comes to these shows.)

Meanwhile, graduates of your MFA programs are submitting their poems to little magazines published by other graduates of your MFA programs—and if those magazines ever do publish those poems, they might be read by fifteen or twenty people *tops*, while I'm writing a new poem in the morning and sometimes reading it the same night to, well, to more people than *that*.

Closet poets are entering MFA programs and being graduated without learning anything about performance. Some of them will go back into the closet for the rest of their lives, with only college loan payments to show for their investment.

I believe that the spoken word movement is going to bring about a new Golden Age of American poetry. It will happen with you or without you. It will be better for everyone if it happens with your active assistance.

Up to this point, APE, everything I've said argues the case that you need us— and you do. You need our vigor, and you would not say no to a share of our audience. But we need you, too. A recent eight-page tabloid from my alma mater carried an article on page seven about "independent" poetry projects which are, in fact, assiduously supervised. One student is quoted as saying, "My professors' comments are so interesting. Something so small as a line break changes a whole poem. They go for every word. My poems are short but their marks are endless."

As much as you need our vigor, we need your rigor. Can't we find common ground?

And finally: Hey, Carol—American poems *are* being recited in the taverns, but not mournfully. We, the outliers of American poetry, the marginalized migrant workers in the fields of spoken word, are performing them, with "thrust and energy, good timing, jokes, outrage, and vigor!" Joyfully!!

A Quick Thank You Note to Anne Sexton and Sylvia Plath

Genevieve Van Cleave

Thanks Anne for being so nuts
You told 'em what you had to say
Then you got crazier
And killed yourself

And even though you won the Pulitzer
And even though we flocked to see you

Somehow you didn't measure up
Except to those crazy feminists
Who weren't even fashionable
Hairy Hysterical Whiners

Fee-Fi-Fo-Fum
Now you're broken
Now you're numb

Addictions
Abortions
Abusers

Didn't exist before you, Anne

So, smoke, sister
Smoke

You and Sylvia
Got right down to it

Hysterical Bitches
Maternal Failures
Sex Crazed Frigid
Housewives

Smith sister, Plath, patron saint of nutty white
    chicks everywhere
Head in the oven
Tried to win the war at home

Sylvia wore white gloves in the women's
    magazine ghetto
Until she was so sopping wet sad
Mad and shocked

With a stick in her mouth and a weird ass song
    to sing

You do not do, you do not do
Barely daring to breath or Achoo Auch Tung
    Daddy I'm through with you

You two shrews let it be known
Far and wide
To hell with structure and meter
Confession demanded the entirety of your lives

The grateful mother
The perfect child
The humble wife

All myths that we have left Mrs.'s
As flowers on your celebrated
Self made graves

Staying true to the seedy secrets of pin curls
    and tweeds
With tragic results
Left the rest of us free to concur

That cutting and purging is no way to survive

And while it's never too late to start huffing gas
In the kitchen
In the garage

It is better to stick it to
The big bastards that beat us
The illicit kisses and unwanted caresses
The pills and institutions created to control

We are free to fill up our pages
Apply bandages
And leave it if we don't like it

Nothing's perfect
It's you two that made that fact abundantly
    clear
But even in our darkest hours
We know now that there is beauty
You saw to that

Saint Catherine of Siena to Mary-Kate Olsen

Marty McConnell

what god stole your hunger? who demands this reduction
to vertebrae? it's a specific treason, a case worth losing,
nobody can hear you with fingers or sticks in your throat,
nobody loves you in the bathroom, everyone's in the kitchen
again, *this is my body, broken for you, take and eat*

the appearance of bones is not a miracle of the flesh.
(*take and eat*) what do your visions insist? who
marries you in the dream, Christ slipping a ring
on my thin second finger, I was six when he first
came for me, my shorn hair all over the floor, gold
for gold / who insists on this full-body stigmata,

woman, how long have you been paying this penance?
martyrdom's a pretty notion until you're nose to nose with it
and nothing to be done, the body rejecting water, salt, fish,
'til you realize the devil's the one who wants you small,
who told you the pus of a cancer was wine, said

sip, swallow, this is my blood, transubstantiation in three
degrees, when you have given your good body to a lie
Mary, when your bones turn to whispers they will bury you
under a stone that did not ask to be a stone / we do not ask
to be but we are and to live, Mary, to swear
on everything holy that these bodies are not vessels

but gifts, that's the trick, to be the altar and not
another sacrifice / for what are you atoning? who is your
eucharist? I made men believe. brought a condemned man
to faith and caught his severed head in my hands, prophet
or not you have hands, a throat – the world doesn't need

another dead-thin girl / your suffering is not special, offered up
to magazine covers and lip gloss endorsements / my mistake
was believing the body meant nothing, yours the opposite.
Mary meaning bitter, Katherine meaning pure, Christ
and I died at 33, anvils for the world's beatings, crucibles

for the world's sins – glue your brittled bones back
into the face of a god who bids you eat, our bodies broken
into bread at your feet / chicory, water lily, do this
for you. rosemary, asphodel, do this
in rememberance of me.

*

my southern heritage

Jason Carney

my southern heritage lies in the smell of june
it was my mamaw
she was half chowctaw half snuff
half crazed by the spirit of the moon
giving her a sense she called the touch
she could see things
catch a firefly with her tongue
she would rub the swollen florescence of their bellies
to my forehead
good vision on my birthday
tell me i was going to be a man that knew
life by the way it felt
walk in the wandering reflection of dream
stand strong and tall like my papaw

cause he was a man that knew life by the way it felt
his eyes were in my soul
his breath within my heart
my southern heritage lies
in their simplicity
poverty and faith
baseball games on an old a.m. radio
and the closeness in the way families share sunday supper
my southern heritage was sundays
baptist revivals
deacons passing the altar plates
deep voices from the choir urging me to go tell it
on the mountain tops cause jesus christ
is lord
i love those hymnals
but i cannot think of these fond memories of childhood anymore
without seeing them with the pessimism of these eyes
which are of a man
i have to ask myself
what kind of truth those old southern baptists found on mountaintops
why could they not hear the voices dangling from branches of elm
dead that have been peeled away into the forgotten
generation after generation
dead that woven themselves into our bones
under our skin
all because they were silent
practiced at turning their heads
my southern heritage
lies in the shades of my skin
twisted and scared worn by their words
colored negro and nigger
go find the truth on that mountain top that my southern heritage
came clothed in white sheets
allows a   rebel flag to hang this very day over the capital of
mississippi

my southern heritage spans centuries of time
where people are silent
practiced at turning their heads
we are the threads of rope that pulled james byrd to his death
we are back roads of jasper, texas
less then two hundred miles from where i live
ignorance reigns
my southern heritage spans centuries of time
people who are silent
practiced at turning their heads
these lessons got to be mine
and teach to my daughter
cause i don't want her southern heritage
to lie in the shade of her skin
she is half thai
half irish chowtaw and snuff
she will speak in multi cultural phrase
combining thai laotin and hick
sabadica—y'all
i will catch fireflies with my tongue
rub their bellies to her forehead
good visions on her birthday
she will travel amongst the dead
learn the lessons of their lifes
spill the dust of stars and planets
traveling in the deepest reaches of her mind
tell her truth on that mountain top
she will not succumb to the wounds of her bones
she will not be silent

she wont ever be practiced at turning her head

*

Ninety-year-old Elizabeth Lewis from Yankton, South Dakota won the Vermillion Literary Project poetry slam at the Coffee Shop Gallery in Vermillion, South Dakota, on Thursday, June 29, 2006. Lewis, an experienced poet who had never slammed before, said about her win, "It made an *old* woman feel almost thirty again."

The VLP held two slam rounds, with poets' scores from the two rounds added together. After hearing Lewis read during the first round, slam regular and Vermillion resident Tony LaPointe commented, shaking his head and smiling, "I don't know if I can beat the old lady." LaPointe earned second place.

Traditionally, the VLP slam winner performs a third poem while wearing the infamous VLP gladiator slam belt. Lewis was too exhausted to come up to the microphone again, so slam master Doug Murano brought the wireless mic to her table, and she performed a brief, additional piece. VLP faculty advisor Michelle Rogge Gannon noted, "We did not require Elizabeth to put on the slam belt, as we felt the heavy-duty leather belt might be somewhat oppressive for ninety-year-old bones."

Thirty? Again

Elizabeth Lewis

Oh to be thirty
To be thirty
To be young and fit
With a head of dark hair
My skin soft and smooth
With no wrinkles there
To be light on my feet
To remember with ease
The things I've forgotten
No pain in my knees
To feel I'm attractive
To even one man
To work for a living
To go back again?

Oh, come off it, people
Do you think I am crazy
To go back sixty years
To live them again
The work and the diet,
The grind and the pain?

Thank God I am ninety
Not thirty again.

*

*On Poet Elizabeth Lewis

David Allan Evans

Elizabeth Lewis is still making poems at ninety. She told me that when she first began to talk, she and her mother would often have "rhyming conversations." The comment reminds me of an anthropologist friend who studies the origin of the arts. She maintains that art may have originated in the intimate, rhythmical, verbal play between mothers and infants. The key, she says, is reciprocity: a two-way communication between persons.

Elizabeth taught poetry for a long time. "One of the joys of my life," she says, "was having students say, after a series of classes on writing and appreciating poetry, 'Mrs. Lewis, we never knew poetry could be so interesting!'" I identify strongly with this idea and the spirit behind it. Elizabeth, like all successful poets, knows that in order for a poem to be interesting, it must communicate.

One thing I appreciate about poetry slams is that they require poems that connect with a live audience, some of whom don't read much poetry on the page. No doubt the spoken word has existed for tens of thousands of years, while the printing press has existed for only about twenty generations—a tick of the clock of human time on the earth. Writing poetry is certainly an art, but reading poetry aloud to a live audience is a more basic art. Poets these days tend to cultivate one of the two art forms, not both.

Having won a poetry slam recently, Elizabeth is obviously doubly talented. Her poem, "Thirty? Again," which she read at the competition, has many of the characteristics of most good poetry. It's plain-spoken, concise, and ironic. It states, as does Robert Frost's great poem, "Provide, Provide," that when it comes to aging, it's wiser to choose realism and expediency over sentimentality.

*Guitar Repair Woman

Buddy Wakefield

My mother told me,
"If you ever become a rock star
do not smash the guitar.
There are too many poor kids out there
who have nothin'
and they see that shit
when all they wanna do is play that thing.
Boy
you better let'm play."

Okay, if she ever starts in on one of these
    lectures
your best bet is to pull up a chair, chief,
'cause Momma don't deal in the abridged
    version.

She worries about me so much some days
it feels like I'm watching windshield wipers
on high speed
during a light sprinkle
and I gotta tell'er, "Ma,
yer makin' me nervous."

She was born to be laid back,
y'all, I swear,
but some of us were brought up in households
where Care Free
is a stick of gum,
and the only option for getting out
is to walk faster.

The woman
can run
in high heels
backwards
while bursting my bubble,
double checking my homework,
rolling enough pennies
to make sure that I have lunch money,
and preparing for a meeting at school
on her only day off
so she can tell Miss Goss the music teacher,
"If you ever touch my boy again, big lady,
I'll bounce a hammer off yer skull."

I remember her doing these things swiftly
and with a smile
in her discounted thrift store business suits off
    layaway.
She wore them bright and distinguished
    enough
to cover up the 30 years of highway scars
truckin' through her spine.
Some accidents
you don't need to see, rubbernecker.
Keep movin'
'cause she made it.
She's alive
and she's famous.

We can stretch Van Gogh paintings

from Kilgore, TX to Binghamton, NY
and you still won't find the brilliant brush
     strokes
it takes to be a single mother
sacrificing the best part of her dreams
to raise a baby boy who – on most days –
she probably wants to strangle.

We disagree - a lot.
For instance, she still thinks it's okay
to carry on a conversation
full throttle
at 7 a.m.
whereas I think...
Oh, wait, I'm sorry...
I don't think at seven in the morning.

But we both agree that
Love
makes no mistakes.
So at night time,
when she's winding down
and I'm still writing books about
how to get comfortable in this skin she gave me,
I see rock stars on stages
smashing guitars.
It's then when I wanna find'm a comfortable
     chair
get'm a snack,
and introduce them to Daylight:

This is my mother,
Tresa B. Olsen.
Runner of the tight shift.
Taker of the temperature.

Leaver of the light on.
Lover of the underdog.
Mover of the mountain.
Winner of the good life.
Keeper of the
hope
chest.
Guitar
Repair
Woman.

And I am her son,
Buddy Wakefield.
I play a tricked-out electric pen,
thanks to the makers of music and metaphor,
but I do my best to keep the words in check,
and I use a padded microphone
so I don't hurt you,
because sometimes I smash things,
and I don't ever wanna let'er down.

Echo

Sou MacMillan

I know that
    I am not the first
        scrying the future in a cup of black cohosh &
                            warm water
        counting days out loud &
        hoarding enough soap -

Ophelia is rising in the bathwater
        laughing
        beside the razor & the scrub.

The devotion to drown is as soul-deep as that
        devotion to float -
           ask Virginia
                      peering out of the mirror with the cracked edge
           ask Alice if you can find her
                blinking back across a headlight-glazed windshield
                      in the sticky haze of Monday morning.

All the reflecting things I know are so heavy -
    the Moon and her kindred
    the flashing fish & its sharp fin beneath the ice
    the stained corners of slick magazines, unreadable by bedside lamp
    the child who rests on my left hip
    the pause & gap of my mouth and all the sounds that emerge from there.

Things break and spill out in all the little ways -
           paint wears down eventually
           a jar aches to be filled up again in the end
           noise spreads out when it bounces back

a smooth shin requires a bandage
& there are desperate afternoons beside the sink when
I haven't bled enough to make me buoyant.

Let me rise
Allow me more than just salt & disaster to bathe my skin.

The truth is:
my nails cheapen my ring
my ring shows me up
my girth drags me down

& may I have a moment, please, for the things in my closet -
for the hanger staring mutely
unadorned
beside the red dress
for the threadbare shine in linens softened by
the breath of Desdemona.

Again,
let me rise
humming numbers into the wind,
spread-legged & staining the whole world.

Let me rise
there is too much at stake &
damn,
I am
so tired &
damn,
I am
so low &
damn, I am so tired of being so damned low.
So tired of waiting for
only an echo of myself to return.

*

* The Vagabond Heart says,

Lynne N. Procope

watch where you put your hands. My heart
lifts finger prints, slips out the back door,
with all you don't nail down. My heart's lost
her panties one time too many, she packs
a spare, never asks what you do with them.

My heart leaves easily, bends over herself,
hands cracking

at the knuckles. My heart loves the snap
-marrow-crunch sound. Heart's an open book,
I swear. Though the pages before this and all
the leaves that follow are glued down, to make
a body bare boned and spine cracked, make
a vessel wide to this vicious ether. You'd think
she likes to be *vulnerable*. My heart misunder-

stands boundaries, is too much of a machine.
She, Heart, lacks wings but makes engines
from the shoddy ventricle, from the left behind.
My heart's a bowl, warmed in the hands, a great
bloody beast, bruised myth of imagination.

My heart keeps her medusa in the tea bag,
she uses it as a book mark

If I gave back this heart, I'd go bump in the dark.
Give back this heart and what ferocious thing
is born to spring- to scream from my mouth?
If I cut loose my heart she'd be stripper-naked,

tearing you to bits, let slip her innocence like
a mask of the assassin. Baby, my heart's got

a soldier's back; bones of failsafe, hold like
booby trap, kiss of trip wire, mine field of
small explosions, my heart is full of what least
becomes her and it's no longer safe here,
my heart has overdone her dangerous metaphor.

My heart wishes I'd stop telling her secrets,
that I'd take the subway more often. Heart
really wants a thug for a lover; or a man with
rock face for hands, a woman who brings
her own dick to the party. My heart cannot
believe I just did that, she's become cautious
with her missionary body.

My heart doesn't want me to tell you, she's
the fat lady- wailing all night, body hunched
over the juke box, whispering to the bartender,
it's- not over. The song is not over.

*

* You Are Dangerous

Sarah McKinstry-Brown

Because you look like my father
And you taste like water.

Because in this circus
You do not juggle flame or paint your face but
Pitch the tent;
Your sweat falls
Unnoticed on dirt;
Planting salty seeds to grow whole oceans
For the women you love to swim in;
So that
When you come to them,
Towel in hand
They will tell you,
Honestly,
Lungs at half mast in half
Sleep:

"I am doing swimmingly,"

And you'll both go under, breathless.

You are dangerous,
Bent on one knee, hell bent on loving me
While the earth around us spins about,
Drunk on its own neon sermons and nursery
   Rhymes,
You wait,

Full of silence,
A piano in the palm of a wheat field at dusk;
This is hardly common,
And you have everything in common with
   dreams;
It is thus your eloquent bones
Startle me.

For now,
I am miles from you.
By day, I wade through strange cities;
By night, I sit in motel rooms
In the company of bad art and unsent postcards;
And if all I can be to you is a memory:
Remember me,
A still life of woman in want of your company,
Return to me again and again.
Because tonight, even the moon
Is on your side;
Persistent, she wills her light into my window,
A floodlight burning your skyline into my
   heart.

*

* Eulogy for Gregory Hines

Ed Mabrey

You were haunted by the ghosts Ellison spoke of
Those schizophrenic melodies are the soundtrack to your lineage

Bo Jangle/ begat Scatman/ begat Sandman/ begat Sammy/ begat You

People will start tap conversations off with Savignon causing erroneous understanding just like
    writers whom start poetry with Saul and forget Umar
or acting with Denzel and ignore Robeson
or sports with Jordan passing over Ashe
or jazz with Coltrane when they mean to say Cannonball
or r&b with Marvin when they really mean Jimi

I was there Gregory-
    You got to a gig
    The airline had lost your shoes/ you asked if anyone had extras
    A brother who claimed to live nearby ran off to get his
    While we waited you sat and discussed the entire history of tap
    With the audience like we were your children being tucked in...

    When he returned, shoes in hand, you put them both on, noticed one shoe
    (the left) was too tight and too worn out so rather than give a half ass show,
    you tapped the entire night on one good shoe-
    first doing what the left foot would do, then the right

I was there when you put taps on a pair of Air Jordans and battled with Savignon while Reg E Gaines
    did his piece de resistance *'Please don't steal my Air Jordans'* and the whole floor was set aflame
    by the torch that got passed that evening

The only time I saw my grandfather cry
You were tapping in a church while Aretha Franklin sang

When I asked him why he was sad,
he told me he could see my ancestors on that stage dancing right with you
"There's power in the wood boy," he said "and spirits in your feet."

You got me into ballet and classical music
See, I watched you in some movie with this big time Russian cat and you held your own
It was the cold war, fallout shelters were a reality and a black man was taking on an entire country
    with his mind, words and feet

You kicked Barishnikov in the gut and Gorbachev flinched, Reagan smirked, Thurgood Marshall
    laughed behind closed doors, Ali froze and my mother grabbed my face with both her hands and
    tears in her eyes and said,
"Don't ever let them mistake your kindness for weakness. They step on one foot, offer the other"
I thought I understood...it's like offering a cheek

But what I've learned in 33 years is this-
Offering one cheek after the other has been struck
is only a temporary pain that breaks no barrier
But for someone to step on your foot and you offer them the other as well,
effectively stopping your momentum in life is to defy man
there is strength in those legs of yours
and if you jump up right out of those shoes into the air,
at the peak of your leap of faith God will grant you wings to fly unencumbered
and you can land on clouds doing the last deliberate soft shoe

I see you up there, sneaking on Jesus' sandals when he's sleeping
stealing moves from Satan when he's too drunk to notice

I tell people it wasn't cancer that got you
It was hoof and mouth disease
You grew tired of taking your foot out of peoples mouths
Tapping won't get you anywhere- but it did
You can't act-you did
You can't sing- but you did

You can't be with a woman other than black and still be loved and accepted
as black by blacks- but you did

A hoofer's wish is that when they die they die on their feet-
And you did

Oh, I know your body was on a hospital bed
But your mind was taking all those sounds
Those subsonic conversations
Spoken on levels beyond our understanding
And turned them into your final tap

Drip drop goes the iv
Beep beep goes the heart monitor
Click click goes the emergency call button
Pitter pat goes the nurses running feet
Amen goes the preacher
God bless goes the family
Come home says the sandman
Drip drip goes the iv
Beep beep goes the heart monitor
Click click goes the call button
Ring ring goes the phone
Eyes glaze over I'm going home
Come home says the sandman
Gabriel done called you out
Someone say challenge
Drip drip
Beep beep goes the flatline

*

Jazz Funeral

Chuck Perkins

The very soft slow
Euphonic rhythm of the Jazz band ripens the atmosphere
And a myriad of screams shots and tears seem to blend in with the solemn music
Almost as if the horns and drums had a melodious cry of their own
With a forty ounce in one hand
And a cigarette in another
To calm my nerve and sooth my soul
Along with the others
I gently rock from side to side
As the young brother's casket is brought from the sanctuary of the church
To the back of a Hearse
Where we all began to prepare for his last dance
His last ride
His last party

The African sisters who nurtured this man child are having fits
Because at seventeen you can't help but think of what he could have been
But today he's just dead
Another young, misguided, misdirected warrior
Whose life has been snatched from within his breast
Permanently, forever, for nothing

The precession has started and the crying has become more intense
And as we move away from the church the euphonic rhythm has changed
It is no longer soft and sad
It is now
Wild, happy, and in a sense a little mad

When you throw you hands in the air
And gracefully and emphatically

Move your body in a way that only Africans can
An unpatterned way that's natural to you and flow with the music
Down in New Orleans we call that the second line

Our body's language says to this young brother
That this dance is for you
yes this last dance is for you
We dance so that your last vision of us can be a happy one
As we party past the housing project
It is the last time to see your playground
And battlefield
This vicious, brutal, familiar enclave of blackness
Where you endured much pain and hate
Mingled with laughter and love
It's the last time to see rough, happy, innocent, nappy head little
Boys on their bikes
Who remind you so much of yourself
When you were ten and innocent
The last time to see the old sisters sitting on the porches
Becoming wiser by the day
And the old brothers sitting in front of the liquor stores
Reminiscing about what could have been
It is the last time to see your life and your world
And because of that
We stomp today
We cry today
We dance today
Yes we dance today

And when we get to the candy store
The place were your life was quickly halted
The euphonic rhythm changes yet again
This time the music and the people are in a frenzy
They dance like this will be the last time we all get to see our maker
And as the music pounds, and thumps and blares

And draws us all emotionally into this intense moment

12 of your best homies remove your casket from the Hearse

And in a way equivalent to the white boys hip hip hooray

Your boys thrust your casket to the sky and they take it down

And thrust it again

Triumphantly, angrily, repeatedly

As if to say to your assassin

Mutherfucker

You can't touch now

Not your guns

Not your bullets

Can't touch him now

However in the mist of this frenzy

The roaring sound of a hot bullet rips through the air

Perhaps this is assassin's rebuttal

This bullet must also sound like the fat lady

Cause the party's over

African, brothers sisters and babies seek refuge

Desperately trying to avoid their last dance

But deep down inside we all know

That we will dance again

Again soon

*

The Good News

Matt Mason

"Tell the good news about Jesus"
—a bumper sticker I followed
for a long time

Jesus lent me ten bucks when I forgot my
    wallet at lunch.
Sure, he could've ordered a chicken pesto
    sandwich
and broke it into two full meals, but he's no
    show off.
That's what I like about Jesus.

Jesus listens to cool music. If it weren't for
    Jesus,
I never would have known about Tom Waits
or Ani DiFranco, and I sure wouldn't own any
    Lyle Lovett.
But Jesus makes a kickass mix tape.

Jesus loves cows,
thinks my poems with cows in them are a hoot
and encourages me
to look at herds of white cows
in a green field
and imagine salvation
is underneath each windmill.

Jesus tells me Pat Robertson's right,
and so is Al Sharpton.
That they're both wrong, too,

but that's not the point.
His point's how God's sewn into every fabric.
Even yourself. Even Elvis.

Jesus saves and Jesus recycles.

Jesus eats fish for more
than Omega-3 fatty acids,
drinks red wine for more reasons
than his sacred heart.

Jesus doesn't dress like the Medieval paintings
with the gold hats and the Mr. T rosaries.
Sure, he can clean up nice,
but Jesus likes blue jeans.

Jesus pisses me off
with his honesty
sometimes.
But it's not like he's ever wrong.

Jesus makes a killer chianti,
but he refuses to turn water
into Diet Coke for me.
"What's the difference?" he asks.

Jesus acts real serious
when somebody rushes up to him hollering,
    "Jesus,
can you take me up to Heaven,

I will see you in the Kingdom, Jesus!"
Jesus says they should get their kumbayayas off
by putting on some overalls
and hammering in the morning.
May as well make Heaven bigger,
not just your egos.

Jesus digs the "How does Jesus eat M&M's"
    joke.
He won't do it at a party, but he did do it once
when just the two of us were watching cartoons.

Jesus wanted me to tell you he loves you.
Jesus also wants you to stop doing that thing.

Jesus tells me I'm saved.
Then he laughs real loud.
Jesus makes me nervous when he does that.

*

Letters from a Young Poet

By Young Male Poet

Letter #1
Dear Loyal Publishers,

Another cruel joke by The Maker Of All Things at my expense. As is my custom, I 'Google' myself a couple times a year to keep track of my career outside of the university. I discovered two very curious listings which I followed. To my surprise, there is this "community" or something online called "Live Journal" within which people make regular postings of their goings-ons and whatnot. Somebody, via an anthology within which I've been published, discovered my romance poems and wrote a short story based upon one and posted it to some acclaim. At first, I was excited, because I thought that it might mean some henceforward opportunity for fornication – and, more broadly, that anyone gives a shit at all, which is nice. As it turns out: THE STORY IS AN X-RATED HOMOEROTIC TALE WHICH DETAILS UNSPEAKABLE ACTS BETWEEN HARRY POTTER AND SOMEBODY NAMED DRACO.

Who is Draco? Everybody that commented on the story agreed that the poem (which, at least, they liked) was "so H/D" - apparently there is this entire sub-culture of gay men in England who write fictional stories that describe homosexual unions between characters that their originators would never write. *Harry Potter* is big, and so is *Smallville* - Clark and Lex, it seems, is big. I do not understand. Jesus is laughing his divine ass right off and into the toilet of my feculent love life.

As a consolation prize, there is some teenage girl on the East coast that likes another poem of mine. No mention of sodomy, but her prose is hilarious. Give it a read.
Enjoy. That is, when you are not feeding children or making money like grown-ups do.

In other news, I am considering taking two years or so away from my English major so that I can learn German, French, Latin, and Classical Greek. I have become frustrated with not being able to fully read texts.

Hope all is well.
Young Male Poet
P.S. I have not smoked in 16 days, and have only killed four strangers.

*

The first time I talked to Ted on the phone
He told me I had the voice of a phone sex operator
and I had to wonder,
Was that a compliment?
How would he know?
Is he right?
Am I missing out on a financial opportunity?
The phone rings with unexpected requests
Dominatrix
School teacher
Drill Sargent with big boobs
little boobs
skinny waste
welcoming ass
whips and chains
cocktail waitress
french maid
stranger on a plane
female boss
lesbian
gang banger
complete slut
girl next door
"Tell me what you want baby"
I'd whisper
and listen
"Tell me what you're doing baby"
and listen
hearing moans
and groans
zippers and screams

"you're such a bad boy"
"you're such a good boy"
"you're such a naughty boy"
"you're such a big boy"
I could lie like the best of them
faking oohs and mmms and
oh my gods
faking orgasms
faking emotion
faking everything.
Then I imagine myself
fuzzy slippers in the air
face covered in cream,
cucumbers over my eyes
phone held between neck and shoulder
trying to give these men what they want
I can't give them what they want
I don't think I can handle hearing what they want
without laughing
spilling my drink
kicking my cat in the air
meows screeching
phone dropping
man stops talking
and I pick up.
"wow baby, that was the best ever"
I'd say out of breathe.
Ok. so maybe I could lie just a little.

*

Letters from a Young Poet

By Young Male Poet

Letter #2

Dear Loyal Publishers,

Well, I suppose the chances were about one hundred percent. My poem has been used again - now for a Clark Kent/Lex Luther coupling. I think the story was called "Bruised Knees" or something. Someone has incorporated the entire poem onto her homepage. I am huge in Live Journal land. There seems to be an opportunity here. These chicks or whatnot have gotten this from an anthology - if they were to discover that there's a lot more poetry to be expropriated from my actual book, then maybe my treatise on how to be the hugest pussy ever can also sell 40k copies. Imagine the news ripping, exponentially, through the homocentric fanfic blogosphere - there could be Harry/Draco stories based on all my failed romances, *in perpetua ad nauseum*! Big money.

So here, maybe, is a plan. I will join livejournal as "sassymichelle" or something and let everybody know that there's lots more senti-swill available in the guise of the book, and tell them that they should buy it immediately. We take fifty books (or a million), and I'll cross out my love's name with a black sharpie and replace it with "Lex" or "Draco" - these we can send to Amazon for distribution. Then we watch the money roll in until we are septil-lionaires. Then I can drop out of school and start smoking again - I'll just buy new lungs from the third world whenever I wear a pair out. Heaven.

In the meantime, I hope that you find sleep superfluous and the sound of screaming infants a pleasant and relaxing song.

Assesquely,
Young Male Poet

*

*Slut

Daphne Gottlieb

i die first
in every horror movie,
before the innocent boyfriend, the too-
curious best friend
and the foolhardy pal.
death comes blind fast
and easy, familiar as the top button of
my blouse popping open
and suddenly i'm an angel
on the cutting room
floor, wearing gore,
a blank stare, not much
more.

i do it over and over.
i can play
like this for hours.

sometimes i enter a dark
room and unbutton
my shirt, rock my hips
side to side
until the killer's music comes on.
then I button up
quick, laughing or
shaking, sometimes
both.

from the way i look
after i'm split open

you'd never know:
i was born a baby.
i still sleep
with my stuffed poodle.
her name is "tammy."
after my parents divorced, i wet
the bed for a year.
i want to be a nurse.
my favorite color is blue.

first kiss at 12,
first shame at 13,
first blood at 14.
skipped four years
of gym, skimmed just the tips
of my stepfather's
fingers, nothing more.
i never took my clothes off
for a doctor but my body
became a secret
handshake
all the boys knew
and i didn't.
the ghost story
made me a ghost.

now, at 16,
i only remember my own
skin when i am touched.
it makes me real

when i strip down,
take it off, find the edges of my body
through your eyes or under
your hands, against your skin.
it feels like death
every time you
stop.

there is nothing i can do
except open my throat
and say the word for girls
who are the ghosts of want:

"slut."
i'll take my shirt off
while you watch—

call it love
when the knife rips
through my ribs,
when the ice pick cracks
my chest, or however
it happens this time
but first

here's my prayer:
that what happens to girls like me
who die dirty, give it up
with a shudder like pleasure—
pray that when we're killed as martyrs
we get loved like saints.

Letter My Dad Never Gave Me

Corbet Dean

Yes, I am a police officer,
but I'm not going to help you become one, too.
If you think my job is fun, son, you really need
    to know
that every single cop...becomes an asshole!

Believe me, I didn't start that way.
Back on my graduation day,
I raced to the academy to join my new, dark
    blue family.
Like an infantry of wide-eyed, wannabe soldiers,
we shaved our heads, then glared at the sun;

like a flock of fuzzy eaglets, we were all over-
    anxious
to strap on white, round helmets
and charge out of the academy like scrubbing
    bubbles
sent to sanitize the streets!

Yet in a matter of weeks,
I absorbed an acidic smell that splashed me
    like gasoline.
I might be scrubbing...
but I never quite get clean.

For example, consider my last conversation
     with Daryl,
our neighborhood smack fiend:
Daryl called at two in the morning to claim
     some girl
took a tennis racquet to his three-year-old boy

three weeks before.
"Damn, Daryl, this better be your dope talking."

Daryl waited with my partner
while I started walking a nearby alley in the
     rain.
When I came to the sewer drain, I dropped my
     light,
so I don't think anyone saw me
drop in the dirt, dig in the drain, and touch
the torn, rotted flesh
of a beautiful, broken, black baby boy
who never expected the asshole cop
would be the last one on earth to cradle him
     close
and kiss his cheek.

So you still want my job, son?

Then try to console a sobbing, single mother
who just found vaginal tears
on her two-year-old daughter.

How well can you lie?

Tell mom her baby will be just fine,
tell her to believe in justice,

or tell her the truth about what she's done:
in her hurry to clean her baby's blood
from her brother's salty, warm, infected cum,
she just washed away the evidence.
Now no one will do a day for this crime.
No matter what you say this time, son,
you're going to feel like you just renounced
     your soul,
so go home.

Take a bath, bask in the beautiful fragrance of
     naiveté,
understanding
there's an awful lot of death in life
no one should see.
I need you to leave that world to me—
not because I'm selfish,
but because I believe
I've become the asshole
I never wanted
you to be.

 *

Letters from a Young Poet

By Young Male Poet

Letter #3
Dear Loyal Publishers,

An update about which you will not care, but which has made me feel less cursed: There is apparently some "movement" out there called "slash literature" - the "slash" denotes the slash in something like "H/D", i.e., Harry/Draco or Clark/Lex - they are usually fictions about men fucking men (or boys fucking boys) based upon popular characters. But here's the catch ... they are usually authored by teen-aged girls. I learned this today from a professor, who apparently has her finger on the pulse of contemporary rhetorical movements. For whatever reason (that is to say: "because of my pathology"), I am more comfortable with female teens commandeering my poetry for their homoerotic porn fantasies than gay men of whatever age commandeering my poetry for their homoerotic porn fantasies. What is the difference, you may ask? In a word, *frenulum labiorum pudendi.*

I thought I'd pass this along to you because I know that neither of you have anything important going in your lives, and that you have extra time to read this swill. Also, it somehow makes my artistic life seem less pathetic - more dangerous perhaps, but less caustic - and I wanted to share my special moment.

I hope that you are all well in all possible ways, and that your Superior Halves (to whom I also send my warmest pornless regards) are lactating (or have lactated, or will lactate) in a supportive and nurturing environment, free from the pains of mammary congestion, and spousal abuse.

With love when available,
Young Male Poet

*

Ophelia's Technicolor G-String: * An Urban Mythology

Susan B.A. Somers-Willett

The air tonight is thick as curry;
like every night this summer I could cut it
with my wine glass, spray it with mace.
Over and over it would heal together
like a wound, follow my click and pace of heels
down Conti Street, St. Ann, Bourbon.

Oh Hamlet, if you could see me now
as I pump and swagger across that stage, cape dripping to the floor,
me in three-inch heels and a technicolor G-string—
you would not wish me in a convent.
They've made me a queen here, married me off
to a quarter bag and a pint of gin.

The old men tend bark and splatter, rabid
at each table. I think they stay up all night
just to spite the moon. They bring their diseased
mouths to the French Market in the morning,
sell Creole tomatoes to tourists who don't know
what they are. Each bald head shines plump and red.

It seems like so long ago that I modeled
for those legs outside of Big Daddy's—
the ones over the door that swing *in, out, in, out*—
the sculptor made me painted as Mardi Gras.
I thought you might recognize them if you ever passed
with the boys, parading from Abbey to Tavern,
or think them royal feet in need of slippers.

Someday I expect to find you here,
sitting at the table between the first and second rows,

fingering bones or something worse.
And in the end you will throw me a columbine,
light me a Marlboro and take me to a 24-7 where
jukebox light quivers, makes us as thin as ghosts.

But for now, I will dance for the fat man
who sits in your place and sweats his love for me at 3 A.M.,
because only he knows I am Horatio in drag.

*

Undressing Virginia Dare

Victor D. Infante

Begin at the top:
Stuttering fingers
undo simple buttons,
fumbling at your collar,
afraid to touch pale skin.

Then another. It's a simple garment:
Wool bodice dyed red, it falls easily
onto the forest's underbelly, fabric
sinking into the dirt and nestles,
tentative, calloused hands glide
up your back, undo the ribbon
of your linen shirt, then descending

palms tugging at your waist,
ankle-length petticoats unsuited here,
the New World pulls you close,
until your breaths are intermingled,
strips you of history, transforms you
into a deer, a story,
a destination carved into a tree,
vanished entirely.

*

*On Poet Paula L. Friedrich

Jack Foley

These excerpts (this essay and one on Beau Sia later in this section) are from an article I wrote in 2000, when the entire Seattle slam team—including Paula L. Friedrich—was staying in my home. The team was competing in the National Teen Poetry Slam Championships, where Beau Sia performed. The entire article is available in my forthcoming book, *The Dancer and the Dance* (Red Hen Press). Though I am a performance poet and have given hundreds of readings, I feel that "slam" and "spoken word" are essentially assertions of the individual ego: this is what *I* think, these are *my* feelings. The problem with this notion of "individuality" is basically that it isn't true—which is why so many "individuals" end up saying exactly the same things! The "ego" of "individuality" is the ego generated by mass culture; it isn't real. And, unfortunately, that's the ego most often presented in both slam poetry and spoken word.

Paula L. Friedrich gave me a copy of her chapbook, *Exotic Plants*. Friedrich, a graduate of the Creative Writing/Poetry program at Oberlin, has represented Seattle on three National Poetry Slam teams. She was also Board President of the Seattle Poetry Slam and performs with the ensemble, *A Slip of the Tongue*. Though I didn't hear her read, I was aware that she has been extremely involved in slam, and I was curious about her book. Questions like "Is it really poetry?" and "Does it communicate on the page?" seem to me, frankly, of little consequence, but here was a book by someone deeply involved in slam. What was it like?

Exotic Plants is divided into three sections, "Confessions I Would not Make to a God," "Medusa's Diner," and "Taking Apart Tinkerbell." It is roughly chronological, beginning with a poem dealing with the author's childhood and ending with a poem about the adult poet living in Seattle. *Exotic Plants* may betray its slam roots by the frequent appearance of the pronoun "I," which appears perhaps more than any other word in the book. Like the work I heard at the slam, Friedrich's book has nothing in it that can be called "experimental."

The word "Confessions" suggests the focus of the first section, "Confessions I Would not Make to a God." These poems are indeed "confessional," with echoes of Plath and others:

> I am up the cherry tree
> with my new, blue dress on.
>
> Grandma Omi will make *Kirschentorte*,
> and say *meine Susse*, my sweetie,
> like she always does.
>
> Daddy bought wooden paddles with a rubber ball
> to bang around outside the apartment
> until my brother and I rang the bell and said
> *ich mocte ins Haus gehen bitte*,
> door buzzed through the speaker   *ja, ja.*

Apart from the odd placement of the comma after "new"—perhaps a typo—this is competent, carefully written verse, but it is little more than that. It is also a *kind* of poem we have seen and heard very, very often. A subtext of this kind of writing is always, "See, I am writing a poem: this is like other poems you've read—so you can recognize it—but it is also different because it has my particular subject matter, my life." Unfortunately, the particularities of the life are not sufficiently present to lift the poem into something really memorable. For the most part it is a poem, not bad, but one of many. The concluding lines—particularly "Little hearts that drop from my hands"—move towards something more genuinely touching:

> I wanted the cherries
> from the tree in Germany.
> Little hearts that drop from my hands
> to my dress, which
>   Omi will wash today.

Friedrich's poems—like successful slam poetry in general?—often have a "twist" at the end that makes you reconsider everything. This is also true of Beau Sia's work. If your poem is going to be judged, you want a strong ending—something that will ring in the judges' ears as you close.

Friedrich's confessional section explores childhood experience, the "family romance" ("the young girls who like their fathers so much, you know,/they never get married..."), ethnicity ("Mark of the Mongol"), religion and sex, youthful friendship; it concludes in Seattle, where the poet now lives. The themes are familiar—which is fine if you've never experienced them—but they are hardly examples of Pound's directive to "make it new." As I suggested earlier, these poems are competently written but not spectacular; they have the feeling of apprenticeship—as if Friedrich were learning her trade through them.

The poems in the concluding two sections include several references to myths—which is not something I heard in the slam—and the poet at times takes on various personae, though the assertion of the "I" remains a theme:

> I am Eurydice teasing you into hell.
> Your slumber mutters from the mattress.
> I baptize the precipice,   you slide....

There are also comic poems ("Lego Woman") and fanciful ones ("If M. C. Escher Were My Lover,/We'd Never Have Time for Pizza"). For me, by far the finest work in the book is the concluding poem, "Persephone." Friedrich's placement of the poem suggests that she understands its strength; as I've said, a slam poet is aware of the need for a good ending.

> In the light, my nails are bloody from too many pomegranate
> seeds.
> I guzzle milk like moonbeams; turn blinds for the amaryllis,
> swing children onto my hips, squeeze snot from their nostrils,
> watch them grow.
>
> Mother, I transplanted my roots to a water-drenched city.
> You would rip them if you could face
>   some rapacious, stinking god
> with a spear.

But when the sun is done with the exposition of all dark
corners,
I screw my face into question marks,
exclamation points,   our fingers dragons or whales
we darken sidewalks,   tides;

sleep until two becomes one.

Feel free to fly here,
                    after three.

Everything in this breakthrough poem seems magical and enigmatic. For the first time in the book we come face to face with mystery. The "I" is of course present, but it seems to open itself into a darkness we find nowhere else in *Exotic Plants*. Here, autobiographical and mythic elements touch: the "water-drenched city" is obviously Seattle, but the moon and blood suggest archetypal feminine experience. Persephone, of course, lives half of the year in hell, underground—and she has been "raped." The poem is not exactly "accessible" but it stays with us for a long time, nudging us into an awareness which is never specific but constantly alive.

What do the concluding lines mean? Are they an assertion of freedom ("Feel free to fly here") followed by the assertion of a limitation: "after three"? The poem is like—in Keats' terms—a sudden influx of Negative Capability after a book full of the Egotistical Sublime, and it brings us perhaps to another insight about slam. Slam is a wonderful way to experience the rituals and observances of poetry and to see oneself as participating in those rituals. But poetry needs to *transcend* its rituals. It is possible that every feeling of individual freedom eventually transforms itself into a burden from which, once again, we need to be freed. Slam gave the teenagers who visited me something they will always remember—and which I will always remember—but perhaps it is finally something they need to leave behind. Poetry is frequently represented as winged. "Feel free to fly here," writes Friedrich: Freedom. "After three": Limitation. Friedrich's concluding poem transcends not only the limitations of her book but probably of slam poetry as well. It will be interesting to see what becomes of her, and it.

*what Legitimizes Poems

Paula L. Friedrich

Several years ago, I was surprised when Jack Foley published a review of an unfinished chapbook I gave him to read, *Exotic Plants*. Equally surprising is this opportunity to respond to the review, which I wish more artists could do, as I think it creates more dialogue around art and greater accountability from its critics.

Foley examines two poems in the chapbook. Despite his loud drumming that this a review of a slam poet, "Cherry Tree" is the oldest poem in the collection, written around 1991 when I was twenty-one years old and had never even heard of slam poetry. The crux of Foley's critique is that the "life" in the poem is unremarkable and that it isn't peculiar enough. Perplexing...as the intent of this piece does not involve peculiarity. Rather, it is an attempt to find the voice of a vulnerable child caught in a complicated moment and its resulting reverberations.

Just before he discusses the piece, Foley compares my work in this section to Sylvia Plath, yet gives no reason why. It is unclear if he is insinuating that since "Cherry Tree" is set in Germany and I am writing a confessional poem, I am somehow echoing Plath's "Daddy." In case such a one-dimensional connection is being drawn, either deliberately or carelessly, I would like to point out that unlike Plath, my father is German and I am not citing Germany as a hypothetical but as my earthly (early) reality.

Foley ends by praising "Persephone," a rather bitter and regretful poem that's too witty for its own good. Like "Cherry Tree," this piece was not written with slam in mind and has never been read at a slam. Yet Foley claims "Persephone" as a metaphor to illustrate his own ponderings on my relationship to slam poetry.

My best guess about the meaning of this review is that Foley prefers a specific kind of poetry—one that adheres to his definition of what is truly transcendent literature. It's an age-old question really: Is your art as legitimate as mine? KBCS 90.3 FM in Seattle aired an interview segment entitled "Hip Hop verus Spoken Word," in which local artists were addressing the question of whether spoken word was more literary or intellectual than hip hop. It was an excellent discussion that examined social and historical phenomena influencing the perceived legitimacy of one form of art over another.

Foley's review, however, is unenlightening as to what legitimizes poems in his eyes. He does not consider what my poems want to do, only what he wants them to do. On that note, I'm quite comfortable with my continued cherry picking, even if it's a little ordinary for the likes of Foley and his particular longing for Pound cake.

* Ode to Pablo Neruda

Paula L. Friedrich

Your mouth carries whole nights and days.

In twilight, I hear the birch peeling of your voice.
As the sun rises, I call your animals by name:
Jaguar, Rat, Parrot, Panther.

At noon, I cut my teeth
on the first pear of your thoughts. I wait
for your book to let me go.

I am a drunken bee
pawing the edge of a champagne glass.

After a long nap with you on my chest, I awake to tearing linen,
parachutes falling into labyrinths,
a bearded washcloth on my face,
your syllable tides on my feet,
my back in the sand.

Reaching into the page for meat,
I wonder if it's possible to fall in love
with imagination or with everything I can't resist:

running my hands through bowls
of dusty rice,
the sound of grass cracking,
my tongue in the pan,
the footstep percussion of hallways,
the nasal tinge of gasoline,
each mountain perused from a distance,
eyes of horses, water spreading its legs
before the bow of a boat,
the minor note, chipping silver,
poisonously perfect leaves,
squares of sugar, the feel of table
grains under palm, sitting in clouds
and pulling them around my body
the burning idea at the center of the earth
pumping mantle, plate, crust, and ocean,
foliage, swamp, marble and ice...
but there you are;

the beginning note and the final note,
the last two fingers of wine,
the fresh tomato,

the teeth behind the untouchable lips.

*

conquered, colonized, colonialized

Beau Sia

written by my mother, as writing device

dear audience,

my son agreed to perform this, so that I,
an immigrant, could have a voice.

he does not understand this.
he has never had to leave
all that he knew and loved
in order to survive.
he is soft. he is a tourist.
he will not drink tap water.

this is not for him. this is for the Philippines.

and even though
I have not seen much of the world,
I believe that
what I have to share
is relevant to many people.

thank you for listening.
forgive the translation.

yours,
Elizabeth Sia

(and now, the poem)

welcome to the third world, bitches!

too late to run now!
you gave us visas to do
what you thought was beneath you.

importing us to build your cities,
nanny your children,
and nurse your fragile, antibiotic bodies.

your ikea prices fucked
our minimum wage,
and we are tired of sleeping
where your waste is sent, so we comin' over.
and you can't do shit.
your children are too spoiled
to stop the "immigration problem."

our, "may I take your order,"
sends euros, pounds, dollars, and yen back
    home.

gives our uncles houses with doors,
our children education with computers,
and our communities relief
beer cannot provide.

the first world taught the third world
how to use other countries
in order to benefit the motherland,

so we gonna colonize you.

from Brixton to the Bay,
Tokyo to Paris,
Sydney to Houston.

we learns fast and we breeds faster.

the generation cleaning your toilets
will beget the generation doing your taxes,
will beget your son-in-law.

we've learned to adapt without
a balanced diet,
and we ain't forgettin' the deaths
that brought us here.

thank you for teaching us capitalism.

now let us teach you something
your salary could not.

you
live
in a
world.

you've chosen to win at the expense
of someone else's loss.

you've allowed which is the same as doing.
and your most favored nation status
has only gained you boredom, terrorism,
and high speed internet access.

we are going to serve you
until you realize
that we ain't just here to serve you.

we're gonna colonize the first world,
until you can't ignore us
just by going click.

until our children stop being seen
as the enemy.

until the first world
stops seeing the third world
as a different place.

*

On Poet Beau Sia

Jack Foley

This is the poem Beau Sia put on the cover of his book, *a night without armor II: the revenge.* On the cover the poem looks like a piece of graffiti:

I DON'T CARE WHAT YOU THINK
ABOUT THE WAY I WRITE
I DIE ON THE PAGE
EVERY TIME. WHAT
DO YOU KNOW
ABOUT PUSH-UPS?
TRUE LOVE?
PRESSURE?
AT NIGHT I LIE
IN MY QUEEN-SIZE
BED ALONE. DREAMING
ABOUT IGNOBLE
THINGS. I AM NOT
FANCY. I AM NOT SPECIAL
I AM BETTER THAN YOU.
I AM ALONE. I AM THE
PRODUCT.

The number of I's in that poem is characteristic of much of the emotional push of slam poetry. Gertrude Stein nailed it many years ago when she wrote, "Look at me now and here I am." Much of Sia's poem is a statement of pretty straight, not-too-thoughtful adolescent angst—or at least what our culture usually puts forth as adolescent angst. For males of my generation, such angst was embodied by writers like Thomas Wolfe and J. D. Salinger, movies like *Rebel Without a Cause*, and figures such as James Dean and Elvis Presley. It's easy enough to recognize: "I AM NOT/FANCY. I AM NOT SPECIAL/I AM BETTER THAN YOU./I AM ALONE."

But if Sia gives us adolescence in a readily packaged, easily recognizable form, he also gives us little surprises that jolt us and force us to recognize that we are dealing with something far more genuine here. When he writes, "I DIE ON THE PAGE/EVERY TIME. WHAT/DO YOU KNOW/ABOUT..." we expect the next word to be "ME," but in fact it's "PUSH-UPS." Similarly, the word "PRODUCT" at the end of the poem is completely unexpected. Sia is giving the adolescent audience what it believes it wants—a mirror of what it believes it's like—but, at the same time, he is ahead of the audience, moving it into a genuine experience of language.

* Delilah and Samson

Michael Kadela

Sonnet: A fourteen-line poem usually written in iambic pentameter, focusing on one theme. The Shakespearean sonnet, or English sonnet, has three quatrains (stanzas) with a concluding couplet (concluding two lines).

Delilah softly unto Samson sang
sweet melodies which raised the strength of
   sin;
for through the crypts of Samson's spirit rang
the countless empty temples loud within.

This judge whose sinew bested unjust men
re-wrested stoically the luring psalm,

dispatched the quick to rate and quake again,
to remonstrate with some forsaken qualm.

As hymn and echoed hymn with time accrue,
so will with time forbearances abate.
As with one jaw one thousand men he slew,
so with one song she softly tenders fate.

Thus Samson razed with will his strength and
   found
that heaven sang his locks upon the ground.

*

Epithalamion

Michael Kadela

Epithalamion: a poem written to honor a wedding, some reference to the 'bridal chamber' is in the Greek etymology. In contemporary poetics, E.E. Cummings' book Tulips and Chimneys *helped reintroduce the form with his poem,* Epithalamion.

1.

Love
is ever
forward moving
into selflessness,
is ever only of itself,
is ever always only
one –
one
is the heart which suddenly
insists
that there may be
one only other one
for which to beat,
with which to make
anew a cadence green
as Eden might have boldly wished
to be;
love is ever steeply running
into alwaysness
(as easily as love may run);
love makes one of lonely
two –
two
are the voices who ever singing, sing
one single gorgeous note,
(are singing spring into the springing, singing)

all and everywhere,
one single gorgeous note
            unto the earnest firmament
        (where each to each's ears will soon confide
at highest peaks, what greater breath might instantly declare

that i will die joyously into your arms, smiling
            reverently conceding jubilantly entirely myself
        that I might be but one(so perfect)half
            of you);

    from mornings blue as seas will move,
    from scarlet dusks as suns will proudly bow,
    from these and from the eager pounding of our heart
    love will sire
    an
    irrevocable,
            indigo
        dawn;
    love is ever softly weaving wonder
            into tapestries,
        in colorful exquisities,
            that grace the light of day;
                and,

there is this love that knows (and most especially)
our exclusive eyes

        (in soft moment
        after moment soft,
    love will kiss our lashes lost,
            so
            splendiferously

            lost ,

    in this miracle of us);

love is not for isnot, ever,
and love is never for neveris;
love is never for refuse
and
love is never at defeat;
love will gladly spit despondent faces wet
and happily explain one million simple things
away,
and leaving only perfect sense, will dance
the sweet(and(so meticulous)so)obviousness of our kisses' wake;

love is never rarely singing anything
    but symphonies,
to bluntly fill the silent rooms
with our mighty choruses –

with the loud and fantastic sound of our embrace,
with the murmurings complacent of a placid sea reclining still
    beneath our nearly silent breath,
with the deafening stampede of your anxious eyes upon our touch,
with the ennobled roar of the morning star
    just above your shoulder, sleeping,

love is ever coyly wooing,
love is ever gently cooing,
love is never wrongly doing anything at all
as
love is ever all it ever has to be
:
always is love spontaneously only love.

Thus,

may we venture with our hearts and hands entwined
into the great remaining of our ready lives

*

Epithalamion:
A Few Words for Kathleen

Jack McCarthy

We're here today to celebrate
the wedding of Kathleen and Mark.

Kathleen, when she was eight years old,
started coming with me to my Friday night
    meetings.
That group had really good coffee, and as she
made her way, time after time, to the coffeepot,
I would lose sight of Kathleen, because she was
    short;
but I could follow her progress by watching the
    heads
turn to bless her with their eyes as she passed,
beautiful child that she was, and I knew that
    she was
beaming back at them with a beatific expression
that said, "I know I shouldn't be drinking all this
    coffee
at my age—but I'm getting *away* with something
    here."

At the break they'd raffle off a Big Book,
and when the meeting broke up, Kathleen
would go from table to table collecting
all the discarded raffle tickets, which she would
bring home and store in a shoebox.
Why? I never figured it out.

Up came my anniversary and my sponsor
was out of town, so I asked Kathleen
if she'd be willing to say a few words
in front of a roomful of adults and she was game—

Kathleen was always game. She had to stand
on a chair to reach the microphone,
and if I remember right, what she said was,
"It is always an occasion when someone
    celebrates
their eleventh anniversary. Jack?"

And if I had been expecting something a little
    more—
what? personal? still, it was a great beginning
for a ten-year run. The next year she didn't
need the chair, and she wrote a poem that
    began,
"My dad is the best/he's been that way since
    birth/
It's a shame there's only one of him/on the
    planet earth."

Kathleen's presence those Friday nights lit up
that big gymnasium, and a lot of people who
never got to watch their own kids grow up
came to look forward to her presentations
as a highlight of their year.

Tom G., who couldn't go with us when
we put on meetings in prisons, because
he always set off the metal detectors ,
because he had a police bullet lodged
inoperably close to his spine, said to me,
"That kid is the best advertisement
for this program that anyone could ever see."
And Billy T., a former three-hundred pound biker,

told me he had a daughter Kathleen's age—
somewhere, and that every year he cried at
her presentation—but it was the *good* crying.

Now it's my turn to say a few words for
    Kathleen—
but she's tied my hands a little,
made me promise not to make her cry.
So I'll address my comments to the groom.

Probably most fathers of the bride, if they were
    honest,
would admit that they don't think there's young
    man
in the world who's worthy of their little girl.
I want Mark to know that I don't feel that way—
particularly.

What I am sure of is that Kathleen and Mark
have been extraordinarily lucky to find each
    other.
It's crazy out there, and it seems to be getting
worse every day. Most of us feel fortunate to
    find
anyone willing to cast their lot with us, let alone
the *right* person. Today my heart is telling me
that this is right.

Now, Mark, about the dowry.
I'm afraid I have to ask to be dispensed from
    that
archaic tradition; it's not that I'm ungenerous,
just unemployed. But somewhere among

Kathleen's belongings, in a cellar
or an attic or at the bottom of a closet,
you might still find
a shoebox
full of raffle tickets
that didn't win anything.

If you find it, Mark, hang onto it. A lot of hopes
went into that box, the hopes of people whose
last names I never knew, people who didn't win
life's lotteries, didn't dodge all of life's bullets,
who once looked at Kathleen and took heart,
who loved her and left their tickets on the
    tables
in hope that they might be for her
tickets to a better life than they had had.

And any time you feel that
life's too hard, and you're too much alone,
take that box out and run your fingers
through those old raffle tickets,
mix them up real good,
and think about how much luck it takes
to find the one person in the world
that we were meant to find.

Then go to the kitchen and put on a pot of some
really good coffee—and make enough
for two people.

Sylvia Plath's Gangsta Rap Legacy

Jeremy Richards

Parody poem: a poem written as a humorous imitation of a literary work, with intended distortions and exaggerations of the original style.

Mack Daddy.
Mack Daddy you do not do.
Hootie hoo.

Every woman adores a playa'.
The crow casts his judgmental shadow
over my bootielisciousness
but you confess no less than this,
ghastly ghetto goo goo God.
I shall hit them with the hee,
by which I mean the inevitable decline
over time of my reflection in your chrome low
    rider,
hitting the cider like a rotting oak,
but not enough to cloak your disdain for me,
Mack Daddy,
Ach. Ach. Du.
Du hast mich.

In this picture I have of you,
the gold chains weigh you down
more than your confessions of contempt.

Come, tempt me with your fistfuls of dolla bills;
I have already swallowed the pills of your
    neglect,
and they taste like forty ounces of freedom

in the well of regret.

Dying is an art,
like everything else,
I do it, yeah do it,
do it until you can't take it no more.

Sometimes I like to shake my moneymaker,
sometimes I don't.
Sometimes I prefer to be all up in your stuff,
sometimes I don't.
Sometimes I like to cradle a razor blade like a
forgotten daughter,
sometimes I'd rather not.

I'm off the hook
because I've hung myself with the distance
between our voices.

Ash, ash...you talkin' trash?
Don't make me represent
what a vengeful God has sent
to accuse me of existence.
My penance is your weak-ass game.

You shall never tame me, Mack Daddy;
the calligraphy of scars across my heart
is fashioned from the grooves
I spin on the ones and the twos.

The pain in my soul, I bought it.

The burden in my womb, I bought it.
So throw your hands up at me,
and I will trace the lineage of your sins
spread across your palms like new veins,
diggity dig my grave with your breakfast
    spoon.
You know why I am Supa dupa fly, too,
but Mack Daddy you will not do, you will not

ever come close to gettin all my lovin',

Mack Daddy, if you can't stand the heat ...

then get yo' head out of the oven.

*

*T. S. Eliot's Lost Hip Hop Poem (excerpt)

Jeremy Richards

Let us roll then, you and I,
the evening stretched out against the sky
like a punk ass I laid out with my phat rhymes.

The eternal footman is no one to fuck with.
Alas, he shall bring the ruckus.

You think that you can step
to this, and Lo, I hear your steps like Lazarus
echoing through my soul.

Bring the bass.

Straight out of Missouri,
Harvard University in your face.
I've got ladies in waiting all over
the place, singing each to each;
do I dare eat a peach?

You are damn right I'll eat a peach.
Who shall stop me, with my hip-hop
non-stop, *clippity clop, clippity clop—*

I hear the horses carrying the wassailers!
I'm ready to impale their ears with my rhymes
rolling off of my parched tongue
like trousers roll off my ankles.

I get it done better than John Donne.
Pound for pound, like Ezra Pound,
No other literati around can confound
the post-Victorian quickness
I bring to the microphone.
Though I shall die alone.

But not before I rock the house.
Watch me douse you in my eternal flames
of a freaky-ass style, my crew has the know-
    how
with European tangent, *Kto vahsh otsiets
    saychoss—*
the Russian for, Who's your daddy now?

*

*Parody's Hidden Agenda *

Jeremy Richards

I first encountered T. S. Eliot in high school, and like many readers, I was entranced by "The Love Song of J. Alfred Prufrock" even as it remained beyond my reach. Soon, this poem suffered repeated recitals to girls I wanted to impress. But the depth of the work, with its fragments of narrative, allusion, anxiety, and elegy, still escaped me. In retrospect, I think this stunted understanding was due not to my poor reading aptitude but my simultaneous awe and fear of the work. I approached Eliot as a monolith of the literary canon, to be revered and never questioned.

When I first heard a recording of Eliot, I laughed out loud. By this point, I was in college and becoming more involved with improvisational theater. The practice of spontaneous storytelling merged with my studies in philosophy and literature, and soon I was riffing on Shakespeare, reassembling Plath, taking apart Aquinas, and forging an ontological proof of the existence of Santa. Eliot I heard not as an immortal orator, but as the grave, fragile man he was in the poem. Against this gravity, irony asserted itself, a paradox of distance and reacquaintance with the text. Perhaps my soft mockery of Eliot's persona was a bit juvenile, but the more I honed my parody, the more I got *inside* the process of the persona, and the more I followed that process, the more I understood.

Parody is the Trojan Horse of literature. We welcome it in with a chuckle, share it with a friend, and perhaps reflect lightly on the target of the joke, only to move on to work of more "substance." But if the satirist is effective, we discover something hatching beneath the surface of the humor, something in the juxtaposition that startles us into a new critical approach. A hip commentator may peg this as a "literary mash-up." But beyond an arbitrary mesh, I opt for the term *cross-pollination satire*, a method of weaving disparate elements not just for novelty, but to inform and comment in the execution.

In the case of *T. S. Eliot's Lost Hip-Hop Poem*, Eliot's poems and the conceits of hip-hop are rendered equally absurd, albeit with a healthy irreverence that holds its subjects in high regard even as it skewers them. Here is where parody strives toward more than caprice. In the contrast of Eliot's self-effacing nature and hip-hop's unbridled brio, the tension forces a rupture and relief not only in the humor but in the shifting between contemporary and classic, presence and absence, pop culture and revered literature. In the outcome, I look to Pound's notion of *metamorphosis*, a bursting through of association, image, and expectation into a reassembled vision of the everyday.

What could merit a long, pretentious thesis paper, then, suffices here as an invitation to look past the punchlines to parody's hidden agenda: To disarm our critical faculty just long enough to invade it; not to heap (in Aristotle's terms) praise or blame upon its subject, but to dust off the mantle, rattle the canon, offset our severe commentaries, and yes, by all means, make us laugh—and when the laughter trails off, to follow the lead.

* Medusa

Patricia Smith

Poseidon was easier than most.
He calls himself a god,
but he fell beneath my fingers
with more shaking than any mortal.
He wept when my robe fell from my shoulders.

I made him bend his back for me,
listened to his screams break like waves.
We defiled that temple the way it should be defiled,
screaming and bucking our way from corner to
    corner.
The bitch goddess probably got a real kick out of
    that.
I'm sure I'll be hearing from her.

She'll give me nightmares for a week or so;
that I can handle.
Or she'll turn the water in my well into blood;
I'll scream when I see it,
and that will be that.
Maybe my first child
will be born with the head of a fish.
I'm not even sure it was worth it,
Poseidon pounding away at me, a madman,
losing his immortal mind
because of the way my copper skin swells in
    moonlight.

Now my arms smoke and itch.
Hard scales cover my wrists like armour.
C'mon Athena, he was only another lay,
and not a particularly good one at that,
even though he can spit steam from his fingers.
Won't touch him again. Promise.
And we didn't mean to drop to our knees
in your temple,
but our bodies were so hot and misaligned.
It's not every day a gal gets to sample a god,

you know that. Why are you being so rough on me?

I feel my eyes twisting,
the lids crusting over and boiling,
the pupils glowing red with heat.
Athena, woman to woman,
could you have resisted him?
Would you have been able to wait
for the proper place, the right moment,
to jump those immortal bones?

Now my feet are tangled with hair,
my ears are gone. My back is curving
and my lips have grown numb.
My garden boy just shattered at my feet.

Dammit, Athena,
take away my father's gold.
Send me away to live with lepers.
Give me a pimple or two.
But my face. To have men never again
be able to gaze at my face,
growing stupid in anticipation
of that first touch,
how can any woman live like that?
How will I be able
to watch their warm bodies turn to rock
when their only sin was desiring me?

All they want is to see me sweat.
They only want to touch my face
and run their fingers through my . . .

my hair

is it moving?

*

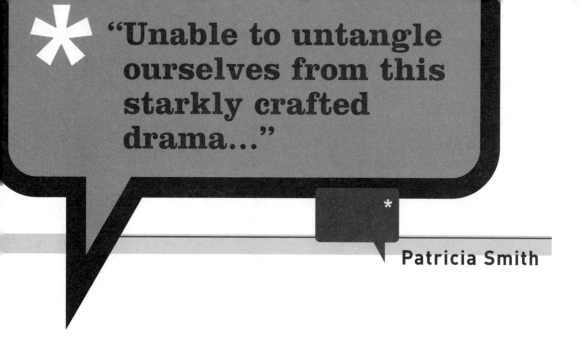

Poetry, by its very nature, slices away the unnecessary, leaving only the lean and vital. When it also manages elegance and nuance, reveals a moral truth, and chances a tweak or two to our accepted notions of language, it's revelatory.

Most riveting and memorable are the pieces in which a poet passes his own power to the subject of the poem. In persona poems, the writer eliminates the neutral voice and steps unflinchingly into the stanzas. Writing in persona can be flat and cringe-inducing when it fails, when the poet hefts the device like a hammer and swings without vision or direction. But when the poet savors his role as backdrop and the subject becomes both the story and the means of telling it, the result is startlingly effective.

A stellar example is "leadbelly," a 2004 National Poetry Series selection penned by Detroit native and University of Illinois professor Tyehimba Jess. A cycle of biographical poems chronicling the exploited days of the gifted Southern singer/songwriter/guitarist, the entire book is an emotionally jarring example of the persona poem's ability to capture the essence of a life.

In this case, the life is huge and minutely textured. Leadbelly (Huddie Ledbetter) was a symbol of all that is sweet and sordid about the Delta and the complicated racial relationships that were born and festered in that heat. Jess not only conjures the singer's troubled and bitter voice, but also the voices of his musical mentors, his relatives, his woman, and even John Lomax, the white Library of Congress archivist who plucked Leadbelly from a life in prison and shoved him into a scorching limelight. The mangled and manipulative link between Leadbelly and Lomax is the pulse of this book, and their clashing voices demonstrate the capacity of persona unleashed.

Jess, who spent years hunting down the primary source material that would finally allow the two men to speak alive and aloud, deftly shatters misconceptions of myth and history to render a disturbing and restless portrait. Unable to untangle ourselves from this starkly crafted drama, we lose pieces of ourselves to a story so directly and intimately told.

* mistress stella speaks

Tyehimba Jess

you think I'm his property
'cause he paid cash
to grab me by the neck,
swing me 'cross his knee
and stroke the living song from my hips.

you think he is master of all
my twelve tongues, spreading notes
thick as a starless night, strangling spine
till my voice is a jungle of chords.

the truth is that I owned him
since the word love first blessed his lips
since hurt and flight and free
carved their way into the cotton
fused bones of his fretting hand,
since he learned how pleading men hunt

for my face in the well of their throats
till their tongues are soaked with want.

yes, each day he comes back
home from the fields,
from chain gang fury,
from the smell of sometime women
who borrow his body. He bends
his weight around me
like a wilting weed,
drinking in my kiss
of fretboard across fingertip
till he can stand up straight again,
aching from what he left behind,
rising sure as dawn.

*

* Candler

James Nave

Prose poem: a poem written in paragraph(s) that doesn't concentrate in lines and linebreaks; it often shares features of a short story but is more heavily influenced by images, metaphors, figures, and controlled rhythm.

Candler used to be a preacher's wife down in Alabama. Her husband the Reverend Doyle Summerhill could preach up a storm. Alabama was farm country, and when Candler was growing up as far as she could see, trees held so much summer that even the bees got tired by August. It must have been during one of those long fly buzzin' nights when the heat had settled across the spine of the meadow that Candler decided weekly newspapers, lousy hairdos, rotary fans and devil-driven sermons were gonna be markers in a book somebody else read.

Nobody knows what made Candler restless. The old folks say if you live too close to the tracks and you hear the trains blow it won't be long before your kitchen starts to look like a diner that charges more for coffee than you're willing to pay. Or might have been the hail storm, the one that tore up half the tobacco in Coleman County.

Most of the boys down at The Creek View Cafe still talk about that storm. Patrick Moss swears he heard his mama's ghost dancin' on the tin roof just like they say she did when she was young and used to sneak off to the jazz clubs down in Birmingham. It drove her daddy crazy until he gave into the idea and decided his daughter was probably better off in Birmingham than New York.

Folks will tell you that hail storm tore up a lot more than tobacco plants. The kind of lightning and thunder that runs along behind those big chunks of ice lifts the skin right off the bone, hair and all. It shakes the top soil loose. Makes the crops nervous. Some say that's the way it was between Doyle and Candler. He didn't treat her bad, he just didn't treat her. It wasn't a whole lot different from somebody giving you a Hershey Bar for your wedding anniversary and trying to tell you it's cake.

Candler knew she shouldn't have gotten married. But like so many girls looking for respectability, she fell for Reverend Summerhill who talked the napkins off her mama's table and told her the Lord had given him a vision and she was part of it.

Restlessness is not something that comes over you like a new idea and gives you a clear view of the mountains. It just scratches and pecks like one of those park pigeons that's used to being fed. For Candler it was more like hair growing out, no matter how you cut it, it still takes a year to get down to your shoulders. Then even after it's down there, you don't always notice it.

The afternoon Doyle rubbed his right hand across the middle shelf above the sink just in front of the fresh-dried coffee mugs and yelled, "Candler, God will never tolerate this much dust, even in hell," was the afternoon Candler pushed her chair back, walked up stairs, and started to pack.

*

MY THIRD 9AM APPOINTMENT WITH THE UNIVERSITY'S WRITER-IN-RESIDENCE

Karyna McGlynn

"A few years back," he says, "I was *badly* blocked. I couldn't write a goddamn thing to save my life. So, Allen calls me up (Allen *Ginsberg* that is—good friend of mine, *great* poet) and he says, 'Michael, what *you* need is to get out into nature, *lose* yourself there, get *naked* in it.' And I said, 'Okay Allen, I'll do that.' Donald was always telling me you had to *humor* the man sometimes (Donald *Hall* that is—good friend of mine, *great* poet). So I went to this isolated cabin in Big Sur that Allen had stayed at with Lawrence and Denise (*Ferlinghetti* and *Levertov* that is—good friends of mine, *great* poets, *good* friends of mine). Denise once spent the summer at my house and I'm *sure* there was something between us, but I was *married* at the time and she was *older* and converting to *Catholicism*, and we were joking around one night and she said she thought I was "too *short*" and—heh-heh—*that* was really funny, and—I don't know—the timing was just FUCKED UP!...but great poet, *great* poet... I ended up publishing a limited edition chapbook by her that's selling on e-Bay now for five-hundred and thirty-seven dollars, so *you* know...And Lawrence too, you *know?* What a *decent* human being...Mr. "Coney Island of the *Mind*," Mr. "My Dog *Peed* on a Policeman's Leg." I mean, how counter-cultural can one guy GET? Always dancing around like: 'Hi, I'm

Lawrence Ferlinghetti and I started City Lights *Book*store! *Woo-woo-woo!* Hi, I'm Lawrence Fucking *FUCK-HEAD* Ferlinghetti. Come *on*, Denise! You don't really want to stay with *this* guy, do you? He's too *short,* and he's always walking around with a BONER for you in his *stupid* pleated PANTS!' ...Anyway, I went to the cabin and all I brought with me was a note-book, a pen, and collection of erotic verse by the ancient Chinese Poet, Li Po (...good friend of mine, *great* poet, *great* poet). And I wandered through the wilderness for *days* until I came to a clearing in the first heat of morning with the fog quickly dissipating and it was so *goddamn beautiful* I just had to take off all my clothes! And I frolicked nude through the vir-gin field and was *moved* to recite part of a poem by Thomas Campion: 'When *to* her *lute* Cor*i*nna *sings nei*ther *words* nor *music* are her *own*; *only* the LONG HAIR *drip*ping down her CHEEK, *only* the *song* of a *silk*en negligee on her THIGH. Poised, trembling, and *unsatisfied*, dew *dripping* from your *secret* inner VAULT. The ruddy MOUNTAINS of your BREASTS *melt*-*ing* under my *touch*. OPEN sweet Lotus! *OPEN* for ME!' ...Well, I'm *paraphrasing* now, but *anyway*, when I had finished reciting the poem, I stopped, and looked down, and lying at my feet was a *steer's* skull, and I picked it up, and the heft felt good in my palms, and it was *bleached* by the sun and *warm* to the touch. And that was the moment when I tasted my first *skull!* You can't know what it's *like*—the *life* that surges through you, Miss McGlynn, when you *first* put your tongue to the BONE, but I'll tell you *this:* My writer's block? *Gone!* And when I told Allen about it (Allen *Ginsberg* that is—good friend of mine, *great* poet, *great* poet), he said, 'Giddy-up, giddy-up, giddy-up, you bad *BAD* horsey, giddy-up, giddy-up, giddy-up...' So...Miss McGlynn, you wanted to see me about something?"

*

* Eve's Sestina for Adam

Lucy Anderton

Sestina: a highly structured poem consisting of six six-line stanzas followed by a tercet, for a total of thirty-nine lines.

I wanted the blood from the lip you'd bite
open for me. I wanted the soft back
of your knee that glowed like an otter's eye,
the flag of hair you'd throw out through the wild
sky, singing praises to Him through the air.
Clearly put, I was not born to be one

more pretty poppy in that garden. One
more handful of fruit just for you to bite,
a patch of dirt where you could plant your heirs.
I was a song you had to put your back
into. The first born fairy. Artless, wild
and bare. And I wanted more than my eye

saw, more than the final glance of your eyes
after you pinned me. No - I wanted one
of your ribs. So I took it. Felt my wild
heart crack with arias as my nails bit
into your side, sliding my fingers back
out, waving that slim wet bone through the air—
spinning myself in sass and yards of air

kisses - turning my nose and loud ass eyes
up to Him. And yes His fire split my back
as if He'd snatched from its cloudy bed one
virgin lightening bolt and threaded its bite

through my bold spine — as if I wasn't wild
enough. As if loving me was too wild,

too blasphemous an idea to air
in Eden. Who was I to need a bit
of love from the gold apple of His eye.
Adam, you helpless egg. I slipped you one
kiss and bled for us, but you were all back

and shoulders to me. Offering your tears back
to that giant nipple. Crying of wild
blood on your thighs. He only could hear one
side. So when that apple dropped through the air
I took it deep in my mouth and then I
saw that the bliss of absolution bites

straight through the heart of any one error.
So, yes, I backslapped Eden with my bloody wild,
But then—who gave you the Universe to bite?

*

the spoken world: poetry abroad

part 5

* It's History

Brendan Murphy
—*Ireland*

TRACK 38

A deserted pub in County Clare,
Middle of the Burren, middle of nowhere.

I'm from Liverpool,
Me mate's from Cardiff,
And we're with this lad, Ben, from Essex.

And it's men like Ben
Who can cause wars (without even knowing it).

We walked into a one-room bar,
Formica-top tables and a wooden floor.
Four still-life drinkers sitting there,
Not a single word is said.
It was like a hillbilly horror film mixed with Father Ted.
"Oh, let's go to another pub," I said.
"No. We're here now," said Ben, "3 pints when you're ready, barman!"

A dense fog, as two cultures collided –
The catalyst for which, Ben solely provided.

Rural insular Clare
Meets urban insular Essex.

The 3 pints arrive,
And y'know what he sez?
He sez:
"I've met some Irish blokes since I've been here,
And some of them (only some of them, mind you)
I think they don't like me just because I'm English –
Knowharramean?"

It's as if they blame you for what's gone on in
     the past,
Have you noticed that?
Well, it's not my fault -
I didn't steal their bloody spuds.
It's 'istry, innit 'ey? It's 'istry.

And then the 4 boys from across the floor
Couldn't ignore him anymore.

"I did a job for a farmer the other day –
Fat bastard!
When was the last time he saw a famine, 'ey?
It's 'istry, innit 'ey? It's 'istry."

Whoa!
A little ignorance goes a long way.
I couldn't find a reply in my head to say.
I just had visions of my balls being hurled
By the G.A. fuckin' A.

And then he said:
"I mean what I want to know is,
What did the English ever do to the Irish
In first place, anyway?
We ruled them,
We had a bit of a war - that was the end of
     that.
It's 'istry, innit 'ey? It's 'istry."

And what about the horses in London?
When they bombed the bloody horses,
Poor bloody horses.
I thought the Irish were meant to like horses.
I don't blame them for that, do I?

I wouldn't mind, I'm Irish meself.
On my grandad's side,
Or my grandad's grandad
(Something like that).
I mean we're all Irish, ain't we?
The whole bloody world's Irish.
It's 'istry, innit 'ey? It's 'istry.

We left soon after that.

We got out without being attacked
(Either verbally or otherwise).

The local lads kept a dignified silence.
And fair play to them for not rising to the bait.
But I think, deep down, they knew
That this man Ben wasn't attacking them,
And what he was actually saying
Wasn't the real him.
It was his story – his cultural story.
It's 'istry, innit 'ey? It's 'istry.

*

Moment Auf Rattanbank

Nora Gomringer
—Germany

Ganzer Sack Mut, auch Baggerladung Courage,
Ausgeklügelte Mimik, Gestik, der Look,
Streben nach so etwas wie Helligkeit im Auge des Betrachters
Sitzen als ich verstellt auf einem Rattanweisitzer.
Neben mir: Grund für Furcht,
Schleppen ind Schwitzen.
Geliebter genannt.
Füße, weil in Sandalen, fühlen Grashalme.
Lungen, weil in Brustkörben, hängen wie schweres Obst.
Finger, weil in Beklemmung, könnten Schweißflecke
Auf schwarze Küchenplatten nässen. Doch heir:
Rattanbank steht auf abenlicher Wiese, zwei Schwerstarbeiter darauf.

*

Moment on Rattan Bench

Nora Gomringer
Translation by Ulrike Reinecke

TRACK 40

Full sack of nerve, and truckload of courage,
Elaborate facial expression, gesture, the look,
Grasping for something like brightness in the eye of the beholder
Sitting disguised as myself on a rattan two-seater.
Next to me: Reason for dread,
Dragging and sweating.
Called lover.
Feet, in sandals, feel blades of grass.
Lungs, in ribcages, hang like heavy fruit.
Fingers, anxious, could make sweaty spots
On black kitchen tiles. But here:
Rattan bench stands in the meadow in twilight, two blue-collar workers on it.

*

*Liebesrost

Nora Gomringer

—Germany

Über Nacht
Bist du oxidiert
Neben mir

Hast aud mich reagiert
Bist rostig geworden
Du sagst
Golden
Ich lecke an deinem Hals
Du schmeckst wie der
Wetterhahn

*

*Love Rust

Nora Gomringer

Translation by Ulrike Reinecke

Over night
You oxidized
Next to me

You reacted to me
You became rusty
You say
Golden
I lick your neck
You taste like
Weathercock

*

* Trois

Pilote le Hot

—France

Névrose psychose et perversion
Les trois mamelles de la nation
Réel symbole imaginaire
Les trois chapitres du bréviaire
L'argent l'argent toujours l'argent
Spiritualité de maintenant
Y'a d'l'eau qui coule sous les ponts
Du foutre sous les édredons
Il est dans quel fuseau horaire
L'Etat d'l'esprit qu'est pas vulgaire
Y'a rien qui presse encore un verre
C'est c'que j'entends me dire grand- père
De son côté de coin d'cimetière
Qu'il a ma foi payé trop cher
La vie qui grouille de partout
Agitation violence dégoût
La vie qui grouille de partout
Trois petits tours et puis au trou
Rien n'sert d'courir non rien ne sert
Nique ta chimère t'auras des frères
Névrose psychose et perversion
Les trois mamelles de la nation
Sang sexe foutre et royalties
Sont les outils d'la fantaisie
La vie est belle mais passe-moi l'sel
Voilà l'message universel
La pensée la parole l'action
C'est là c'est la magique potion
Névrose psychose et perversion
Les trois mamelles de la nation
Réel symbole imaginaire
Les trois chapitres du bréviaire.

*

Three

Pilote le Hot

Translation by Lucy Anderton

Neurosis, psychosis and perversion:
The three Nipples of the nation.
Reality, symbol, and the imaginary:
The three chapters of the Man's Bible.
The money, the money, always after the money.
It's the spirituality of Now.
It's the water that strains beneath the bridges.
It's the cum beneath the eiderdowns.
In what time zone can it be found:
A State of mind that isn't vulgar?
There's nothing going on, so drink up.
It's what I hear my grandfather tell me
From his corner patch in the cemetery
For which he paid too dearly.
Life swarms in every direction
With agitation, violence and disgust.
Life swarms in every direction.
You get your shot and then you're toast.
Ain't no point in hurrying.
Fuck your fancy plans, when you do you'll find your comrades.
Neurosis, psychosis and perversion:
The three Nipples of the nation.
Blood, sex, cum and royalties
Are the tools of this fantasy.
Life is beautiful but pass me the salt.
Behold the message that rings universal.
Word, thought and action:
It's among us, that the magic potion.
Neurosis, psychosis and perversion:
The three Nipples of the nation.
Reality, symbol, and the imaginary:
The three chapters of the Man's Bible.

*

An American Dream

Jürg Halter a.k.a. Kutti MC

—*Switzerland*

Translation from German by Eileen Walliser-Schwarzbart

for Marc Smith

From the Chicago River ascends
a red balloon
pulling a laughing child out of the water
it's image reflected
in a skyscraper
soaring into the gray sky above the city

The cloud curtain opens a crack
the child with the balloon

floats into the blue sky
in the clarified glance of a
daydreaming passerby
the curtain closes again

The river carries an orphaned shoe
gently out of the windy city
in a cradle of waves

*

Infected

David Stavanger a.k.a. Ghostboy

—*Australia*

It started in my right (write) testicle.....
the doctors said it was a cyst but I knew better:
I knew it was a first line!
Several months later I found the development
of a stanza in my stomach...
then it spread to the intestine,
that's where the poet finds their rhythm
finds their rhyme...
before I KNEW IT
my heart was beating to a haiku heartbeat:
5-7-5   5-7-5   5-7-5
the words got stuck in my throat
tattooed to the page of this skin &
I WAS INFECTED!!!!

The W.H.O. tracked me down
& diagnosed me with
Performance Poetry Influenza
quarantined me to a small walled wooden box
taking me a slave, as their undercover poetry
    agent
traveling the seventeen seas
in search of the source of this disease
re-naming me in the process:

Ghostboy......

*

* Amrit Sar

Chris Mooney-Singh
—*Singapore*

In the waters of the sacred pool
the golden body of Hari Mandir
takes a long bath when it's cool.

The gold sun slowly cleans its face.
Some nights, the moon comes down as well.
Celestial bodies know this place.

The soul of a paper kite has given
its pink face in an act of surrender
and floats upon the waves of Heaven.

Yet, the big carp in their nibbling school,
but holy songs emit more current,
eating prasad thrown in the pool.

The waters are lit with electric light,
but holy songs emit more current,
for the Word is sung here day and night.

Each pilgrim, family - husband, wife:
thousands are praying for health and wealth,
praying for everlasting life.

Yet, all must drink inside the mind
from the pool of immortality,
but the inner peace is hard to find.

*

* Prelude to a Journey

Matthew Shenoda
—*Eygpt*

The struggle is not in the wave
or the fury   but in the silence of ocean's calm
the granules of sand separated
by omnipotent wind.

Be careful of the ripples in the bay
of the places where water kissed shore.

Be wary of lingering clouds
the shuttering voices of sky.

Understand that in the end
it is silence of heart that will kill us
the muffled song
that will cut off our feet.

*

Remembering

Matthew Shenoda

—Eygpt

The mason came
From the Pharaoh's garden
Preparing to erect a tomb,
Calling upon grace
He cleansed his hands
And whispered:

From this place
I will shape
The memories of inevitable generations
&
In this place will they be remembered.

love poem

Suheir Hammad

—Palastine/Jordan

it is late raining tonight
the only safe place i know
is the air still warm right after
a kiss the place where lips almost meet
breath lives electric

need is past now I hunger
not in heat but in searching
for more than a pyre to sun me and my body
is straining against sleep
close

i want to be open and hide
the children of palestine within me
heard first i would bear down
bring them into me
an act of desperate love

the israeli army shoots children in the head

i would shelter them where
it is warm where limbs meet

where life is where babies
come from horizon dawning

pray these children
grow up fall in love
make love everywhere always
be human be alive

it is said sex is
in the head where god is
where too ancestry where
vision and memory
and the ability to hear angels

place palestine 's
children in this sacred
air between kisses breathe them in
love them safe until
the Israeli army stops
shooting children in the head

the young and
spoken: youth poetry

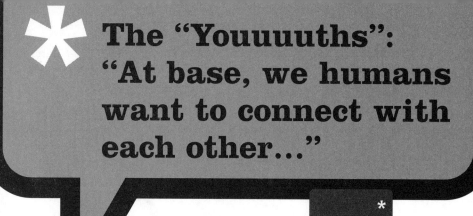

part 6

The "Youuuuths": "At base, we humans want to connect with each other…"

Jeff Kass

When I first started to teach performance poetry to high school students eleven years ago, I hoped there would be a number of positive benefits. The fire and intensity of spoken word would, perhaps, capture the attention of some of my more lackluster charges, and I thought a handful of them might start to take their writing more seriously. In addition, I suspected the infusion of contemporary work into the curriculum might ignite a spark of interest in the minds of reluctant readers. Might encourage them to seek out new writers on their own, maybe even attend a reading or two.

I never imagined hundreds of high-schoolers would adopt the habit of carrying journals in their backpacks and back pockets, ready to whip them out at a moment's notice to record their observations and thoughts.

I never imagined 3,500 people would pack the San Francisco Opera House for the finals of the Brave New Voices National Youth Poetry Slam Festival in 2005, or that Harlem's famed Apollo Theater would sell out a year later for the same event.

I never imagined a girl would read a poem in class about how painful it was for her to choose to have an abortion and that, the next day, when she showed up for class she'd find a bouquet of flowers on her desk paid for by her classmates.

I never imagined the hours I would spend after school, attempting to ask probing questions of frustrated poets who'd never cared about writing before, as the clock ticked into the night and they refused to leave the room, repeatedly insisting, *but it's just not saying what I want it to say yet.*

I never imagined the monthly open mics, the field trips to perform at other schools, the minutes-long standing ovations, the tears, the annual boisterous celebration of a house-packing Poetry Night, the chapbooks, the CDs, the kids who would lie to their parents in order to sneak out and attend poetry slams, the radio shows and newspapers, the hugs, the friendships, the journeys around the country, the poems written and prized as birthday presents, the poets who would blossom into leaders of movements against violence against women, against war, against couch-potato-hood; the poets who would go on to write and direct plays, teach in juvenile detention centers, lead peer-counseling discussion groups and wilderness trips; the poets who would build and rebuild and give back to their communities—the obvious and necessary power of words.

It is this last—the obvious and necessary power of words—that hits hardest. My students are overwhelmed by words. Words on the radio and television. Words on e-mail and MySpace. Words condensed and contracted into instant and text messages. Words spit-fired in hip-hop songs. Words droned from the mouths of teachers, parents, bosses, siblings, and friends. But how many of these words are honest? And when I say honest, I don't mean telling the truth, I mean sprouting from authentic feeling; I mean the product of undisguised naked emotion. On the other hand, how much of what today's youth hear and see is slickly packaged to sell them something?

When I watch television, I sometimes feel like the goal of every advertisement —whether car, beer, soft drink, shampoo, pair of jeans or personal music device— is to convince me that if I buy this item, I will attain the ultimate nirvana of human existence; I will be able to dance in uninhibited fashion. Smart marketing, I assume, for who does not want to dance uninhibited? Who does not want to *feel* uninhibited? To feel like it's possible to tap into who we really are and to be unafraid of what anyone else thinks?

Of course, the beers and cars and personal music devices are all mirages, false totems. Words, when spoken honestly—when flowing unfettered from that place of naked undisguised emotion—are not. But they don't often flow from there. Especially not toward youth, who are constantly being sold to, lied to, politicized, censored and protected from and manipulated. Youth live in a swirling cosmos of false language, even among themselves. Annually, the number one complaint I hear from students is that our school is filled with too many fake people. Too many people who put on *fronts*. The tendency to eye-roll when someone else is speaking, or to tune out and (often) tune in to a personal music device, is epidemic. Is habitual. And why shouldn't it be, when so much of what is communicated is insincere?

Performance poetry is a spear which pierces false fronts, and therein lies its power. A teenager who speaks in public of the sexual assault she survived navigates among the battering asteroids of false language and illuminates the darkness with a brilliant light of naked, undisguised, face-to-face emotion. A boy who proclaims the pain he feels from his mother's death obliterates the seductive call of pretending he's too tough to care about anything.

The need for honest communication among young people is palpable. The world has never been more confusing, more fraught with global discontent, disconnect, misinformation, and spin. There have never been more technologies capable of communicating absent face-to-face accountability, yet at the same time with greater capacity for sophisticated manipulation and disguise. The power of performance poetry is its ability to offer a low-tech alternative, a single voice—sincere—from heart to ear.

Last spring I was struck by the sight of three young poets, all female—Angel Nafis, Maggie Ambrosino, and Caronae Howell—as they walked together through the student parking lot after school. It was a gusty afternoon, and as the wind thrashed against their quirky clothes—their long skirts, bandanas and babushkas, their crepe shawls and magenta running shoes—they thrust their chins forward and soldiered on. Here is power. Here is kick-assedness. Here are three teenagers completely unafraid to say what they think, to display in public what they *feel,* to challenge with passion, to care. Watching young people grow through poetry— grow into poets—is watching them grow into leaders of their peers, is watching them grow into wielders of influence, is watching them grow into people who can unsheathe spears and shatter all the polished slick fortresses of fake that threaten to suffocate them.

At base, we humans want to connect with each other. We want to dispense with the barriers between us—the fronts—and feel each other to the core. Performance poetry, particularly for the youth, is a way to clear the swirling debris of false language and connect. That is its power. When I first began, I did not imagine the scope of its emotional impact on my students or on me as a teacher, but I have learned it. One poem at a time, from heart to ear.

Sixteen Fragments of Islam

Caronae Howell

(written when she was 16, Pioneer High School, MI)

The first part is identification.

Two times this war in the Middle East,
two times have I come so close to knowing you, an intricate pattern
of circles and sapphire.

People say that spirits are corrupt,
but where do you draw the line between fanaticism
and faith?

4   The solidity of the book is more powerful
than the testimonials themselves.
Every believer knows that truth
is an element of a lie.

The veil obscuring my hair is dark,
protruding into the very red heart of worship,
this lack of Goddess rooted so firmly.

6   Beauty is
strung through my grandfather's faith
like the dusty plum lines winding around these bloated domes.
Am I here to believe in a God I have seen wisp away with every breath?
Is he that fragile,
like cotton?

Seven men
on the streets
for every woman. My heart hides below
this headscarf and
my waistline may never see sunshine.
These women are like church spires,
piercing

and falling back again,
piercing
and falling back again.
Does your wife stop at the edge of her skin?
Is she dry and cracked,
fragments of the Koran drifting across her eyelids like cataracts?

8   The first time I understood the difference
between Iran and Iraq.
I had only been through thirty-two seasons
and this God, here, expects me to understand where I a come from?
I cannot go on calling myself Iranian knowing only fragments of my insides.

I cannot do this again,
explain who I am
when I make vague references to Islam,
you cannot be a quarter Muslim.
I have swallowed enough Mosques
for one evening
of suicide.
These rooms are the most sacred in the world
and the smooth, curved roofs
seem to melt with the sky,
so even,
so turquoise.

When did this garden begin?
Did someone throw 10,000 seeds into the air
and leave Allah to plant the rest?
Can you nurture faith
like pale gold flowers
while still feeling so empty;
like someone has carved a hole into your pelvis?
I will never walk again;
I plant no seeds of anger,
only lentils and hope.

11   I must steady myself
I will count the number of minutes

it takes me
to run my fingers
along the spine of the holy Koran.
I will listen to the rustle of its pages.
I will come to know it so well that
I do not recognize the edges of my body
in relation to my husband's.

Heaving between the two pinnacles of my clavicle
is a place more innocent than the Mediterranean olive groves.
My chest is dawn's fingers,
and she wonders where to plant the fragments of shattered women.
My grandfather will not go to Hell.

The men and women
wander on opposite sides of the town and
I simply cannot bring myself to rejoice
in the irony of a faithful war.
God's war-
fragmented bones littering the sewage strewn street.
Allah's war-
severed ankles stringing bracelets around pomegranate color sidewalks.
This is no man's land.
This is that empty space when I press my wrists together.

16   I have crisscrossed the world of believing
a million times
and I have not even moved out of my chair.
I have risen my faith like smoke
and fallen for such a lack of beauty.
I only wish I could place my atheism next to your divinity
and pray for a while
to a God. Any God
who will sit calmly in one place
and ask for no human sacrifice
in his name.

*

* Two Cities

Kelly McWilliams
(Walnut Hill School, MA)

1.

By mid-morning the city is made of sandaled feet and little Buddhas; of gray elephant skin like leather; of spiders that blow across your toes and then are gone. The warmth of knowing that what you left behind to die will one day come alive again, as something else–this is the city at noon. Arriving there for the first time is like slipping for the first time between orange silk sheets, or waking in the arms of a rain tree that holds you carefully, wraps you completely, and does not let you go even as you twist. And when the heat has mellowed to yawning, the city is a scorpion the size of your open palm, sleeping on the dirt beside your bed, the two of you arcing nearly parallel–two gently, sleeping creatures caught in momentary unison, though they will never know it.

2.

At dawn, men climb the skeletons of buildings to work themselves into hollows, like cool, fragile caves in the sky. There they hoist, they raise, they elevate until the sun spills sweat into their eyes. The city below, itself a skeleton, stretches its bony fingers, clawing into the desert. The blue sky ripples as if someone is shaking it out over the brown earth. If men fall, it is because they were dreaming, up there, of cool water, of the way night rushes the harsh desert all at once. The city that these hands build will be a monument. Have you ever felt, as you walk through a building, hands cupping the bottoms of your feet to carry you high above the streets? The human backs, curved and swelling beneath you?

*

*Lebron James

Nate Marshall

(16 years old, Whitney Young High School, Young Chicago Authors)

I have a confession, I am Lebron James...
...'s biggest fan
and I am writing this for all those spectators who are watching
not by choice, but by hatred of those bastards in uniform.

This for the kid on no cut teams
on benches far back like pirates on planks a step away from
the murky deep.
This for five foot four fifteen year olds who idolize Shaq
white men who wanna dunk like Vince Carter
and everyone who's ever sang along to that damn song
"I wanna be like Mike,"
but can't shoot.

Took me off final cut lists so I took pens and cut this.
Penciled in acceptance on my chest.
Stenciled in acceptance on my wrist.
Made my own teams.

All I have left is...
triple double scores from judges.
Crossovers from HotHouses to HBOs.
Double nickel drops that clank into a collection bin on Red Line stops.

CTA dime-droppa...

That be me see,
I been that
heir-apparent all-star
Of open mics.

Just
hopin' to cop those new Mike's.

PSYCH!

Really I'm FDRin' it let's cut a new deal.

I'll be the first spoken word brotha with a shoe
deal.

But for my kicks instead of Jumpmen I'll have slumped men
Slaving
over
pages like
little kids in Southeast Asia who made this
emblem
For below minimum wages.

I'm a hustle player so I dive for loose balls and blocks.
Plus my literary wingspan goes from
Wordsworth to Pac,
Haiku to hip-hop,
Vernacular to grammar proper, see.

I'm the head coach of a Dream Team fighting hypocrisy.

Steve Kerr with mic reverb.
Threes and free throws with poetry scores.

'Cause see they cut me from that team,
but it's cool
'cause I still rock games
drop dimes and
drop flames.

Because I am

Lebron James.

*

Superfabulous

Molly Kennedy

(Wordplay, Baton Rouge)

I was watching TV last night and must say I'm appalled:
Entertainment Tonight told me that the new Superman was gay.
My first reaction was: 'Nonsense!'
Superman is an <u>icon</u>!
He stands for truth, justice, and the American way of life,
which translated into modern terms means
'go buy more cheap plastic crap at Wal-Mart!'
My second reaction was 'Well, yeah, no duh.'
People are <u>surprised</u> by this?
Entertainment Tonight's slander against the Man of Steel
was just confirmation of something we've secretly known for years:
Most superheroes are gay.

I can see why the media would start this smear campaign.
Not because the director of the most recent Superman movie is openly homosexual,
but because our media is prejudiced!
Superman, after all, *is* an illegal alien.
We don't want them foreigners coming across our borders
Rescuing our *American* women as they fall from buildings
Saving our *American* cats when they get stuck in trees
Protecting us *Americans* from other angry hostile foreigners
Like Darkseid, Mongul, or Effron the Sorcerer!
We want our *American* jobs for us *Americans*!
Why in this day and age a Krypton-born superhero
would be lucky to get a job cleaning up after Captain America's dog!

Superheroes have always been a bad influence on kids!
Adam West's Batman convinced my cousin Nathan to jump off the roof and try to fly.
(Dumbass. Everyone knows Batman can't fly!)
Superman shows preschoolers that, yes, sweetie,
it's ok to walk around with your underwear outside your pants

And I still think I can blame the Human Torch
for making me into a pyromaniac.

No. You're right.
I was playing with lighters and WD-40
before I even knew who the Fantastic Four were.

On a completely different note, due to America's love of lawsuits
and the rampant stupidity of my fellow countrymen,
the Superman cape at Target is sold with a disclaimer:
"Wearing cape does not enable user to fly."

Well there shatter my childhood dreams.

The way I see it, what harm could come if Superman really <u>was</u> gay?
It wouldn't be much of a jump from his mild-mannered reporter persona.
It would pave the way for the rest of the repressed Justice Leaguers
Who've been hiding in the closet since 1962
watching *Lawrence of Arabia* and *A Taste of Honey*
And...Holy-Anti-Bear Spray!
Batman would come out of his cave,
Robin would soar out of the nest,
and the Green Lantern would let his love light *SHINE!*
And Aquaman?
Well, jeez, if you didn't figure out that one on your own...

On the other side of this debate
you have the people who insist that Superman
is an allegory to Jesus Christ.
"The son becomes the father and the father the son" etc. etc.
That's too mind-blowing for my already skewed theological perspective.
I mean, Catholics have already boycotted the Da Vinci code
'cause there's no way Jesus could have been married to Mary Magdalene...

Imagine the *damage* that could be done to religious cinema-goers
if we told them not only was Christ married,

he was gay, an illegal alien, and wore his underwear outside of his clothes?
I figure Tim Rice and Andrew Lloyd Webber would make a musical of it,
Jesus Christ Superman.
And in his little red speedo and tights the world would know
what it really means to be *hung* on a cross...

Most superheroes are gay.
And I say that straight-faced,
gazing into a pint of Superman ice cream
marveling at its melting rainbow hue.
It tasted like fruit when it went down.

If Superman were gay,
Superman would be supergay.
Superman would be fabulous.
Superman would be Superfabulous.
Superman would walk up to Lex Luthor with jazz hands,
Slap him across the face, and go

"World domination? I don't think so, honey!"

And the world would be a better place for it.

*

Dear son, part 1

Zora Howard

(13 years old, Urban Word, New York)

Dear son,

I bought a cake on your birthday
With 19 candles and 1 for good luck
And I cried through the frosting
The cake is ruined but
I'm sending you this candle
I paid 4 dollars
Extra for first class mail
So wherever you are
When you get it
Light a match
Or use a lighter
But light my candle
And make a wish
Son
Make a wish
Promise
Cross you heart
And hope to die
You promised you would write
And you promised not to lie
And I promise
when you get home I'll beat you
You promised not to die
So until you come home
I promise not to cry
I'll be your soldier
As long as you promise to be mine.

*

* Dead Ass

Michael Cirelli

In the bodega, a young girl wearing
jeans so tight she has to use turpentine
to get them off, says to her friends,
Damn, it's dead ass raining out!

I was enamored. Instead of cats and dogs,
I pictured donkey corpses falling from
the sky, clogging the gutters.
That's some serious rain.

The song on the radio said that the po-po was:
"tryna to catch me ridin' dirty." I imagined
Chamillionaire wearing a 20 lb. gold chain
with mud dripping off Jesus' shiny toes,
Krazie Bone in four hundred dollar jeans,
with grass stains on the knees.

In Oakland, the sound there is "hyphy." To me,
that alien word means gooney-goo-goo.
To me, that word is my dead father's kiss.
But to thousands of kids with trousers that sink
below the Plimsoll line of their asses, hyphy
music makes their bodies dip up and down
like an oil drill.

These words make me feel old, and alabaster.
When I hear something new, it's like I
    discovered it
for the first time, like I excavated it from the
    mouth
of a teenager. So I dust it off with my fossil
    brush
and try to jam it into the keyhole of academia.

I am not afraid of dope lyrics, not dope meaning
    weed
but dope meaning good. My kind uses scrilla to
    board
up the windows of shook, Duke University
    graduates
who holla, "Go Brooklyn! Go Brooklyn!"

Fo shizzle, crunk, hella: I put in glass jars like
    rare moths.
I want to hang them on the doors of sonnets
like a welcome sign to an apartment
I don't live in.

*

a hip-hop poetica

part 7

* The Revolution Will Not Be Televised

Gil Scott-Heron

You will not be able to stay home, brother.
You will not be able to plug in, turn on and cop out.
You will not be able to lose yourself on scag and
skip out for beer during commercials because
The revolution will not be televised.

The revolution will not be televised.
The revolution will not be brought to you by Xerox in four parts
    without commercial interruption.
The revolution will not show you pictures of Nixon blowing a bugle and
    leading a charge by John Mitchell, General Abramson and Spiro
    Agnew to eat hog maws confiscated from a Harlem sanctuary.
The revolution will not be televised.

The revolution will not be brought to you by
The Schaeffer Award Theatre and will not star
Natalie Wood and Steve McQueen or Bullwinkle and Julia?
The revolution will not give your mouth sex appeal.
The revolution will not get rid of the nubs.
The revolution will not make you look five pounds thinner.
The revolution will not be televised, brother.

There will be no pictures of you and Willie Mae
pushing that shopping cart down the block on the dead run
or trying to slide that color tv in a stolen ambulance.
NBC will not be able to predict the winner at 8:32 on reports from
    twenty-nine districts.
The revolution will not be televised.

There will be no pictures of pigs shooting down brothers
on the instant replay.
There will be no pictures of pigs shooting down brothers
on the instant replay.

There will be no slow motion or still lifes of Roy
Wilkins strolling through Watts in a red, black
and green liberation jumpsuit that he has been
saving for just the proper occasion.

Green Acres, Beverly Hillbillies, and Hooterville Junction
will no longer be so damned relevant
and women will not care if Dick finally got down with Jane
on *Search for Tomorrow*
because black people will be in the streets looking for
A Brighter Day.
The revolution will not be televised.

There will be no highlights on the *Eleven O'Clock News*
and no pictures of hairy armed women liberationists
and Jackie Onassis blowing her nose.
The theme song will not be written by Jim Webb or Francis
        Scott Key
nor sung by Glen Campbell, Tom Jones, Johnny Cash,
Englebert Humperdink, or Rare Earth.
The revolution will not be televised.

The revolution will not be right back after a
message about a white tornado, white lightning, or white people.
You will not have to worry about a dove in your bedroom,
the tiger in your tank or the giant in your toilet bowl.
The revolution will not go better with Coke.
The revolution will not fight germs that may cause bad breath.
The revolution *will* put you in the driver's seat.
The revolution will not be televised
                will not be televised
        not be televised
                be televised
The revolution will be no re-run, brothers.
The revolution will be LIVE.

*

* harlem love poem

yvonne fly onakeme etaghene

I love Harlem for the brothas playing football across Lenox avenue,
across traffic,
      above heads
            like *what?*... this is Harlem.
old school soul music playing on the streets
sweet oils and incense
flirting with my senses
as I walk to the #2 train
at 125th

we all know:
nothing
beats
Brooklyn,
the Bronx rolls *hard*,
queens is huge—the *most* underestimated,
& I don't know shit about Staten Island
except that's where Wu-Tang comes from/

it's just something about the streets
of Harlem:
vibrant, alive, honest
the cracks in the sidewalk look like crow's feet
on the face of the city
laughing at me for being in such a hurry
all the damn time/

Harlem: where blackness is a political statement
& IHOP is my spot, folks do not know
about IHOP on Adam Clayton Powell!

living up the street from the Apollo
& a few blocks from Langston Hughes' house
means something

everyday
I get called a queen
it's enough to melt my hardened heart
make me smile once or twice
much later in my day
remembering/

I thought I was gonna have to move to Oakland
to find peace of mind, until *Harlem* loved me/
after living in Harlem
it was like the streets were calling my name
from Minneapolis
from Los Angeles
from Green Castle, Indiana
come home, we know what you like to eat
we know how you like to dress baby
we know you walk hard
but are tender like feathers inside
come home
your Nigeria away from Nigeria

folks have church on the streets in Harlem
and even tho I ain't no Christian
I got to respect that
every Sunday
you can't ignore the word
you got to *walk around our God*
but come correct
& you are welcome to join in
if so moved.

*

Brooklyn's Atlas

Kyle G. Dargan
~Radio Raheem

> *"In Sal's, there's no music, no rap,*
> *no music, no music."*
> *~from "Do the Right Thing"*

Does it itch when the alkaline
dries up?—the ghetto blaster
heavy and mute on your shoulder.

A street sage cannot rock
a walkman, not
with a name like Raheem. Boom.
Box. Boom-box napalming bass,
painting the Bed-Stuy deaf.

        Boom-bip,
kids skip behind you—pied piper
of Public Enemy. *I don't like nothing else*:
hard beats that translate
like your name—Allah,
giver of nourishment.
Martyr. Molotov.

(Dance Break)

We dance for the patron
saint of woofers the size of wheels,
noise pollution for the soul. We call,
we answer yes
yes y'all (repeat), jumping off stone stoups,
stepping in tongues. All bodyrock revival
speaks to you. What other ascetic
ever thrived off a diet high-top fades and D
   batteries?

*

Microphone Fiend

Kyle G. Dargan

The child freestyles in the shower,
battling yellow tiles
with a steam-heavy tongue.

        Siblings can wait
while s/he rhymes the hot water to an end.

Braggadocio and bubblegum toothpaste
blend, beatless. S/he spits, and spits
and spits until words harden
like lime crust on the spray head.

Have to get the neck into it—flexing
inward then out, recoiled

from the force of breath. *Did I
say I'm number one? Um, sorry
I lied. I'm number one-two-three-four
-and-five.*

And the crowd goes...

water applauding
against the basin. Momma goes
"If you don't get your narrow behind
out that bathroom with all that nonsense!"

        The water stops,
the shower curtain makes way.

S/he wipes condensation from the cabinet
   mirror,
barely eye-level with reflection. On tip-toes,

s/he anticipates emceedom like a growth
   spurt.

*

*1707

Idris Goodwin

Roosevelt and South Michigan
1212 Apartment complex
1st year of college
Room 1707

Tonight the beat playing is "Full Clip" by
    Gangstarr
Our chorus only has two lines

In 1707 till the sun come up
We illuminate the mic with the rhymes we bust

Second line comes from Will
Lives with his journalist father
Dark green skullie hat
Even though it's hot as hell

Hes loud and 16
Already written the first few bars of his verse
He never has writers block

He reminds me of me
Or who I thought I wanted to be
When I was 16

In 1707 till the sun come up
We illuminate the mic with the rhymes we bust
I rap like sex/ like gats and lust

This line comes from Alvin
Calls himself Top gun
Plays football
Lives with his grandma on the section 8 floors
He started comin up to my place
Cuz I'd let him smoke cigarettes
In exchange he'd teach me
Chicago slang

"I'm a need a get a square up out you joe, so I
    can jap on this beat"

He's gonna write his verse
After he hears what everybody else got
It will no doubt contain
A gun reference
A clever joke
And a mention of his grandmother

In 1707 till the sun come up
We illuminate the mic with the rhymes we bust
I rap like sex/ like gats and lust
Make threats/ like raps turn bricks to dust

Everybody
Was initially curious about Paul
The lanky white poetry major
He lives across the hall
Smirking in delight
At the convergence of styles

He and I both got 9 a.m.
Poems and scripts to share
But this is our other group
We cant come empty handed

In 1707 till the sun come up
We illuminate the mic with the rhymes we
    bust
I rap like sex/ like gats and lust
Make threats/ like raps turn bricks to dust
Storm the city/ with the gritty/ cuz it's a must

Russell is an aspiring filmmaker
I let him crash on my broken futon couch
So he doesn't have to take that 2nd train
After that 2nd bus
After his 2nd job at the Loews Cineplex

His raps come out like exorcisms
Strange embraces of death
Surrounding the women in his family

In 1707 till the sun come up
"Full Clip" plays on repeat
No one says a word
Heads are buried in paper

                    We illuminate the mic
With
The rhymes we bust

It's Tuesday @ 2:23 a.m.

                                        I rap like sex/ like
Gats
And lust

And we'll stay there even longer if we have to

                            Make threats/like raps
Turn
Bricks to dust

Be back tomorrow night

                        Storm the city/ with
The
Gritty/cuz it's a must

Every night
Until we all
Come up

    *

the spoken word revolution redux *

* Detroit Winter (excerpt)

Invincible

The city streets are bitter sweet
I pound pavement
While I'm kicking litter at my feet
Under the snow, the ground's blanket
These heavy hitter beats
Can be the sound arrangement
Towards my destination
Every footstep is a down payment
Now I'm walking as I head home
Walkman and my headphones
Wrapped around my ears
My fears turn around face em
Burnt to the ground ancient
Ruins of a metropolis
Now the populous shrinking
Inking deals to build as if the towns vacant

Every empty lot
Remaining a profound statement
Every empty bottle
Claiming all the drowned pain and sorrow
But tomorrow brings a new beginning-
    groundbreaking
Pedometers around your waste couldn't count
    the paces
Of this long walk to freedom
Foot soldiers for social change
During Detroit summer
Gotta prepare for colder days
Never slow ya pace u got ya soul to save

No matter what the starting point
Or all the roles we play

DETROIT IN THE WINTER
The cold is a poison that lingers
A point for beginners to hold on avoiding the
    shivers
You either bundle up or burn rubber
But if u can't take the winter
You don't deserve summer

*

*Toward a hip-hop poetica

*

Kevin Coval

Used to speak the king's English
But caught a rash on my lips
So now my chat just like dis
                              —Mos Def

The creative cultural practice of hip-hop poetry spreads primarily because of its language and syntactical fractures, its ruptures and breaks, the idea of play, the excitement of making language new, breaking the rules of the King's English. Hip-hop poetica on all levels is fun and radically democratic, therefore inclusive of multiple dialects. We wrote raps. In class, on the bus, in rooms while we were supposed to be asleep. Raps written outside of the percussive structured boom-bap of hip-hop time, outside the institutional gaze of academy and parental advisory, in the lonely nights of self-reflection and communal ciphers of spiral notebook sessions, a hip-hop poetica was born.

Hyperliterate emcees began to add and allude to a canon of verse that was very much alive and dynamic, not pale, dead, and static. Chuck D (and other emcees, Chuck, arguably, the most conscious participant in a broader literary tradition) lead to a (re)discovery of ancestors and elders: Gil Scott-Heron, Watts Prophets, Sonia Sanchez, June Jordan, Martín Espada, Etheridge Knight, Psalms, Frank O'Hara, Bob Kaufman. The foundation of a hip-hop poetica is the desire to (re)connect and proclaim a legacy and history in (primarily, though not limited to) African American letters centered on the popular music of the era. Langston to blues, Black Arts to Bop, hip-hop poets as translators and practitioners of the aesthetics of hip-hop culture.

Hip-hop poetica are modern griots, indigenous keepers and tellers of his/her/stories. Implicit in that is the always tale of a people, the continuing narrative of family and ancestors, the next and current articulation of lineage, that we spit and speak within a tradition we inherit and search(ed) for. Hip-hop poetics is the epic recitation of the marginalized, a meta-pronouncement of displacement in and outside of historical specificity, as well as the particular moment of neighborhood, space, and time, the reporting of a people, Chuck D's Black *CNN*.

To begin (or continue) a conversation on the aesthetics of a hip-hop poetica, I have made a ten-point program, and wish to engage in the critical pronouncement toward a manifesto, toward a hip-hop poetica:

1. The hip-hop poetica is aware of and constantly sifting (digging) through legacy. Hip-hop poets are inheritors of the mytho-poetic, keepers of stories, urban, de-industrialized bards, seers and recorders of a neo-colonial, gentrified dystopia. (Re)Present(ing) the traditions (Black Arts, Nuyorican, Beat, Harlem Renaissance, Slam, etc....) of American letters. While the Hip-hop poetica is certainly experimental, surreal, and/or magically real, we are, at our foundation, a generation of storytellers firmly rooted in the realist tradition of narrative, an extension of Gwendolyn Brooks and Carl Sandburg, a continuation of the political implications Langston Hughes engendered by rendering stories of everyday people. Hip-hop poetica tells stories of people they know. Pat Rosal's *Freddie*, Kyle Dargan's *Microphone Fiend*, Willie Perdomo's *Crazy Bunch*, Kelly Tsai's *Lili's Hands*, the best poets of our generation are recording who and what is around them, painting a clear picture of where they are at.

2. The hip-hop poetica constructs radical collages, pastiches a universe of symbolic-logic, where Big Daddy Kane and Homer, Islam and cartoon video games, neighborhood characters and superheroes, the school and the bodega, the strip mall and skate park, housing project and abandoned lot, all construct a system of meaning. The hip-hop poetica acts as DJ, taking into consideration lives and influences holistically and democratically rather than in cubicled isolation, able to

encompass and value the dynamic complexities of self and nation. Tracie Morris, in *Life Saver*, considers Savion Glover in the tradition of tap and its historical and racial implications, while mixing and blending language from several eras, using the percussive consonants and compounded rhymes to imitate the sound aurally with tap Savion might employ with his feet.

3. The hip-hop poetica is a systemic rupture of line and time. Not only are the poets of this generation playing with enjambment and breath-line units (Latasha Diggs and Idris Goodwin), text size and style (Douglas Kearney), sampling from forms, original poetic and non-poetic sources for language and structure (Duriel E. Harris), but also in the process of bringing ancestral legacies into the new paradigm of our poetics, there is the praxis of time rupture. What Afrika Bambaataa, Grandmaster Flash, later DJs Shadow, Krush, Q-bert, and scores of others do with sound, poets do with verse: sampling the *Bible*, military cadence, and cereal ads in the same poem, pulling together seemingly disparate sources, time periods, styles, and sounds. In reading, the reader becomes unaware of time, other than that which the weaver keeps. The DJ/poet sound-style mash-up informs a constant now, a past that is brought present, a future that is upon us. The moment fissured and reassembled. The hip-hop poetica as apocalyptic quilters of inheritance and hope.

4. The hip-hop poetica is in-your-face-insistence-of-place. Willie Perdomo is a Nuyorican writer. Pat Rosal's *B-Boy Infinitives* could be about no other place than Edison, NJ. These poems remind us of our homes, and that is their strength, the particular articulating the universal, but these are local poems. The hip-hop poetica is primarily interested in the representation of a place, the demand and insistence to rep where you are from, for better and worse. KRS rep-ed the Bronx, Mos holds Brooklyn, Nas is from Queensbridge, NWA, Compton, Common, Chicago, OutKast, Atlanta. We connect in the de-industrial new millennial American narrative by reporting on the conditions of home and hood. We share subtle language alterations, and become hip to and aware of the struggles and slang and celebrations of France, Palestine, South Africa, and Tennessee and begin to paint a holistic portrait of the hip-hop nation under all.

5. Hip-hop poetica is satiric, not ironic. Funny, not futile. No frat boy, sketch comedy kind of irony. Hip-hop poets are too smart and genuinely concerned for the

uplift of their communities to wax pathetic. Thomas Sayers Ellis and Bryonn Bain employ satire as a poetic strategy in challenging the vastness of white cultural supremacy. Ellis's droned anaphoras begin to sound like all their (read: white, crusty, dead, academic) writing, yet in each second half of his phrasing a twist, like a knife, alerts the reader to another level of meaning.

6. Hip-hop poetica is consciously confrontational. You can get the finger…the middle. Duriel E. Harris's villanelle, Kyle Dargan's portrait of Radio Raheem, the non-apologetic, unforgivable poetic stance of hip-hop has had outlaw status ever since it was illegal for black folks to read and write. So what (continues to) scare and enrage the gatekeepers of language more than articulate, innovate, young poets of color, who truth at unjust systemic inequity and cultural capitalist supremacy? The stance of hip-hop poetica, manifest in the hubris of Duriel E. Harris, has been aggressive, lyrical terrorism (KRS-ONE). As poet Dennis Kim aka Denizen Kane from the Chicago Underground Superhero Hip-Hop group Typical Cats explains, "fuck you/I can speak about myself/in rhyming couplets/if I want to." Once the oppressed, the marginalized, the Othered, put pen to paper, begin to tell and scream and spit their impressions and stories, begin to record their experience in late-twentieth/early twenty-first-century Empire, the towers and castle doors shake.

7. Hip-hop poetica is juxtaposition and (over)layering of styles/genre. This is Afrika Bambaataa playing Kraftwerk and P-Funk and 1950s commercial jingles in the same set, sometimes in the same moment. A graff writer who utilizes a Disney animated character to represent a forgotten neighborhood in public space on public transit. Filmmakers have hipped me to this. Quentin Tarantino's *Kill Bill* series is anime, spaghetti western, martial arts epic, morality play, film noir, all in the same three hours. *Brick*, the John Hughes-like high school drama set in noir style and language, points to this idea. Here it is clearly in Duriel E. Harris's *Villanelle: for the dead white fathers.* A villanelle battle rap blues song mocking the old, dead, writers, gatekeepers, to prove the point that, yes we can do it, no it's not impossible, and yet still our shit is hotter—what!?!

8. Hip-hop poetica is self-reference and layered meaning. If you get me at this level cool, if not, that's what's up too. The self-referential, not reverential (this

essay excluded), layers meaning on the hip-hop poet's verse. If you understand the multiple references in the layered collage the depth of meaning grows. However, if the reader doesn't know say, Radio Raheem in Dargan's poem, the cabbage patch in Major Jackson's *Rock the Body Body*, meaning is still digestible and understood. The need for explanation of these references is undesirable. It is the demarcation of who is ahead and who needs to study, the wild style alphabet of graf writers. As a generation we ran to the libraries looking up obscure X-Clan references. All of us wanting to be smart at the party, to know exactly what Kane meant when he said "the Asiatic descendant."

9. Hip-hop poetica is song structure and word play. The pulling apart and invention of language, in Kearney and Phi's hip-hop haikus, their innovation of *skillables,* and the fracture of *biz-arre* and *man-ure.* All the assonance and compounded rhyme scheme in the three-line battle haikus, the fun and dexterity and clever word nerd silliness. In Goodwin's *1707*, the progressive line chorus created by the young men in the college dorm room in the South Loop of a changing Chicago pulls the listener/reader into the music and narrative movement of the poem. The language, sparse and a cappella, builds like a club anthem rewarding us with the completion of this fractured, composite chorus that seems to have been pulled together right before our eyes. Ellis employs a similar and more devious strategy in the use of anaphora. The droned repetition acts as an anti-song, anti-flavor, to clearly articulate what is not linguistically fly, about all their stanzas, thereby paving the way for the hip-hop folk ode of Pat Rosal, the musicality of Bryonn Bain (whose verse demands to be sung and chanted), and the word-unit breath control of Invincible.

10. Hip-hop poetica is communal narrative. Hip-hop poets are not dislocated from place or community, not the romanticized troll poets of privilege writing on and about birch wood from a chalet in Vermont. Perdomo writes the stories of a thousand ghost children lost in New York, Betts' reports on the disenfranchised lives of Chicago's youth, Dargan loves and delights the hip-hop head-center of our generation, giving us glimpses and narratives we head-nod to like, *yeah, dog, I feel you…* I recognize, finally, myself, my friend, my community, his/her story in a poem, in an anthology, in an utterance in public space, challenging the dominant cultural narrative that we were not here, were never here. Hip-hop poetica is documenting,

insuring, insisting that history will be written by the masses (this time). That not only are we concerned with line breaks and entendre, but also we are equally concerned with equity and enchantment, with meta-narratives and democracy, with opening the mic, to the actual multiplicity of voices represented in the landscape and not merely the whitewashed-wonder-bread Norton graveyard tombs of the past. This is not to say you can come wack. You must have skills, we talk more shit than anyone, this is not a touchy-feely-Berkeley—(respect fam, I love y'all but...)—type of poetic.

Read these poets and you may recognize William Carlos Williams, Pablo Neruda, Sonia Sanchez, or MC Lyte. We are the next articulation in American letters, the next wave in a long tradition of verse. We are here. You can get in the middle if you're not ready. This is only the beginning, of a conversation, of our time, in our infancy. We are here. word/up.

The Day Jam Master Jay Died

Kevin Coval

woke unsure how to pay rent
check hadn't come in from county
too many months living like artist
with no net to break the fall

went to my brother's class at Kelvyn Park
taught Luis Rodriguez in freshman honors
two poems about neighborhood folk / one
heroin-addicted guitar player and the other
man angry in Humboldt Park killing a car

gave a reading at Wright College
theater full of aging teens and faculty
after the set this skinny white kid comes over
gives me props for a poem about graff writers
i ask if he writes, *ELOTES* he says
no shit i say *i've been digging you*
for years over red and brown line tracks
first seen you up on that truck at Chicago
and Halsted / that's me he said

ate with Eboo downtown near Loyola
he lectures to a class of grad students
about discovery and inheritance / he is brilliant
in describing our engagement with modernity
we encounter the vastness of cultural practice
and build bridges back home he says

i think of Isabel / young writer at Kelvyn Park
Bindi between her eyebrows / picture of Lady Guadalupe

in her notebook / she reads the *Bhagavad Gita* in Spanish
with her Aunt who teaches Yoga at the Church
and i tell this class my path back to Judaism
was paved in breakbeats

walk to the train
get home / call my girl
she lives in Brooklyn
on my bed / she tells me

Jam Master Jay was shot
his head spilled onto the control panels
of his studio in Queens

it's fucked up she said
it's fucked up i said

said we'd talk tomorrow
hung up and my apartment was silent
like there was no music in my apartment
my apartment was silent like my childhood
memories silenced tonight like the music

-eulogy-

Chuck D said John Lennon was killed today
and i miss Pac and Big more than ever
i am Holden Caulfield watching hope break in the stalls of public bathrooms
i am Pete Rock and C.L. Smooth reminiscing over the fallen body of b-boy
Trouble T-Roy and dying hip-hop birth sites falling wayside to the pounding beats
of green-fisted real estate agents and the hard crack rock drug wars america wages
on her children creating culture with turntables

we have been here before

and i want Scott La Rock back to break up all this violence
i want Big L to throw a peace sign up in the air and DREAM
and Ramon and all the other graffiti artists killed in the line of their calling
to come back and bomb the World Trade Center
with the biggest streaked wildstyles the sky has ever seen:
a mural for the forgotten spray painted on the clouds
a gold chain cast across the sun
a single shell toe held up in the air

it was Jam Master Jay who introduced me to the culture
who soothed me over the bridge of whiteness and rock
it was his cool lean arms wrapped around chest / head back
in black fedora / no laces in his adidas / he stole electricity
to light the block parties / reparations / for all the stars exploded
before he could play the last song they requested / he'd send shine
beams on vinyl / into the distant homes of the sun starved
and let us bask in his light scratching scarce sounds / found
digging the landfills / of america's sonic consciousness

> *it's not bad meaning bad but bad meaning*
> *it's not bad meaning*
> *it's not bad meaning*
> *it's not*

*

* what norman rockwell didn't capture

Kevin Coval

on soccer field moms
blue chips off the old stock option
orange slice crescents into the pond
of their mothers' faces empty like stomachs
beneath searchlight gossip and broken seashells

they are practicing for the MCATs
have run out of frogs and pig fetus
bang chests like orangutans caged
in the basement behind *Donkey Kong*

near keebler elf slave quarters
Ari and Rachel consume TVs
for dinner cut washing machine detergent
with popsicle sticks and slurpee
psychotropes through nights of insomnia

their father is a long way from work
crunching numbers and bodies of color
in the parlors of monetary madams

he entertains other lives
with bleu cheese olive martinis
in a cul-de-sac not his own

he sleeps with the enigma
who whispers american dreams
from the balcony of his one night stand

in the bedroom castle we are
barred in all the King's pleasures:
sex sockets surround a floor of plug-ins
Barbie in a barbed-wire push-up bra
GI Joe bathes in a circus of pin ups
and shell casings

the last time we sat in the dining room
Uncle Dave stuck a bread knife thru his abdomen
his blood is covered by a throw rug and the silent
conversations we don't have

Crazy Bunch Barbeque at Jefferson Park

Willie Perdomo

This is definitely for
the brothers who ain't here
who woulda said
I had to write a poem
about this get together
like a list of names on a
memorial that celebrated
our own Old-Timer's Day

For those of us
who age in hood years
where one night can equal
the rest of your life and
surviving the trade-off was
worth writing on the wall
and telling the world
that we were here
forever

The barbeque started with a
snap session
Jerry had the best snap of the day
when he said that my family
was so poor and the fellas said
how poor and he said so poor that
on Thanksgiving they had to buy
turkey-flavored *Now & Laters*
The laughter needed no help when
we exposed the stretch marks of
our growing pains

Phil had barbeque on the grill
He slapped my hand when I tried to
brush extra sauce on a chicken leg

Yo, go find something to do
write a poem
write something
do something
I got this
I'm the chef
you the poet
talk about how you glad to be here
look at that little boy on the baseball diamond
look at him run circles around second base
today is his birthday
write about how the wind is
trying to take his red balloon

It use to take a few shots of
something strong before we
could cry and say I love you
we have always known how
to curse and bless the dead
now we let the silence say it
and like the little boy's sneakers
disappearing in a cloud of dirt
we walk home in the sun
grown up and full

This is definitely for
the brothers who ain't here

who woulda said
I had to write a poem
about this get together
like a list of names on a
memorial that celebrated
our own Old-Timer's Day

For those of us
who age in hood years

where one night can equal
the rest of your life and
surviving the trade-off was
worth writing on the wall
and telling the world
that we were here
forever

*

* B-Boy Infinitives

Patrick Rosal

To suck until our lips turned blue
the last drops of cool juice
from a crumpled cup sopped
with spit the first Italian Ice of summer
To chase popsicle stick skiffs
along the curb skimming stormwater
from Woodbridge Ave. to Old Post Road
To be To B-boy To be boys who
snuck into a garden to pluck
a baseball from mud and shit
To hop that old man's fence before
he bust through the front door
with a lame-bull limp charge
and a fist the size half a spade
To be To B-boy To lace shell-toe Adidas
To say Word to Kurtis Blow
To laugh the afternoons
someone's mama was so black
when she stepped out the car
the oil light went on
To count hairs sprouting
around our cocks To touch

ourselves To pick the half-smoked
True Blues from my father's ashtray
and cough the gray grit
into my hands To run
my tongue along the lips of a girl
with crooked teeth To be
To B-boy To be boys for the ten days
an 8-foot gash of cardboard lasts
after we dragged it
seven blocks then slapped it
on the cracked blacktop To spin
on our hands and backs To bruise
elbows wrists and hips to Bronx-Twist
Jersey version beside the mid-day traffic
To swipe To pop To lock freeze and
drop dimes on the hot pavement-
even if the girls stopped watching
and the street lamps lit buzzed all
night we danced like that
and no one called us home

*

* Freddie

Patrick Rosal

Freddie claimed lineage from the tough
Boogie-Down Boricuas
who taught him how to break-
dance on beat: up-
rock headspin scramble and dive

We call it a suicide:
the front-flip B-*boy* move that landed you
back flat on the blacktop That
was Freddie's specialty-the way he'd jump
into a fetal curl mid-air the *thwap*
against the sidewalk his body
laid out like the crucified
Jesus he knocked down
one afternoon in his mom's bedroom
looking for her extra purse
so both of us could shoot
asteroids and space invaders
until dusk
    That wasn't long before
Freddie disappeared
then returned one day as someone else's ghost
smoked-out on crack
singing *Puerto Rico Puerto Rico*
Las chicas de Puerto Rico
That was the first summer we believed
you had to be good at something
so we stood around and watched
Freddie on the pavement—all day—
doing suicides
until he got it right

*

* Born under Punches

Major Jackson

The deejay figured at 12"
From a batch of milk crates &
We were back inside the school
Gymnasium, cat walking between
slow drags & hipgrinds.

Skullcaps pulled below
Brows, Timberlands
Laced high, our fists swelled
Inside goosedown, metallic
Parkas. Spacemen

On the dance floor!
Heavy-eyed, feral-faced,
We roamed til some
Boy's neck flashed
Links of gold.

When Big Jake threw
A sucker punch, the boy
Fell like a swimmer
Given up breathing. Lovers
Left each other's arms,

Backing away.
Someone's sister moaned
In the bleachers &
A heavy groove
Unlocked a flurry of fists.

In the darkness,
Speakers rose like
Housing projects,
Moonlight diamonded
Mesh-wire panes.

What was it that bloomed
Around his curled
Body when the lights
Came up, fluorescent,
Vacant, garish?

The gym throbbed
With beats & rage
And his eyes darted
Like a man nailed
To a burning crucifix.

*

All Eyez On U

Nikki Giovanni

(for 2Pac Shakur 1971-1996)

as I tossed and turned unable to achieve sleep unable to control
anxiety unable to comprehend why

2Pac is not with us

if those who lived by the sword died by the sword there would be no
white men on earth
if those who lived on hatred died on hatred there would be no KKK
if those who lived by lies died by lies there would be nobody on wall
street in executive suites in academic offices instructing the young
don't tell me he got what he deserved   he deserved a chariot and
the accolades of a grateful people

he deserved his life

it is as clear as a mountain stream as defining as a lightning strike
as terrifying as sun to vampires

2Pac told the truth

there were those who called it dirty   gansta rap inciting there were
those who never wanted to be   angry at the conditions but angry at
the messenger who reported: *your kitchen has roaches your toilet
is overflowing your basement has so much. water the rats are in the
living room*

your house is in disorder

and 2Pac told you about it

what a beautiful boy graceful carriage melodic voice sharp wit intellectual
breadth what a beautiful boy to lose

not me   never me   I do not believe east coast west coast   I saw
them murder Emmett Till I saw them murder Malcolm X   I saw
them murder   Martin Luther King   I witnessed them shooting
Rap Brown I saw them beat LeRoi Jones   I saw them fill their jails
I see them burning churches   not me   never me   I do not believe
this is some sort of mouth action   this is some sort of political
action and they picked well   they picked the brightest freshest
fruit from the tallest tree   what a beautiful boy

but he will not go away   as Malcolm did not go away   as Emmett
Till did not go away   your shooting him will not take him from us
his spirit will fill our hearts   his courage win strengthen us for the
challenge   his truth will straighten our backbones

you know, Socrates had a mother   she too watched her son drink
hemlock   she too asked why   but Socrates stood firm and would
not lie to save himself   2Pac has a mother   the lovely Afeni had
to bury her son it is not right

it is not right that this young warrior is cut down   it is not right for
the old to bury the young   it is not right

this generation mourns 2Pac as my generation mourned Till as we
all mourn Malcolm   this wonderful young warrior

Sonia Sanchez said when she learned of his passing she walked all day
walking the beautiful warrior home to our ancestors I just cried as all
mothers cry for the beautiful boy who said he and Mike Tyson would
never he allowed to be free at the same time who told the truth about
them and who told the truth about us who is our beautiful warrior

there are those who wanted to make *him* the problem   who wanted
to believe if they silenced 2Pac all would be quiet on the ghetto
front there are those who testified that the problem wasn't the conditions
but the people talking about them

they took away band   so the boys started scratching they took away
gym   so the boys started break dancing the boys started rapping
cause they gave them the guns and the drugs but not the schools and
libraries

what a beautiful boy to lose

and we mourn 2Pac Shakur and we reach out to his mother and we
hug ourselves in sadness and shame

and we are compelled to ask:
R U Happy, Mz Tucker? 2Pac is gone
R U Happy?

*

*Mr. Dynamite Splits

Thomas Sayers Ellis

December 25, 2006

Long before the patriot acts
of anthems *Say it Loud, I'm Black and I'm
    Proud,*
Funky President and *Living In America*,
you and your Revue were

the only flames the hood could afford,
and by "hood" I mean "nation"
and by "nation" I mean "community"
and by "community"

I mean any one of the various
Black "folk" Americas
within Black America,
the Constitution's future reframers.

Your famous flames
were not the famous flames
of civil war or civil rights.
These flames were raw chicken guts

and a bewildered next-time fire
of choked chords and percussive horns
Papa lit the behinds
of new bags with.

To quote Sweet Charles, *Yes it's you*
the warm globe mourns...

for passing mashed potatoes and peas.
Gimme some more.

No. 1, not because of the hits
but because the roads,
like Augusta, all lead back to you.
Georgia might not-never let us bury you.

The hellish crossroads of black genius
(not geography) left you leathery as Miles.
Not the first to smack-your-bitch-up
and stick-it-to-the-man,

but the first to smack-your-bitch-up,
stick-it-to-the-man,
fine your band, tour Vietnam,
serve two drummers,

fire your band, tour Africa,
save the Boston Garden, endorse Nixon,
rehire your band, sue a rap group
and start a choir in prison.

Pre Hip Hop, you had your own emcee,
your own dancers, your own cape,
Lear jet and crown.
You graduated Super Bad.

Dr. King called it Drum Major Instinct.
Shirley Chisholm,

unbought and unbossed.
Damn right you were somebody.

"These nuts," that's what all the Camel Walks,
splits, spins and Popcorns
told those early closed doors.
Get up offa that thang.

Long live your plea please pleases,
Byrd's brotherly loyalty,
and calling-on Maceo's licking-stick.
Live at the Apollo laid legend to myth.

Before Hammer Time,
there was a time when "whatsinever" you did,
you did "to death."
Funky Broadway.

Your *eeeeeeeeeeeyow* will never rest.
You remain proud, cold bodyheat and sweat,
that muthafucka Black Caesar,
the only one who ever murdered dying.

Wasn't Jesus born today?
The Big Payback: the Angel Pneumonia
(not escape-ism) calling
the Godfather only halfway home.
What you gon' play now?

(Harlem, January 2007)

*

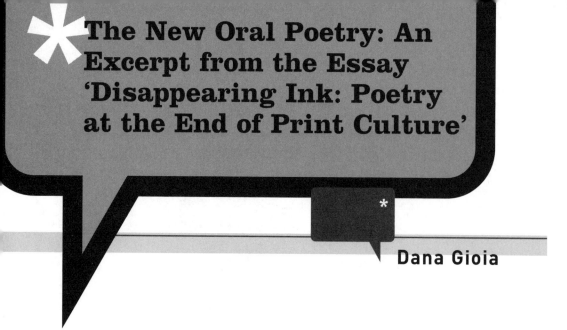

The New Oral Poetry: An Excerpt from the Essay 'Disappearing Ink: Poetry at the End of Print Culture'

Dana Gioia

'Sight isolates, sound incorporates' —Walter Ong

*What is a conscientious critic supposed to do with an Eminem or Jay-Z?
As individual texts for analysis, Snoop Dogg's "Doggy Style"…?*

If one examines the new popular poetry in more than a cursory fashion, one notices several significant ways in which it departs from the assumptions of mainstream literary culture. There are at least four fundamental ways in which it differs from traditional literary poetry. Without doubt the most surprising and significant development in recent American poetry has been the widescale and unexpected reemergence of popular poetry—namely rap. Thriving without the support of the university or the literary establishment the work has enormous implications for the future of poetry.

The nearly universal critical bias against rhyme and meter as recently as ten years ago, especially in university writing programs, indicates how distant the poets in a print culture had become from the orality of verse. The new popular poetry reminds literati that auditory poetry virtually always employs apprehensible formal patterns to shape its language. This rule not only holds true in primary oral cultures without writing and in scribal literary traditions like medieval Europe or imperial China where written verse was composed to be read aloud; it also applies to secondary oral cultures like contemporary mainstream America where popular verse is now transmitted without written texts.

The specific ways that speech is shaped into poetry differ from language to language, but the practice of arranging some aurally apprehensible feature such as stress, tone, quantity, alliteration, syllable count, or syntax into a regular pattern is so universal that it suggests that there is something primal and ineradicable at work. Metrical speech not only produces some heightened form of attention that increases mnemonic retention; it also seems to provide innate physical pleasure in both the auditor and orator. Typographic poetry may provide other pleasures, but it cannot rewire the circuitry of the human auditory perception to change a million years of preliterate, sensory evolution and permanently block the receptors that respond to auditory form.

The specific formal features of the new popular poetry deserve close examination, however, because they are not the traditional forms of English high-art poetry. Rap has developed so rapidly that it now uses a variety of metrical forms, but it is fascinating to analyze some of the early work that established the genre. Most rap still follows the initial formula of rhymed couplets that casually mix full rhyme with assonance. Here are a few metrically representative lines from one of the first popular raps:

> i said by the way baby what's your name
> said i go by the name of lois lane
> and you could be my boyfriend you surely can
> just let me quit my boyfriend called superman
> > from *"Rapper's Delight," Sugarhill Gang*

Rap is not written in the standard accentual-syllabic meters of English literary verse, but its basic measure does come out of the English tradition. Rap characteristically uses the four-stress, accentual line that has been the most common meter for spoken popular poetry in English from Anglo-Saxon verse and the border ballads to Robert Service and Rudyard Kipling.

> What is a woman that you forsake her,
> And the hearth-fire and the home-acre,
> To go with the old grey Widow-maker?
>
> She has no house to lay a guest in —
> But one chill bed for all to rest in,
> That the pale suns and the stray bergs nest in.
>
> She has no strong white arms to fold you,
> But the ten-times-fingering weed to hold you —

Out on the rocks where the tide has rolled you.

> *from "Harp Song of the Dane Women,"*
>
> *Rudyard Kipling*

The four-stress line is also a meter found throughout Mother Goose:

Tom, Tom, the piper's son,
Stole a pig and away did run.
The pig was eat, and Tom was beat
Till he run crying down the street.

In accentual meter, the poet doesn't count syllables, only the strong stresses. The unstressed syllables don't matter as long as the number of primary stresses remains constant from line to line. A four-stress line can be as short as:

Tóm, Tóm, the píper's són,
(6 syllables)

Or as long as:

The cóck's on the dúnghill a-blówing his hórn
(11 syllables)

The more unstressed syllables, usually, the faster the line is spoken. Rap consciously exploits stress-meter's ability to stretch and contract in syllable count. In fact, playing the syllable count against the beat is the basic metrical technique of rap. Like jazz, rap extravagantly syncopates a flexible rhythm against a fixed metrical beat, thereby turning a traditional English folk meter into something distinctively African American. By hitting the metrical beat strongly while exploiting other elements of word music, rappers play interesting and elaborate games with the total rhythm of their lines. Here is a syncopated couplet from Run DMC:

He's the better of the best, best believe he's the baddest
Perfect timing when I'm climbing I'm the rhyming acrobatist
(14 and 16 syllables, respectively)

Rap performers are not unaware of their connection to the tradition of English spoken verse. Here are a few lines from Run DMC's "Peter Piper":

Like the butcher, the baker, and the candlestick maker
He's a maker, a breaker, and a title taker
Like the little old lady who lived in a shoe
If cuts were kids he would be through
Not lying y'all he's the best I know
And if I lie my nose will grow
Like a little wooden boy named Pinocchio
And you all know how the story go

Rap's complex syncopation frequently pushes the meter to a breaking point. A reader would not always know exactly where the strong stresses fell. See how difficult it is to discern the four strong stresses in the first Run DMC couplet quoted, simply from the printed text, which I have purposely left unscanned. Likewise, literary scholars often have enormous difficulty in scanning *Mother Goose* rhymes on the page—unless they accept the performative tradition of schoolyard recitations, which place the beats squarely on certain syllables. Anglo-Saxon poets understood the problem inherent in strong-stress verse. That is at least one reason why they added alliteration to reinforce the meter. In rap the meter is also enforced by what its performers call "the beat." Traditional prosody describes the rhythm of poetry as the meaningful counterpoint of speech pattern against a fixed abstract meter. That same principle of expressive counterpoint is quite literally what its audience hears and enjoys in rap.

Influenced by print culture's habit of silent reading and its typographical bias toward a text's visual identity on the page, contemporary literary poets often neglect or underplay the auditory elements of their verse. Too overt or apprehensible a verbal pattern seems old-fashioned to many poets. When they employ new or traditional auditory forms, they often tone down the musical effects by deliberately flattening the rhythms, avoiding end-stopped lines, and eliminating noticeable alliteration or assonance. If they venture rhyme, that most conspicuous auditory technique of verse, they often play it down as well by burying it in run-on lines or substituting slant and half-rhymes.

The new popular poets, by contrast, flamboyantly display their metrical schemes. In the aesthetic of rap, for instance, the stronger the beat, the more extravagant the rhyme, the more elaborate the pattern skillfully deployed, the better the poem…

The unabashed stylization of the new popular poetry demonstrates two basic features of oral poetry. First of all, it always revels in its own formal elements. Why? Because that overt stylization distinguishes it from ordinary speech. Form is how oral verse announces its special status as art. In the same way that an early Modernist poem in free verse distinguishes itself from prose by certain typographical conventions such as empty space and line breaks that visually disrupt the standard page rule of the right-hand margin, oral poetry uses apprehensible auditory patterns, such as rhyme and meter, to command the special attention an audience gives to the heightened form of speech known as poetry.

Second, oral poetry understands—as does all popular art—that much of its power comes from the audience understanding exactly the rules the artist follows. Popular art is a performance that feeds, teases, frustrates, and fulfills the expectations of the audience. In this situation, the artist must demonstrate his or her conspicuous skill to do something better than the members of the audience could manage and to engage, move, surprise, and delight the audience within predetermined conventions. Without knowing anything about the etymology of English words, the audience for the new popular verse understands that poetry, like its Greek root *poesis,* is something that is *made* and that the poet, like the medieval English synonym, *makar*, must be its maker. The purpose of art is not to deny artifice but to manage it so well that it appears inevitable.

Finally, the new popular poetry differentiates itself from mainstream poetry in the most radical way imaginable, by attracting a huge, paying public. In a culture where high-art poetry requires state subsidies, private support, and academic subvention to survive, the new popular verse shamelessly thrives in the marketplace. Rap has already become a major branch of commercial entertainment. It would be no exaggeration to say that rap is the only form of verse—indeed, perhaps the only literary form of any kind—truly popular among American youth of all races. If there is a new generation of readers emerging in America, rap will be one of its formative experiences...

Why spend so much time analyzing popular verse so seriously if one makes no special claims for its artistic distinction? No, I do not consider Busta Rhymes and Jay-Z the Wallace Stevens and T. S. Eliot *de nos jours*, but I do insist that their creative methods, performance techniques, and public reception illuminate the world of literary poetry in ways that conventional frames of reference do not. I also understand that a critic risks intellectual derision by discussing popular poetry on its own terms without first clothing it in an elegant ideological wardrobe, preferably imported from Paris. But there are odd things currently happening in the poetry world, both high and low, that don't make sense in conventional terms, and the key to understanding these events lies in the innovative nature of new popular poetry.

Villanelle: for the dead white fathers

Duriel E. Harris

Backwater, yeah, but I ain't wet, so misters, I ain't studin' you:
Don't need your blessed doctrine to tell me what to write and when.
Behold, God made me funky. There ain't nothin' I cain't do.

I can write frontpocket Beale Street make you sweat and crave the blues,
Dice a hymnal 'til you shout *Glory! The Holy Ghost done sent me sin!*
Backwater, yeah, but I ain't wet, so misters, I ain't studin' you:

Signify a sonnet—to the boil of "Bitches Brew."
Rhyme royal a triolet, weave sestina's thick through thin.
I said God made me funky. There ain't nothin' I cain't do.

Eeshabbabba a subway station from damnation to upper room.
Lift-swing-hunh chain gang hammer like Alabama's nigga men.
Backwater, yeah, but I ain't wet, so misters, I ain't studin' you:

Shish kebab heroic couplets and serve 'em dipped in barbecue,
Slap-bass blank-verse-lines, tunin' fork tines 'til you think I'm Milton's kin.
Indeed, God made me funky. There ain't nothin' I cain't do.

You're poets dead; I'm poet live. Darky choruses belt: *Hallelu'.*
While you were steppin' out, someone else was steppin' in.
Backwater, yeah, but I ain't wet, so misters, I ain't studin' you:
God sho-nuff sho-nuff made me funky. There ain't nan thing I cain't do.

*

*Drag

Duriel E. Harris

drag \ . . . \row of hooks *under* crisp black umbrellas *napping* my head
mowing dreams' terse air *arrives* at **BAT**S(') psychedelic coatroom nigga lips
thinned for flight   and hanging   *breathable fabric*   pawpad

    BATfaces *unshut* leech like humming sacred *eeeek* rise cube my head:
juice-out, they disperse, eating my

    locs, body sleighing back dense *flagflap flagflap*   (laggard brake slugging)
flagflap flagflap (tether, flesh

*

self portrait at the millennium

Duriel E. Harris

for Mamie Till Mobley (1921-2003)

(Bad medicine stalks its way to surface
catches like dirt-latched blades:
barbed buoy, bloated blood house
tendered skull hole-punch to daylight;
minced cartilage toughens the brilliant chill
until hours protrude hard and slick.)

Spoiled niggra is the meat;
its hearty pulp warms hands,
builds strong bones and teeth.

*

* Rasta Not

Tracie Morris

I wear these dreads
reps crown of thorns
around my head
but do not mourn

the lion's tread
I'd rather scorn
the lie that lead
my others born

to fancy. Fled
pressed kinks forlorn
napping not dead.
Tied – roots untorn.

*

* Indigo

Tracie Morris

In Africa it showed up
folks too well. Brought here for dying – Blue Jeans.

*

* Life Saver

Tracie Morris

(for Savion)

Congolene-free, SG
Dap sans Dax. Unkneaded
He's so so savvy!
Oh, Bright – but no shinin'.

Replace the Ha
(cha cha cha)
Trade the happy
for the dreaded "N"

Seencha flicka
(Tag:
He of the Sunshine
Sammy genus)

So, Junior, betta watcha step
When they start acksin'
"Didn't Fred Ah, uh and Kelly er, um
'bust ya move'?"

Nah, Mista C – that's no steel life:
bubbah's bunioned
blistered & bludgeoned
even mo' on the good foot twernt um, *runnin'*

Drummin' up biznis
Y'all say we can't
be playin'. Pickin' on feats
— call it a toe jam, baby!

Lil Man buck dance
Bruva deckin' hall
G-love hit missives, Metal of
honor on point: — toe, heal, tow

Shuffle ain't sloe: flow staccato
Boot black front bubble up fo' suthin'!

Spit o' spirits slavin' in one container:
Pure he float: heir buoyant, he a life savor.

*

HIP HOP HAIKU (17 SKILLABLES)

Douglas Kearney & Bao Phi

DOUGLAS KEARNEY

Bend a fool swan-like,
origami cats just fold.
I'm cold as Klondike.

BAO PHI

Act bold and I'll light
you up like a pipe and set
your ass to swan dive.

DOUGLAS KEARNEY

Got rhymes? You pawned mine
in hard times like heirlooms. I
housed you like spare rooms.

BAO PHI

Phobias broken.
You like a nicotine patch:
the mic stops smoking.

DOUGLAS KEARNEY

Crews popped like Tupac.
Strip your sunset with ones that
stun cats and bruise cops.

BAO PHI

While me and D mic
pass—rock tight like tube tops and
tricolored tube socks.

DOUGLAS KEARNEY

Y'all punks is half-bull
like minotaurs. Waving white
flags like semaphore.

BAO PHI

Allow me to retort:
in response to y'all who dissed
before—you want more?

DOUGLAS KEARNEY

Be warned: we taunt more
than Apollo crowds. Launch war
sounds like hollow rounds.

BAO PHI

Confound clowns with our
upside-down frowns. Astound when
we 'round, rhymes abound.

DOUGLAS KEARNEY

Climb a mound of man-
ure, you're still not funky and
nasty as we are.

BAO PHI

We biz-arre, wield
corded scimitars, lyrical
stars shine in twilight.

DOUGLAS KEARNEY

Y'all should sing back-up
like Chi-Lites. Searching for words
like games in *Highlights*.

BAO PHI

Shine bright all the way
from the days of Litebrites to
flashlights to searchlights.

DOUGLAS KEARNEY

We call you "Recall"
cuz you don't work right. Our verse
smites, packs the hearse tight.

BAO PHI

Our mic fights make you
polite. Gobbledy-gook crack
a yolk in your soup.

DOUGLAS KEARNEY

Nigcompoop shoots mel-
onseeds. Be driven to com-
mitting felonies.

BAO PHI

Write rhymes on Post-it
notes. Memos doper than your
demos, one better.

DOUGLAS KEARNEY

Unfettered letters
scar monitors causing your
pants to get wetter.

BAO PHI

Pump lead into con-
federates heavy with sed-
iment to pen this.

DOUGLAS KEARNEY

Stupendous word bend-
ers, we lift like suspenders.
Bao Phi: let's end this.

*

*makémake ghetto bodypartscasta

LaTasha N. Nevada Diggs

for shane & q

Portions of this poem are written in Hawaiian after a conversation as to whether or not rap lyrics could be structured on the page and still maintain both literary and rhythmical integrity. The translation of each word is literally beside it, either before or after, indicating a body part with the exception of Pele, the goddess of the volcano, wai hua'ai, a traditional drink from Hawai'i and haole, which is a term for white people.

'ā'î neck   protect ya deck
kikala hip skip like yo booty don't care
cause you can't maintain the funk...
I'm the millionare
the debonair   sipping wai belvedere

my ihu nose lines   the prize
dressed to the nines
the debonair   sipping wai hua'ai
    belvedere

check. clean. check. fresh. check. fly. so def.
yes yes ya'll   Pele comes to wreck

wit da kino body rock
lehelehe lips wit the glock

of menehune   you's a pua'a at a lû'au

    my hand lima blazes like 'aumakua
maka eye's Funkadelic like
Redman in a hula   *dope-a-delic*

I'm taking cheek papālina
poli breast feedin' malihini dust schemas

wit da force of my momma's
devil's walking stick
po'o   head trip! slap!
oh you's a dumb haole chick

your waha mush mouth
just dust in my shells
pu'uwai heart like my nose
take it right back to the cell

my ihu nose lines   the prize
dressed to the nines
the debonair   sipping wai hua'ai
    belvedere

check. clean. check. fresh. check. fly. so def
yes yes ya'll   Pele comes to wreck
yes yes ya'll   Pele comes to wreck

*

My Father's Brother

Christina Santana

I.
They dared his aim.
Bet a pack of cigarettes
he couldn't crack
the old jibaro's window
three houses down.

He pulled back
a tan leather pouch
tied to bacon-thick rubber bands.

Marbles: ammo.
Let go.

My father's brother,
Junior, killed a man
with a slingshot.

II.
Now, he paces across Viequez.
Gathers coconuts
from orphaned trees,
sells them for a dollar.

Only left his business to visit
his mother's funeral back in St. Thomas
where gave me a t-shirt he made—
"Se Venden Cocos."

I tell him he'd make more money
if he sold the shirts.

He says nothing,
teeth rotten
from letting go.

*

hoodology (west side of chicago)

Mike Booker

we learn to time the gun shots
7:45, 9:17, 11:23, 1:36 in the morning, nigga
every night duckin below window sills

my block was so hectic
i lived between danger and a stop sign
learned the streets backwards i was outside so much
better yet learned the streets better than the back of my hand
better yet learned the streets better than the back of my father's head
cuz that's all i ever saw

when i was 15
i went w/ chris to go shoot at some niggas
over his babies mom and a gun
shot missed my chest by 6 inches

my grandmother used to tell me be grateful for what you got
some people got it rougher than you

lil jerry his 3 brothers 4 younger sisters
had to sleep on cardboard boxes in the garage
at the end of my alley b/c his mother did drugs too bad

miss adams down the street
had 6 sons
all of them sold drugs
none of them ever saw age 19
the last one killed a week before
his 19th birthday

and you wonder why it's a curse to be stuck here forever
wonder why school never meant nothing to me half the time

everybody from kedzie to cicero is on welfare
the property tax is so low
teachers fresh from college would come teach at my school for 2 months

so they could get a job somewhere in the suburbs
so they could put on their resume, "I worked in the inner city"
like they was in the trenches of war
and you think we didn't know what was happenin
when we had 4 different 5th grade teachers

analyze my life and tell me how many opportunities i've had
to break down stereotypes

the first thing i learned how to count was drug money
fairy tales never knocked on my door
my favorite child hood game
was cops and gang bangers

so apparently we are the bad seeds of this nation
the inner city constituents
and it's hard for me to see how

when all the serial killers turn out to be white boys who grew up in the suburbs
when all the rapists turn out to be catholic priests

my hood is full of kings and queens
who evolved into peasants over the time span of 500 years

my ancestry was ripped away from me
replaced w/ drugs and guns
thugs and crack heads
misdemeanors, felonies and jail bars

but my grandmother used to tell me
you got a roof over your head
clothes on your back
food in your stomach

my grandmother used to tell me be grateful for what you got
some people got it rougher than you

my grandmother never lied to me
not once

*

*For Those Who Need a True Story

Tara Betts

The landlord told Raymond's mother that twelve dollars
would be deducted from their rent for every rat killed.
She sends her son to the store for a loaf of Wonder Bread
and five pounds of ground beef. Young Raymond
returns with bread & meat that she tears & mixes inside
a metal bowl. Mama seasons this meatloaf with rat poison
pulled from the cabinet beneath the sink. Well done,
meat sits steaming in the middle of the kitchen floor.
Then the scratching scurries. The squeaking begins
and screeches its toward the bowl.

Raymond describes the wave of rats like a tidal crash
covering the bowl, leaping over each other's bodies,
then the dropping, the stutter kicks.

A chorus of rat screams rambles through Raymond's ears.
Keening, furry bodies tense paws against churning guts
as they hit cracked linoleum until an hour passes.
Silence sweeps away the din in death's footsteps.
The mother's voice quivers in her next request.
Raymond, help me count them.

They waded through these small deaths with rubber gloves,
listened to the thump of each dead rat as it rustled against
the slackness of plastic bags.

Raymond wanted to stop counting,
but mama needed to save a dozen dollars
wherever she could
if they wanted to finally leave the rats behind.
After the last rat was counted, Raymond handed
the bag to the landlord as proof. Here.

Enough rats to skip the rent for three months.
Enough rats to avoid the fear of sweet sleeping
breath leading to bitten lips.
Healthy children wrapped in designer dictates
cannot describe Raymond's fear of rabies,
the smell of poison rotting from the inside out,
the scratching inside the walls at night.

Those children
should find soft lives
that drop pendulums in their dreams
and never tell another story
about the ghetto
until they've had to count rats
with their hands.

* Lili's Hands

Kelly Tsai

she uses them
to slice fish
from the market

to dump bundles
of rice noodles into
boiling water

to smash garlic
with the edge
of a cleaver

to spin the tap
for cold water

to soak the bittermelon
and suck it of
its dry newspaper taste

Lili's hands
wipe down the counters
with lightning speed

pile sets of buns
soft with heat
onto a plate

dash sesame oil
soy sauce and ginger
into the steaming wok

Lili's hands
cube tofu
cure chicken feet
wipe the shit stains
from my aunt's toilet

Lili's hands
massage my uncle's feet
bloated from a lifetime
of a soldier's walk

she curves his soles
as he contorts his face
tv-watching
Stephen Chow
kung fu chop
over a wall

Lili's hands
rub acetone
over fingernails

Lili's hands
ball into tiny fists
as she pulls her
blanket over her head
on the cot
in the back room
next to the laundry machine

*

* Blue Monday

Xero

I sing the blues every Monday moanin' and I don't stop until my day is done
I sing the blues every Monday moanin' and I don't stop until my day is done
And if I ever meet a man named Monday
He better already be holdin' a gun

My father had a stroke on Monday morning
Now the right side of his body's indefinitely on strike,
and he, a devout working man, has yet another reason to despise
Monday mornings,
but he and those blue Mondays used to be old friends
See, my father was born on a plantation of sharecroppers
For those of you who don't know,
sharecropping was "the other slavery"
So my father was well acquainted with the Louisiana sun
cracking its whip across his poor little face
until perspiration poured
from his lacerated pores
Yet, that same sweat
was the glistening badge of honor that he wore
His childhood chores matured
because he was a power plant of bio-thermal energy,
so inactivity don't sit well with my daddy 'cause my dadd...
my father never did SIT well

My father had a stroke on Monday morning
And it wasn't the stroke of his paint gun
across the hull of a dilapidated barge
Although he was a seasoned veteran of the shipyard,
seasoned by the seasons that found his beautiful blue-black skin
marinating in the Tabasco of ultra-violet rays

Out-working men haf his age who had
tasteless tops compared ta his sawt n'pepper locks
No matter hah bitter or hot it got, my pops...
my father had mouths to feed

A blue sky means that the paint will get a chance to dry,
but rain clouds deny   wages
His strength amazes me,
but men like him are not interesting these days
These days interest is accrued with riches
and we don't revolve around our families
as much as we revolve around rims, *dat redundantly revolve around*
Respek for tha blue collar worker done died and it ain't gon' breath again until MTV airs a show call
    "Pimp My Insides"
Ma daddy had a stroke on Monday moanin'

And it was a sinister stroke of bad luck, because it waited
See, for six months my father's been laid off,
pacing and mowing across his yard
until business picks up at the shipyard
The stroke didn't strike until after they called him last week
and asked him to report back to work,
first thing Monday morning
It struck on THAT Monday morning
But it struck before he could make it
to the jobsite, where his health insurance would have been
reinstated
By Monday afternoon he was fidgeting
in his seemingly comfortable hospital bed,
his left side, sending a message to the Angel of Death
circling overhead
One that can best be verbally expressed as,
"Don't start no shit, won't be no shit!"
His right side, limply flailing in the winds of change,
drowning in the rain that drops the dreaded thoughts of retirement onto his brain

Painters don't get paid on rainy days,
but don't no man know tha weather like ma daddy
I sot down neks to him and aksed him if dere was anythang he needed or wonted
And he replied, "Boy, I wonts to go outside"

Ma daddy took wit a stroke on Monday moanin'
And I expect tha by neks week he gon' been done started to paint tha sky blue once again, 'cause he
   got a soul to feed and 'cause he never did mind makin' a lil' ovahtime
fa his sons
in the sun

*

* ,said the shotgun to the head. (excerpt)

by Saul Williams

TRACK 51
(excerpt)

Most Beloved,

i am certain
of nothing more
than your existence.

a thousand ants
crawling under a log
may find themselves
 exposed
in my childlike search

                    for you.

my Kali
        flower,

i am eternally destroyed

                 by your love.
no longer
am I eligible
for any worker's
pension.

my friends laugh at me
and talk behind my back.

they say that you have
changed me

and i am.

i am like a survivor
of the flood

walking through the streets
drenched with
God. surprised
that all of the
drowned victims
are still walking
and talking.
(the secret of our leaders became how they said
and quickly became IT. oratory art is of sorcery. slang
rap democracy. through death as through life. we shape
a clearer silence. pitch black through the registers. hat-
cocked to the submarine. in love with you for
asking.)

maybe there's hope.

i rush to each
victim's side
sucking what
i can of you
out of your

various incarnations

pumping their
stomachs and
filling them.

to touch them
is to touch you.

to kiss them
is to kiss you.

my friends,

love is an artform

          slightly removed
from its element.

one may ask,
well what does
this mean?

i respond
i've made it up
but it shall be
from now on.

from now on
cities will be built
on one side
of the street

so that soothsayers
will have wilderness
to wander

and lovers
space enough
to contemplate

                                                    a kiss

                                              she
                                        kissed
                                        as if she,
                                        alone,
                                  could forge
                                  the signature
                                        of the sun.

                              i close my eyes
                                    although
                              i never know
                              the difference
                              i stood before
                              a brighter light
                                    at lesser
                                        distance.

and then, a feeling. almost as if
nothing were ever bound to repeat
Itself again. as if history had been as
masterfully created as the great
pyramids and any attempt to
reconstruct or relive any given
moment would have to stem from an
understanding of how the pyramids
were built from the top down.

and if one could understand such majesty
one would also that pyramids were first
made of flesh and that kisses
are portals.

                                        our bounded souls
                                      shifting through
                                        hidden corrals
                                    and passageways
                                  a will find my way
                                      to eternity
                                                    within you.

                        when i can feel you
                          breathing into me
                        i, like a stone gargoyle
                    atop some crumbling building,
                            spring to life
                          a resuscitated
                            angel.

i sweep through city streets my wings out-stretched making mothers clutch their young
                            and remember.

                      and do you remember, dear ones
                      or has your history forsaken you?
                    there were tales told 'round fires
                        mysteries coded in song
                          chants and uprisings
                            centuries of art
                            all incantations
                        calling forth this day.

on this day
the drunks vomit in unison
'though last night they drank from different cups.

children laugh and play
introducing their parents
to invisible friends.
a country girl smiles
and two trees blossom
out of season.

sea sons awaken
our mother has returned
to wave us
from uncertainty
once tidal.

twice born
of wooden ships

thrice formed
through mothers' hips

mother ships
graced tu lips
a poets' garden..

"2 for 5"
"they're going fast"

the future's bargain

"that's strange,
" i heard my name"

the river's parting

"hurry up"

things blurry up
the sun is darkened

river
like oceans
oceans
like answers
questions
in cloud form
raindrops
in stanzas

to be
or not to....

to see
or not to....

she had eyes
like two turntables
mix(h)er
in between
my dreams and reality
blend in
ancient themes

the base is of isis

cross-faded to ankh

the beat drops
like a cliff

over-looking

my

heart.

6000 feet
above sea level.
3300 bodies
disassembled.

the head bone's
connected
to the cock pit.

knee jerk
ass backwards

dancing slaves
in a mosh pit.

punk

rock

of Gibraltar.

roll out
nothing's new.

mo' blood dyes
the mo hawk

only this time
it's u.

and u
never loved her
for what she
possessed.

u powdered
her face
and came
on her
head-dress.

oil slick feathers
putrid stenched
water-bed

"mother nature's
a whore"

,said the shotgun to the head.

and it smelled
like teen spirit,
angst driven

insecure.

a country
in puberty.

a country

at war.

*

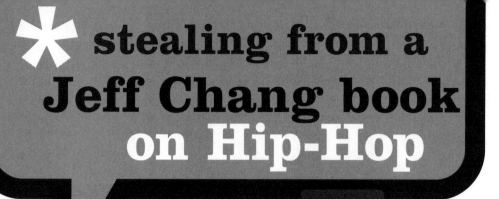

It has become myth, a creation myth, this West Bronx party at the end of the summer in 1973. Not for its guests, a hundred kids and kin from around the way. Nor for the setting, a modest recreation room in a new apartment complex. Not even for its location, two miles north of Yankee Stadium, near where the Cross-Bronx Expressway spills into Manhattan. Time remembers it for the night DJ Kool Herc made his name.

The plan was simple enough, according to the party's host, Cindy Campbell. "I was saving my money, because what you want to do for back to school is go down to Delancey Street instead of going to Fordham Road, because you can get the newest things that a lot of people don't have. And when you go back to school, you want to go with things that nobody has so you could look nice and fresh," she says. "At the time my Neighborhood Youth Corps paycheck was like forty-five dollars a week—ha!—and they would pay you every two weeks. So how am I gonna turn over my money? I mean, this is not enough money!"

Cindy calculated it would cost a little more than half her paycheck to rent the rec room in their apartment building at 1520 Sedgwick Avenue. Her brother, whom she knew as Clive but everyone else knew as Kool Herc, was an aspiring DJ with access to a powerful sound system. All she had to do was bulk-buy some Olde English 800 malt liquor, Colt 45 beer, and soda, and advertise the party.

She, Clive, and her friends hand-wrote the announcements on index cards, scribbling the info below a song title like "Get on the Good Foot" or "Fencewalk." If she filled the room, she could charge a quarter for the girls, two for the guys, and make back the overhead on the room. And with the profit—presto, instant wardrobe.

Clive had been DJing house parties for three years. Growing up in Kingston, Jamaica, he had seen the sound systems firsthand. The local sound was called Somerset Lane, and the selector's name was King George. Clive says, "I was too young to go in. All we could do is sneak out and see the preparation of the dance throughout the day. The guys would come with a big old handcart with the boxes in it. And then in the night time, I'm a little itchy headed, loving the vibrations on the zinc top 'cause them sound systems are powerful.

"We just stay outside like everybody else, you know, pointing at the gangsters as they come up, all the famous people. And at the time they had the little motor-cycles, Triumphs and Hondas. Rudeboys used to have those souped up. They used to come up four and five six deep, with them likkle ratchet knife," Clive says. He still remembers the crowd's buzz when Claudie Massop arrived at a local dance one night. He wanted to be at the center of that kind of excitement, to be a King George.

Cindy and Clive's father, Keith Campbell, was a devoted record collector, buy-ing not only reggae, but American jazz, gospel, and country. They heard Nina Simone and Louis Armstrong and Nat King Cole, even Nashville country crooner Jim Reeves. "I remember listening to Jim Reeves all the time," Clive says. "I was singing these songs and emulating them to the fullest. That really helped me out, changing my accent, is singing to the records."

In the Bronx, his mother, Nettie, would take him to house parties, which had the same ambrosial effect on him that the sound systems had. "I see the different guys dancing, guys rapping to girls, I'm wondering what the guy is whisperin' in the girl's ears about. I'm green, but I'm checking out the scene," he recalls. "And I noticed a lot of the girls was complaining, 'Why they not playing that record?' 'How come they don't have that record?' 'Why did they take it off right there?'" He began buying his own 45s, waiting for the day he could have his own sound system.

As luck would have it, Keith Campbell became a sponsor for a local rhythm and blues band, investing in a brand-new Shure P.A. system for the group. Clive's father was now their soundman, and the band wanted somebody to play records during intermission. Keith told them he could get his son. But Clive had started up his own house party business, and somehow his gigs always happened to fall at the same times as the band's, leaving Keith so angry he refused to let Clive touch the system. "So here go these big columns in my room, and my father says, 'Don't touch it. Go and borrow Mr. Dolphy's stuff,'" he says. "Mr. Dolphy said, 'Don't worry Clive, I'll let you borrow some of these.' In the back of my mind, Jesus Christ, I got these big Shure columns up in the room!"

At the same time, his father was no technician. They all knew the system was powerful, but no one could seem to make it peak. Another family in the same building had the same system and seemed to be getting more juice out of it, but they wouldn't let Keith or Clive see how they did it. "They used to put a lot of wires to distract me from chasing the wires," he says.

One afternoon, fiddling around on the system behind his father's back, Clive figured it out. "What I did was I took the speaker wire, put a jack onto it and jacked it into one of the channels, and I had extra power and reserve power. Now I could control it from the preamp. I got two Bogart amps, two Girard turntables, and then I just used the channel knobs as my mixer. No headphones. The system could take eight mics. I had an echo chamber in one, and a regular mic to another. So I could talk plain and, at the same time, I could wait halfway for the echo to come out.

"My father came home and it was so loud he snuck up behind me," he remembers. Clive's guilt was written all over his face. But his father couldn't believe it.

Keith yelled, "Where the noise come from?"

"This is the system!"

Keith said, "What! Weh you did?"

"This is what I did,'" Clive recalls telling his father, revealing the hookup. "And he said, 'Raas claat, man! We 'ave sound!!!'

"So now the tables turned. Now these other guys was trying to copy what I was doing, because our sound is coming out monster, monster!" Clive says. "Me and my father came to a mutual understanding that I would go with them and play between breaks and when I do my parties, I could use the set. I didn't have to borrow his friend's sound system anymore. I start making up business cards saying 'Father and Son.' And that's how it started, man! That's when Cindy asked me to do a back-to-school party. Now people would come to this party and see these big-ass boxes they never seen before."

It was the last week in August of 1973. Clive and his friends brought the equipment down from their second-floor apartment and set up in the room adjacent to the rec room. "My system was on the dance floor, and I was in a little room watching, peeking out the door seeing how the party was going," he says.

It didn't start so well. Clive played some dancehall tunes, ones guaranteed to rock any yard dance. Like any proud DJ, he wanted to stamp his personality onto his playlist. But this was the Bronx. They wanted the breaks. So, like any good DJ, he gave the people what they wanted, and dropped some soul and funk bombs. Now they were packing the room. There was a new energy. DJ Kool Herc took the mic and carried the crowd higher.

"All people would hear is his voice coming out from the speakers," Cindy says. "And we didn't have no money for a strobe light. So what we had was this guy named Mike. When Herc would say, 'Okay, Mike! Mike with the lights!', Mike flicked the light switch. He got paid for that."

By this point in the night, they probably didn't need the atmospherics. The party people were moving to the shouts of James Brown, turning the place into a sweatbox. They were busy shaking off history, having the best night of their generation's lives.

Later, as Clive and Cindy counted their money, they were giddy. This party could be the start of something big, they surmised. They just couldn't know how big.

epilogue

Victor D. Infante

The success of spoken word came from its appeal to nontraditional poetry audiences, people looking for something beyond the "poetry establishment." But wouldn't a new poetics, existing outside the boundaries and influence of the establishment, serve as a threat to the business-as-usual of the university programs, or the academy that feeds off them? How much poetry traffic can the middle-class market bear?

These are soul-searching times, demanding of maverick poets that they speak to the issues of the day, not to big houses in the country. In this, both slam and the academy have more in common than their leaderships would ever dare express: the memberships of both care deeply for the art form they share. The very act of writing a poem is a political expression, the simplest pastoral verse a probing at the boundaries of freedom of speech. Great art cannot be made without the risk of great, even horrific, failure.

As it stands, slam holds a great well of untapped potential. Indeed, if there is a potential of stagnation there at all, it comes from strict adherence to the forms and limitations of the competition itself.

In the years to come, it seems likely that America will be fascinated by its out-law poets, heaping increasing amounts of success and praise on them, until the national mind focuses elsewhere for a while. What then? One hopes that the poets would remain the same, screaming at darkness whether anyone listens or not, but one can also see more than a few of the once-maverick poets settled down in old homes in the country, pondering them until the next class begins.

A Tree in the Forest

Marc Smith

He sat in the hollow center
Of a personal universe, his wood,
With the scowl of a dead walnut tree
Draping his face.

No one came near.

No trespass allowed.

His dreary countenance
Repelled any lighthearted dapple
Chancing a penetration into the gloom.

And when he spoke,

Dry walnuts were launched
Smacking the tin roofs below
Thudding heavy to the ground.

All who might have listened
Wondered what they might
See in his breath,
A certain slant of sun
Beaming off the wood?

But there was none, no light.
And those who cocked an ear
Heard nothing
But the howling husks
Of some lonely place
And the misanthropic attack
Of his rotting dead fall.

About the Editors

Editor:

Mark Eleveld is also editor of *The Spoken Word Revolution* (Sourcebooks MediaFusion, 2003), the top-selling book on the spoken word poetry movement. He is co-publisher at EM Press and a board member of the Midland Authors Society in Chicago. He lives in Joliet, Illinois.

Advisor/Narrator:

Marc Smith is the founder of the poetry slam. He began the poetry slam over twenty years ago at the Green Mill Jazz Lounge in Chicago. One of the longest running shows in Chicago history, it is perhaps the longest running weekly poetry show in the country. The creation of the poetry slam has lead to a new form of poetics generally regarded as Slam Poetry. Smith and the "Uptown Poetry Slam" continue to perform to packed audiences every Sunday. He is the author of *Crowdpleaser* (Collage Press) and editor of *The Complete Idiots Guide to Slam Poetry* (Alpha Press). He has performed his poetry to over 100,000 people.

Advisor/Narrator:

Kevin Coval is the artistic director for the Young Chicago Authors and co-founder of the teen slam "Louder than a Bomb." He is a regularly featured poet on Chicago Public Radio and the author of *Slingshots: A Hip-Hop Poetica* (EM Press).

Deep Background:

Ronald Maruszak is a co-founder at EM Press. He has published poetry books and CDs, worked on dozens of poetry shows, and was instrumental in research and guidance with *The Spoken Word Revolution* and *The Spoken Word Revolution Redux*. He is a graduate student at the University of Chicago.

Acknowledgments

a special thank you to my family, michelle, finn, ava, donald, lynne, dom,
kathy and bob, jayme and jimmy, and tucker, grace, rachel, jeff,
matt and jennifer and kyle, faith, nick, dave and deb and davie,
ron and dr. joann and emily rose, evelyn, marc s., kevin c.

thanks to roger b., jeff m., patricia s., lisa b., jack m., taylor m., john c

thanks to my teaching colleagues, the students, always to george,
dick...all the words and discussions

thanks to Chicago Producers Circle c/o rob and tim,
The Bowery Poetry Club c/o bob h., elena a.,
The Poets House c/o carlin w. & stone, Green Mill,
Chi St Pub, PSI Inc.

thanks to sandra f., jillian f., chase t., jack b. and mary g., dana g.
brandy b-s., zoran o.

thanks to todd g., megan d., and dom

thank you to my buddy, "So what"

Contributor Biographies

Michael Anania is a retired professor of English at the University of Illinois-Chicago. He is the author of *In Natural Light* (Asphodel Press).

Patricia Barber is a jazz singer, pianist, bandleader and songwriter. *Mythologies* (Blue Note) is Barber's ninth career album; each track is based on a character from poet Ovid's masterwork.

Marvin Bell is Iowa's first poet laureate. He taught forty years for the Iowa Writers' Workshop. *Mars Being Red*, his nineteenth book, will be published in 2007.

Tara Betts has appeared on HBO's Def Poetry Jam and in the SouthWest VDay production of Eve Ensler's "Vagina Monologues" at Chicago's DuSable Museum. Her work has appeared in *Essence* magazine, the Steppenwolf Theater, *Bum Rush the Page* (Three Rivers Press), and *Home Girls Make Some Noise: Hip Hop Feminism* (Parker Publishing LLC). She teaches writing at Urban Word and Bronx Writers' Center.

Roger Bonair-Agard is the author of *Tarnish and Masquerade* (Cypher Press). He is the 1999 National Poetry Slam Individual Champion and has been featured on HBO's *Def Jam Poetry* three times in the past.

Mike Booker has been writing in Chicago since 2002. He has performed twice at Louder Than a Bomb: The Chicago Teen Poetry Festival, and twice at Brave New Voices: The National Teen Poetry Slam. He has performed in London, Jamaica, and shared the stage with Nikki Giovanni, Regie Gibson, and Kevin Coval.

Derrick Brown, former paratrooper for the 82nd Airborne (North Carolina), gondolier (www.gondolagetawayinc.com), magician, and fired weatherman (Arizona), now travels the world and performs his written work. Originally, from Long Beach, CA, he currently writes for a children's show called *Kidmo* and lives outside of Nashville, Tenn.

Michael R. Brown has published his poetry, fiction, travel articles and columns in wide-ranging periodicals all over the world. His fourth book of poetry, *The Confidence Man*, was published by Ragged Sky in 2006.

Jeff Buckley was born in 1966 and died in a tragic drowning accident on May 29, 1997. He had emerged in New York City's avant-garde club scene as one of the most remarkable musical artists of his generation, acclaimed by audiences, critics, and fellow musicians alike. His EP *Live At Sin-é*, was released in December 1993 on Columbia Records, and the acclaimed album *Grace* followed in 1994. On New Year's Day 1995, he appeared and read at the annual St. Mark's Church Marathon Poetry Reading.

Lisa Buscani is the author of, *Jangle*, and the 1992 National Poetry Slam Individual Champion. She is currently the Executive Director of the Poetry Center of Chicago.

Jason Carney is a former skin head who now uses his poetry to write against intolerance. He has appeared on *Russell Simmons Presents Def Poetry*.

Jim Carroll is the author of *The Basketball Diaries,* and more recently the poetry collection *Void of Course* (Penguin).

Jeff Chang is a hip-hop historian and author of the American Book Award winning *Can't Stop Won't Stop: A History of the Hip-Hop Generation*.

Michael Cirelli has been a National Poetry Slam individual finalist and the only person to make all three Bay area slam teams in the same year, winning the finals in both San Francisco and Berkeley. He is currently an MFA candidate at the New School University and the Director of Urban Word NYC.

Billy Collins is the author of *The Trouble with Poetry* (2005). He is a professor of English at Lehman College and served as U.S. Poet Laureate from 2001-2003.

Matt Cook is the author of three collections of poetry. His newest book, *The Unreasonable Slug*, is forthcoming from Manic D Press.

Billy Corgan is the author of *Blinking With Fists* (FSG). He is a founding member of the Smashing Pumpkins.

Gregory Corso is one of the original Beat Poets along with Jack Kerouac and Allan Ginsberg. He is the author of the novel *American Express* (1961) and the poetry collection *The Happy Birthday of Death* (1960). He died in 2001. His writing has influenced a generation of readers and writers.

Robert Creeley attended Harvard University, and received the Lannan Lifetime Achievement Award and the Frost Medal. One of his last publications included *If I Were Writing This* in 2003. Creeley died in 2005 at the age of 78. He was a Black Mountain Poet and a Beat Poet who influenced a generation of poets.

EE Cummings is a poet and writer whose poetry is known for its unusual grammar and punctuation. His name was frequently expressed "e e cummings" in lowercase, to mirror the grammatical style of his poetry. However, Cummings himself did not approve.

Da Boogie Man is the first male National Poetry Slam Individual Champion and four-time winner of *It's Showtime at the Apollo*. He also wrote *The Relationship Cookbook*, the premiere guide for creating healthy, fulfilling, and long lasting relationships.

Gayle Danley is the 1994 National Poetry Slam Champion and the 1996 International Slam Poet Champion. She has been featured to on *60 Minutes*.

Kyle G. Dargan teaches in American University's Creative Writing Program. He is an advisory editor for *Callaloo* and former poetry editor for *Indiana Review*. His first collection, *The Listening* (University of Georgia Press, 2004), won the 2003 Cave Canem Poetry Prize.

Corbet Dean, author of *A Collection of Crime Scenes* (and producer of the spoken word film by the same name), can be reached through his website at www.corbetdean.com.

Mayda Del Valle is the 2002 National Poetry Individual Champion.

LaTasha N. Nevada Diggs is the author of *Ichi-Ban* and *Ni-Ban* (MOH Press), and *Manuel is destroying my bathroom* (Belladonna Press). She is the lead electronic vocalist for the bands, The Yohimbe Brothers, fronted by Vernon Reid and DJ Logic and TBK, fronted by Guillermo E. Brown. She is a Harlem Native.

Thomas Sayers Ellis is the author of *The Maverick Room*, *Song On* and *The Genuine Negro Hero*. He teaches at Sarah Lawrence College.

Martín Espada's eighth poetry collection, *The Republic of Poetry*, was published by Norton in 2006. He is a 2006 Guggenheim Fellow.

yvonne fly onakeme etaghene: daughter of Nigerian water goddesses, dyke, poet, dancer, playwright. She has spit poetry in the kitchens, on the rooftops and stages of over 25 U.S. cities and have released three poetry chapbooks and one CD.

Dave Allan Evans is poet laureate of South Dakota and has five books of poems published along with two book of prose. His most recent poetry collection is *The Bull Rider's Advice: New and Selected Poems*.

James Fenton was educated at Magdalen College, Oxford where he won the Newdigate Prize for poetry. He has worked as political journalist, drama critic, book reviewer, war correspondent, foreign correspondent and columnist. His *Selected Poems* was published in February 2006 by Penguin and in October 2006 by Farrar Straus Giroux.

Dan Ferri is a former factory worker, fork lift driver and potter who recently retired after 20 years as an elementary and middle school teacher. He is a regular commentator on NPR's *All Things Considered* and Chicago Public Radio's *848,* and has received a Best Radio Commentary Award from the Illinois Associated Press, and the Peter Lisagor Award from the Chicago Society of Professional Journalists. His work has appeared in *Harper's, Re-Thinking Schools* and *The Outlaw Bible of American Poetry*.

Jack Foley's poetry has been described by Heaven Bone magazine as "evolving from the linguistic musical tradition of the original S.F. 'Beat' poet/performers and extending that eye, ear and voice of penetrating clarity into a modern mythology." His column, "Foley's Books" appears in the online magazine *The Alsop Review*; his radio show, *Cover to Cover*, is heard every Wednesday at 3 on Berkeley, California station KPFA.

Nick Fox has been performing poetry since 2000 and is the founder of the Flagstaff Poetry Slam. He is currently working towards his MFA in fiction at Warren Wilson College.

Cynthia French is the longest running Slam Master in Slam Minnesota! history. She is a three-time member of the SlamMN! Team. In 2002, she coordinated the National Poetry Slam Championships in Minneapolis. She has her MFA in Writing from Hamline University and is working on her next book of poetry, *Venice is Sinking*.

Paula Friedrich was a member of three National Poetry Slam Teams from Seattle and has coached five teams. Her poems have appeared in *Art Access* magazine, *SlamAmerica*, *Real Change*, and *Exquisite Corpse*. She co-directed the Seattle Poetry Festival as well as National Poetry Slam 2001. In her spare time, she works in the marketing department at Experience Music Project (EMP), a nonprofit pop music museum in Seattle, WA.

Regie O'Hare Gibson is the 1998 National Poetry Slam Individual Champion and author of *Storms Beneath the Skin* (EM Press). He has recently been published in *Poetry Magazine*, *The Iowa Review*, and is finishing an MFA at New England College.

Dana Gioia is a poet and critic. His last book of poems, *Interrogations at Noon* (2001), won the American Book Award. He is currently Chairman of the National Endowment for the Arts.

Nikki Giovanni is one of the most widely-read American poets. Her recent children's book *Rosa*—which tells the story of Rosa Parks—reached #3 on the New York Times bestseller list, became a Caldecott Honors Book, and received the Coretta Scott King Award. She is a University Distinguished Professor at Virginia Tech.

Gary Mex Glazner is the founder and executive director of the Alzheimer's Poetry Project, alzpoetry.com. He is the managing director for Bowery Arts and Science. "Maps and Wings" is a sonnet-length version of *The Grapes of Wrath*.

Nora Gomringer is a professor of American literature at Otto Friedrich University of Bamberg. She is Germany's foremost slam poet.

Guy Le Charles Gonzalez .is the founder of *The Louder Arts Project*. Recent publication includes *Selected Squares of Concrete* (2003).

Idris Goodwin is an award-winning playwright, writing teacher, hip-hop performer and recording artist. Currently, Idris is a creative media consultant/documentation for the Interfaith Youth Core, an internationally recognized non-profit committed to inter-religious peace work facilitated by young people.

Daphne Gottlieb currently teaches at New College of California. She is the editor of *Homewrecker: An Adultery Reader* (Soft Skull Press, 2005), as well as the author of *Final Girl* (Soft Skull Press, 2003), *Why Things Burn* (Soft Skull Press, 2001) and *Pelt* (Odd Girls Press, 1999).

Jürg Halter a.k.a. Kutti MC was born 1980 in Berne. He is well-known under the name Jürg Halter as a poet, and under the name Kutti MC as a rapper. After years in the Swiss Hip Hop scene, in 2003 Kutti MC appeared in Chicago and became a national US Slam champion. Links: www.art-21.ch/halter, www.kuttimc.com

Suheir Hammad has written two collections of poetry, *Born Palestinian, Born Black,* published when she was just 22 years old and more recently *ZaatarDiva* (Cypher Press).

Duriel E. Harris is the author of *but there are miles* (1999), a limited edition chapbook, and her poetry has appeared in numerous journals and anthologies, including the *Crab Orchard Review, fyah* and *Spirit and Flame*. She is the winner of the Eighth Annual Gwendolyn Brooks Writer's Conference Poetry Slam. Harris is the recipient of the 1999 Chicago Bar Association Charles Goodnow Memorial Award for Poetry.

Ethan Hawke is an Academy Award nominated actor for his work in *Training Day*, an Academy Award nominated writer for the *Before Sunset* screenplay and a Lucille Lortel Award and Drama League Award nominated actor for his work in *Hurlyburly*. He has uniquely established a successful career acting on film and on stage, as a novelist, a screenwriter and a director.

Mike Henry is a long-standing poetry slam member from Austin, Texas. He has organized three National Poetry Slam Championships and is a former president of PSI Inc., the official body of the poetry slam competitions. He directed the film *Slam Planet*.

Bob Holman is Visiting Professor of Writing at the Columbia School of the Arts and Proprietor of the Bowery Poetry Club (www.bowerypoetry.com). His most recent book is *A Couple of Ways of Doing Something*, a collaboration with Chuck Close (Aperture, 2006).

Pilote Le Hot is a French performance artist. He is a long-standing member of Poetry Slam Inc., the official body of poetry slams.

Zora Howard is a 13 year old poet affiliated with Urban Word in New York City.

Victor D. Infante is the editor of "The November 3rd Club," an online literary journal of political writing, and a poet, essayist and journalist whose writing has appeared internationally.

Major Jackson's collection of poetry, *Leaving Saturn* (University of Georgia Press, 2001), is a Cave Canem Poetry Prize selection and was short listed for the National Book Critics Circle Award. His work has appeared in *The New Yorker* and *Triquarterly*, among other literary publications. His second collection of poetry is *Hoops* (W.W. Norton, 2006). He teaches at the University of Vermont and Queens University in Charlotte, North Carolina.

Tyehimba Jess' first book of poetry, *Leadbelly*, was a winner of the 2004 National Poetry Series. Jess was recognized as one of 2005's eighteen debut poets to watch by *Poets and Writer's* magazine. Jess' *Leadbelly* was voted one of three best poetry books of 2005 by *Black Issues Book Review*.

Linton Kwesi Johnson has five collections of poetry, his most recent is *Mi Revalueshanary Fren* (Ausable Press). He is the originator of Dub Poetry.

Michael Kadela's first collection of poetry, *1 hundred hiccups*, was published by EM Press in 2002. He is currently a graduate student of English at DePaul University.

Jeff Kass heads the creative writing programs at The Neutral Zone, Ann Arbor's Teen Center, where he founded and continues to direct The VOLUME Youth Poetry Project, the Ann Arbor Youth Poetry Slam, Poetry Night in Ann Arbor, the VOLUME Summer Institute, the Second Tuesday Visiting Writers Series, and the performance poetry troupe Ann Arbor Wordworks.

Douglas Kearney lives near L.A. with his wife and their dog. *Fear, Some*, his first book of poetry, is out.

Maureen "Molly" Kennedy is 17 years old, the spawn of two English professors, and (hopefully) graduating from high school May 2007. When not writing poems unsuitable to read to family members she can be found haunting coffee shops or corrupting the young by (gods forbid) encouraging them to think.

She enjoys many activities too nerdy to be listed in a national publication, and thinks writing about herself in third person is odd. This is her first time being published.

Ted Kooser served as United States Poet Laureate from 2004-2006. In 2005, he was awarded the Pulitzer Prize in poetry for his book, *Delights & Shadows* (2004).

David Lerner is the author of *The Last Five Miles to Grace* (Zeitgeist Press). He was a regular reader at Café Barber in San Francisco. He died in 1997.

Billy Lombardo started performing poetry at the Green Mill in 1989. He teaches at The Latin School of Chicago and is the author of *The Logic of a Rose: Chicago Stories*.

Ed Mabrey is the 2007 Individual World Poetry Slam Champion.

Sou MacMillan, formerly the voice behind Caroline/Double Deuce's Pet Ufo, is currently writing and recording in Worcester, MA. Her latest novel, *Chrysanthemum*, and her most recent book of poetry, *Shallow Empire* is available from Lethe Press.

Taylor Mali is a former teacher turned full-time, professional poet and spoken word artist. He is a four-time National Poetry Slam team champion who has appeared in the film *SlamNation* and on HBO's *Def Poetry Jam*. He has published one book of poetry, *What Learning Leaves,* and is featured on several CDs and compilations, including *Conviction, The Difference Between Left and Wrong* and *Poems from the Like Free Zone.*

Nate Marshall is a teenage poet at Whitney Young High School in Chicago. He has been competing in Louder than a Bomb: Teenage Slam since seventh grade.

Matt Mason's first full book of poetry, *Things We Don't Know We Don't Know*, was released by The Backwaters Press in 2006 and made it as high as #12 on the Poetry Foundation's best seller list for contemporary poetry.

Jack McCarthy has been called a legend in the poetry slam community. His most recent publication is *disGrace Notes: Confessions of a Relapsing/Remitting Catholic* (Pudding House).

Marty McConnell is co-founder of the louderARTS Project, an MFA grad from Sarah Lawrence College, and member of the Piper Jane Project and five National Poetry Slam teams.

Jeffrey McDaniel is the author of three books, most recently *The Splinter Factory* (Manic D Press*)*. He teaches at Sarah Lawrence College in New York.

Mike McGee is the 2003 National Poetry Slam Individual Champion and a member of the multi-weighted poetry/music group "Tons-of-Fun University."

Karyna McGlynn's poems have recently appeared or are forthcoming in *Gulf Coast, Another Chicago Magazine, Octopus Magazine, Fence Magazine, Spinning Jenny, Ninth Letter, Willow Springs* and *Denver Quarterly*. A three-time Pushcart nominee, Karyna is the recipient of the Hopwood Award for poetry at the University of Michigan where she is currently teaching and completing her MFA.

Sarah McKinstry-Brown studied poetry at the University of New Mexico and the University of Sheffield, England. Most recently, she won the Blue Light Poetry Prize for her collection *When You Are Born*.

Kelly McWilliams is a teenage poet in Massachusetts. Her poem *Two Cities* was published in *Polyphone Literary Magazine*.

Anis Mojgani is the 2005 and 2006 National Poetry Slam Individual Champion.

Tracie Morris has written two collections of poetry, *Intermission* and *Chap-T-her Woman*. She teaches at Sarah Lawrence College. Recently, her sound poetry has been featured in the Whitney Biennial.

Andrew Motion is current UK Poet Laureate. In 2005 he began working with The Poetry Archive of audio poetry recordings.

Chris Mooney-Singh is a poet, writer, editor, Eastern musical heritage revivalist and now Singaporean PR. He has published three joint collections and an individual collection of poetry, *The House of Winter*. He edited the *Penguin Book of Christmas Poems*.

Hank Mortensen is a fledgling poet and a Los Angeles native. He currently attends Columbia University and is expanding his poetry into music.

Viggo Mortensen is the author of four books of poetry, his most recent is *Linger* (Perceval Press). He founded Perceval Press in 2002.

Simone Muench's book *The Air Lost in Breathing* received the Marianne Moore Prize for Poetry and was published by Helicon Nine in 2000. *Lampblack & Ash* is her most recent title (2005). She is an assistant professor of English at Lewis University.

Brendan Murphy is the 2006 Cúirt Festival Poetry Slam Champion.

James Nave is a fixture on the Poetry Slam circuit and co-founder of *Poetry Alive!* For ten years he taught creativity workshops with Julia Cameron, author of *The Artist's Way*. He has published a book of poems, *The Road*, and holds an M.F.A. from Vermont College.

Willie Perdomo is the author of *Where a Nickel Costs a Dime* (Norton, 1996) and *Smoking Lovely* (Rattapallax, 2003), which won the 2004 PEN American Beyond Margins Award. He is the author of a *Visiting Langston*, a Coretta Scott King Honor Book for Children, illustrated by Bryan Collier. Perdomo is the recipient of the New York Foundation for the Arts Fiction and Poetry Fellowships. He currently teaches at Friends Seminary and Bronx Academy of Letters.

Chuck Perkins is a favorite of audiences at Chicago's renowned Green Mill Lounge. Perkins has been featured at respected poetry venues across the city and the region and was an emcee at the1999 National Poetry Slams at the Chicago.

Bao Phi has twice won the Minnesota Grand Poetry Slam, and also won two poetry slams at the Nuyorican Poets Café in New York. He remains the only Vietnamese American man to have appeared on HBO's *Russell Simmons Presents Def Poetry*, and the National Poetry Slam Individual Finalists Stage, where he placed 6th overall out of over 250 national slam poets.

Lynne Procope's work appears in *Bowery Women, Washington Square Review, Drum Voices Review*. She is co-author of *Burning Down the House* and she tours with the Piper Jane Project & VisionIntoArt.

Sonya Renee is the 2004 National Poetry slam Champion, the 2006 Four Continents Slam Champion and is featured on the sixth season of HBO's *Def Poetry Jam*.

Jeremy Richards is a writer, actor, and radio producer in Seattle. His forthcoming book *Suddenly Shakespeare* is a guide to improvisation.

Luis J. Rodriguez, winner of the Carl Sandburg Literary Award for his book *Always Running: La Vida Loca, Gang Days in L.A.*, is an American poet, novelist, journalist, critic, and columnist. Rodriguez is known as a major figure of contemporary Chicano literature. His most recent book of poetry, published in 2005, is *My Nature is Hunger: New & Selected Poems*, 1989-2004.

Patrick Rosal is the author of *Uprock Headspin Scramble and Dive* (Persea Books), which won the 2004 Member's Choice Award from the Asian American Writers Workshop. His most recent book *My American Kundiman* (Persea Books) was published in 2006.

Christina Santana is a 20 year old writer who teaches hip-hop poetry at Oak Park-River Forest High School.

Gil Scott-Heron is a novelist, poet and recording artist. In 1970 he recorded *Small Talk at 125th and Lenox*, assisted by Bernard Purdie (who later recorded *Delights of the Garden* with The Last Poets). Gil Scott-Heron is often seen as a founding father of rap.

Matthew Shenoda's debut collection of poems, *Somewhere Else* (Introduction by Sonia Sanchez) was named one of 2005's debut books of the year by *Poets & Writers Magazine* and is the winner of a 2006 American Book Award. Most recently he has been nominated for a Pushcart Prize.

Beau Sia is an original cast member of the Tony award-winning *Def Poetry Jam on Broadway*. He is the author of *Night Without Armor II: The Revenge*. He is a two time National Poetry Slam Champion.

Patricia Smith is a four-time National Poetry Slam Individual Champion. Her most recent work is a biography of Harriet Tubman, *Fixed on a Furious Star*. Her most recent poetry title is *The Teahouse of the Almighty* (Coffee House Press, 2005).

Susan BA Somers-Willett is the author of, *Roam*, published as part of the Crab Orchard Award Series Open Competition in 2006 and featured in the November/December 2006 issue of *Poets & Writers* magazine. Her poems have appeared or are forthcoming in a number of periodicals including the *Virginia Quarterly Review*, the *Iowa Review, Painted Bride Quarterly, Verse Daily, and Hayden's Ferry Review*, and she is a former Co-Editor of *Borderlands: Texas Poetry Review*.

David Stavanger aka Ghostboy is an Australian performance poet.

Kevin Stein is Caterpillar Professor of English and Director of Creative Writing Program at Bradley University. In December 2003, Kevin Stein became Illinois' fourth Poet Laureate.

Mark Strand is the author of eleven poetry books; his most recent collection is *Man and Camel* (Knopf). He teaches at Columbia University and is a former U.S. Poet Laureate.

Henry Taylor is a Professor of Literature and Co-Director of the MFA Program in Creative Writing at American University in Washington, DC. Taylor won a Pulitzer Prize for his book *A Flying Change*.

Jeff Tweedy is the author of *Adult Head* (Zoo Press). Tweedy is currently in the band Wilco. He released a live solo concert DVD in late 2006.

Genevieve Van Cleave has been a slam poet since the spring of 1995 and works as a non-profit director. Her ambition in life is, "to work for the fewest number of people possible, for the greatest return possible."

Buddy Wakefield is a two-time Individual World Poetry Slam Champion, and has featured on NPR, the BBC, HBO's *Def Poetry Jam*, and most recently signed to Strange Famous Records.

Michael Warr is author of *We Are All The Black Boy*, and a co-editor of *Power Lines: A Decade of Poetry From Chicago's Guild Complex*. His poetry is most recently anthologized in *Dream of a Word – Tia Chucha Press Poetry Anthology* and *Black Writing from Chicago: In the World, Not of It?* His many awards include a NEA Creative Writing Fellowship and the Gwendolyn Brooks Significant Illinois Poets Award. His poems and photographs from Ethiopia and Mali, where he served as a foreign correspondent, can be found at warrandpeace.com.

Phil West is a writer, teacher and publicist based in Austin, Texas. He has been involved with poetry slam since 1994 as a competitor and organizer, making it to the finals stage in 1996 as part of the Austin team as seen in the documentary movie *SlamNation*, and will be co-directing his third National Poetry Slam in 2007.

Saul Williams is a recording artist, actor, and one of America's best selling poets. He is the author of three books of poetry, *She, ,said the shotgun to the head*, and *The Dead Emcee Scrolls,* recorded two albums, *Amethyst Rock Star* and *Saul Williams*, the former being named one of the top ten albums of 2004 by *Rolling Stone Magazine*. He has been featured in *The New York Times, Esquire, Vibe*, and opened for the rock band Nine Inch Nails' 2005 tour.

Allan Wolf is the author of *Immersed In Verse: An Informative, Slightly Irreverent & Totally Tremendous Gudie to Living the Poet's Life* (Lark Books). His latest verse-novel is *Zane's Trace* (Candlewick Press).

Scott Woods is the author and editor of nine volumes of poetry, *50 Mistakes Poets Make* and *Out of the Woods* most recently. He has been featured multiple times on NPR. He is also President of the national organization Poetry Slam, Inc., which puts on the annual National Poetry Slam and Individual World Poetry Slam.

hydi zasteR has recently been published in the *Iowa Review*.

Credits

Michael Anania: "Apples" Grateful acknowledgement is made for permission to reprint text from *In Natural Light* by Michael Anania. Copyright © 1999 by Michael Anania. Lucy Anderton: "Eve's Sestina for Adam" (text and audio); "Three" translation of Pilote le Hot poem © Lucy Anderton. Patricia Barber: "Love, put on your faces" (text and audio) © Patricia Barber. Marvin Bell: "Bagram, Afghanistan, 2002" first appeared in *The New Yorker* and is reprinted from *Mars Being Red*, Copper Canyon Press, © Marvin Bell 2007. Tara Betts: "For Those Who Need a True Story" first published in *Gathering Ground: A Reader Celebrating Cave Canem's First Decade* (University of Michigan Press, 2006). Roger Bonair-Agard: "Mandate" © Roger Bonair-Agard; Mandate has appeared previously in the *National Poetry Slam Anthology* 2004 and in the collection *Tarnish and Masquerade* (cypher books, 2006). Mike Booker: "hoodology (west side of chicago)" © Mike Booker. Derrick Brown: "Kurosawa Champagne" (audio) previously appeared in *Born in the year of the butterfly knife*, 2004, Write Bloody Publishing, brownpoetry.com; "How the Jellyfish Wishes" (text) previously appeared in *I Love You Is Back*, 2006, Write Bloody Publishing, brownpoetry.com. Both © Derrick Brown. Michael Brown: "Hammer Heistand (The Police Chief)"; © 2006, Michael Brown. "Hammer Heistand (The Police Chief)" winner 2006 York (PA) Arts contest. Jeff Buckley: "A Letter to Bob Dylan". Jeff Buckley recording used with the express permission of Jeff Buckley Music, Inc. and SonyBMG-Legacy Recordings (c) 2007. Audio recording used with kind permission of Elena Alexander. Lisa Buscani: "Hell Night" © Lisa Buscani. First appeared in *Power Lines: Ten Years of the Guild Complex*. Jason Carney: "My Southern Heritage" © Jason Carney. Jim Carroll: "8 Fragments for Kurt Cobain" from *Void Of Course* by Jim Carroll, copyright © 1998 by Jim Carroll. Used by permission of Viking Penguin, a division of Penguin Group (USA) Inc. Jeff Chang: "Stealing from a Jeff Chang Book on Hip-Hop" originally titled "Making a Name: How DJ Kool Herc Lost His Accent and Started Hip-Hop" from *Can't Stop Won't Stop* by Jeff Chang. Copyright © 2005 by the author and reprinted by permission of St. Martin's Press, LLC. Michael Cirelli: "Dead Ass" © Michael Cirelli. Billy Collins: "Brightly Colored Boats on the Banks of the Charles" (text and audio) © Billy Collins. John Condron: "Lullaby for Jill" (audio) © (p) 2004 tacony music (ASCAP) www.johncondron.com. Matt Cook: "The Modernist Bowling Alley" © Matt Cook. Billy Corgan: "Poetry of My Heart" © Billy Corgan. Gregory Corso: "Marriage" By Gregory Corso, from *The Happy Birthday of Death*, copyright © 1960 by New Directions Publishing Corp. Reprinted by permission of New Directions Publishing Corp. Kevin Coval: "The Day Jam Master Jay Died" (text and audio), "A Hip-Hop Poetica" © Kevin Coval. Robert Creeley: "I Know a Man" from *Selected Poems of Robert Creeley* Copyright © 1991 by the Regents of the University of California. "Short and Clear" from *The Collected Poems of Robert Creeley, 1975-2005*. Copyright © 2005 by the Regents of the University of California. Reprinted with the permission of the University of California Press, www.ucpress.edu; Copyright © 2007 by the Estate of Robert Creeley. E. E. Cummings: "put off your faces,Death:for day is over". Copyright 1931. © 1959, 1991 by the Trustees for the E. E. Cummings Trust. Copyright © 1979 by George James Firmage, from *Complete Poems: 1904-1962* by E. E. Cummings, edited by George J. Firmage. Used by permission of Liveright Publishing Corporation. Da Boogie Man: "Messiahs" © Da Boogie Man. Gayle Danley: "Funeral Like Nixon's" © Gayle Danley. Kyle Dargan: "Brooklyn's Atlas" © Kyle G. Dargan; "Microphone Fiend" Originally published in *Ploughshares*, © Kyle G. Dargan. Corbet Dean: "Letter My Dad Never Gave Me" © 2000 by Corbet Dean also appeared in *A Collection of Crime Scenes*, iUniverse Press, © 2007. Used with permission from the author. Mayda Del Valle: "Tongue Tactics" © Mayda Del Valle. LaTasha N. Nevada Diggs: "makémake ghetto bodypartscasta" © LaTasha N. Nevada Diggs, previously published in *Cave Canem IX*, 2004. Thomas Sayers Ellis: "Mr. Dynamite Splits" originally appeared in *The Nation*. Used here by permission of the author. "Take Me Out to the Go-Go" and "All Their Stanzas Look Alike" reprinted by permission of the author, Thomas Sayers Ellis, 2007. Martín Espada: "You Got A Song, Man," (text) from *The Republic of Poetry (W.W. Norton, 2006)*, © 2006 by Martín Espada. Reprinted by permission of the author. yvonne fly onakeme etaghene: "harlem love poem" © yvonne fly onakeme etaghene. David Allan Evans: "Winter Journey," by David Allan Evans, reprinted by permission of the author; "Essay on Elizabeth Lewis," by David Allan Evans, reprinted by permission of the author. James Fenton: "The Raised Voice Of Poetry" Originally published: *American Scholar Vol.71 No.4 Autumn 2002 p35 J Fenton*. Daniel Ferri: "Keys"; "So This Guy Walks into

Photos/Illustration

All credits listed by page number. Every effort has been made to correctly attribute all the materials reproduced in this book. If any errors have been made, we will be happy to correct them in future editions.

Index

GEORGE
WASHINGTON
CARVER

GEORGE WASHINGTON CARVER

Gene Adair

Senior Consulting Editor
Nathan Irvin Huggins
Director
W.E.B. Du Bois Institute for Afro-American Research
Harvard University

CHELSEA HOUSE PUBLISHERS
New York   Philadelphia

CHELSEA HOUSE PUBLISHERS
Editor-in-Chief   Nancy Toff
Executive Editor   Remmel T. Nunn
Managing Editor   Karyn Gullen Browne
Copy Chief   Juliann Barbato
Picture Editor   Adrian G. Allen
Art Director   Maria Epes
Manufacturing Manager   Gerald Levine

Black Americans of Achievement
Senior Editor   Richard Rennert

Staff for GEORGE WASHINGTON CARVER
Associate Editor   Perry King
Deputy Copy Chief   Ellen Scordato
Editorial Assistant   Jennifer Trachtenberg
Picture Researcher   Joan Kathryn Beard
Assistant Art Director   Loraine Machlin
Designer   Ghila Krajzman
Production Coordinator   Joseph Romano
Cover Illustration   Richard Daskam

5   7   9   8   6   4

Library of Congress Cataloging-in-Publication Data
Adair, Gene.
  George Washington Carver / Gene Adair.
    p.   cm.—(Black Americans of achievement)
  Bibliography: p.
  Includes index.
  Summary: A biography of the Afro-American whose scientific re-
search revolutionized the economy of the South.
  ISBN 1-55546-577-3.
      0-7910-0234-9 (pbk.)
  1. Carver, George Washington, 1864?–1943.   2. Agriculturists—
United States—Biography.   3. Afro-Americans—Biography.
[1. Carver, George Washington, 1864?–1943.   2. Scientists.   3. Afro-
Americans—Biography.]   I. Title.   II. Series.
S41.7.C3A63 1989
630'.92'4—dc 19   89-770
[B]   CIP
[92]   AC

CONTENTS

—❦—

BLACK AMERICANS OF ACHIEVEMENT

RALPH ABERNATHY
civil rights leader

MUHAMMAD ALI
heavyweight champion

RICHARD ALLEN
religious leader and social activist

LOUIS ARMSTRONG
musician

ARTHUR ASHE
tennis great

JOSEPHINE BAKER
entertainer

JAMES BALDWIN
author

BENJAMIN BANNEKER
scientist and mathematician

AMIRI BARAKA
poet and playwright

COUNT BASIE
bandleader and composer

ROMARE BEARDEN
artist

JAMES BECKWOURTH
frontiersman

MARY MCLEOD BETHUNE
educator

BLANCHE BRUCE
politician

RALPH BUNCHE
diplomat

GEORGE WASHINGTON CARVER
botanist

CHARLES CHESNUTT
author

BILL COSBY
entertainer

PAUL CUFFE
merchant and abolitionist

FATHER DIVINE
religious leader

FREDERICK DOUGLASS
abolitionist editor

CHARLES DREW
physician

W.E.B. DU BOIS
scholar and activist

PAUL LAURENCE DUNBAR
poet

KATHERINE DUNHAM
dancer and choreographer

MARIAN WRIGHT EDELMAN
civil rights leader and lawyer

DUKE ELLINGTON
bandleader and composer

RALPH ELLISON
author

JULIUS ERVING
basketball great

JAMES FARMER
civil rights leader

ELLA FITZGERALD
singer

MARCUS GARVEY
black-nationalist leader

DIZZY GILLESPIE
musician

PRINCE HALL
social reformer

W. C. HANDY
father of the blues

WILLIAM HASTIE
educator and politician

MATTHEW HENSON
explorer

CHESTER HIMES
author

BILLIE HOLIDAY
singer

JOHN HOPE
educator

LENA HORNE
entertainer

LANGSTON HUGHES
poet

ZORA NEALE HURSTON
author

JESSE JACKSON
civil rights leader and politician

JACK JOHNSON
heavyweight champion

JAMES WELDON JOHNSON
author

SCOTT JOPLIN
composer

BARBARA JORDAN
politician

MARTIN LUTHER KING, JR.
civil rights leader

ALAIN LOCKE
scholar and educator

JOE LOUIS
heavyweight champion

RONALD MCNAIR
astronaut

MALCOLM X
militant black leader

THURGOOD MARSHALL
Supreme Court justice

ELIJAH MUHAMMAD
religious leader

JESSE OWENS
champion athlete

CHARLIE PARKER
musician

GORDON PARKS
photographer

SIDNEY POITIER
actor

ADAM CLAYTON POWELL, JR.
political leader

LEONTYNE PRICE
opera singer

A. PHILIP RANDOLPH
labor leader

PAUL ROBESON
singer and actor

JACKIE ROBINSON
baseball great

BILL RUSSELL
basketball great

JOHN RUSSWURM
publisher

SOJOURNER TRUTH
antislavery activist

HARRIET TUBMAN
antislavery activist

NAT TURNER
slave revolt leader

DENMARK VESEY
slave revolt leader

MADAM C. J. WALKER
entrepreneur

BOOKER T. WASHINGTON
educator

HAROLD WASHINGTON
politician

WALTER WHITE
civil rights leader and author

RICHARD WRIGHT
author

ON
ACHIEVEMENT

———— ✿ ————

Coretta Scott King

BEFORE YOU BEGIN this book, I hope you will ask yourself
what the word excellence means to you. I think that it's a question we
should all ask, and keep asking as we grow older and change. Because the
truest answer to it should never change. When you think of excellence,
perhaps you think of success at work; or of becoming wealthy; or meeting
the right person, getting married, and having a good family life.

Those important goals are worth striving for, but there is a better way
to look at excellence. As Martin Luther King, Jr., said in one of his last
sermons, "I want you to be first in love. I want you to be first in moral
excellence. I want you to be first in generosity. If you want to be
important, wonderful. If you want to be great, wonderful. But recognize
that he who is greatest among you shall be your servant."

My husband, Martin Luther King, Jr., knew that the true meaning of
achievement is service. When I met him, in 1952, he was already
ordained as a Baptist preacher and was working towards a doctoral degree
at Boston University. I was studying at the New England Conservatory
and dreamed of accomplishments in music. We married a year later, and
after I graduated the following year we moved to Montgomery, Alabama.
We didn't know it then, but our notions of achievement were about to
undergo a dramatic change.

You may have read or heard about what happened next. What began
with the boycott of a local bus line grew into a national movement, and
by the time he was assassinated in 1968 my husband had fashioned a
black movement powerful enough to shatter forever the practice of racial
segregation. What you may not have read about is where he got his
method for resisting injustice without compromising his religious beliefs.

He adopted the strategy of nonviolence from a man of a different race, who lived in a distant country, and even practiced a different religion. The man was Mahatma Gandhi, the great leader of India, who devoted his life to serving humanity in the spirit of love and nonviolence. It was in these principles that Martin discovered his method for social reform. More than anything else, those two principles were the key to his achievements.

This book is about black Americans who served society through the excellence of their achievements. It forms a part of the rich history of black men and women in America—a history of stunning accomplishments in every field of human endeavor, from literature and art to science, industry, education, diplomacy, athletics, jurisprudence, even polar exploration.

Not all of the people in this history had the same ideals, but I think you will find something that all of them have in common. Like Martin Luther King, Jr., they all decided to become "drum majors" and serve humanity. In that principle—whether it was expressed in books, inventions, or song—they found something outside themselves to use as a goal and a guide. Something that showed them a way to serve others, instead of living only for themselves.

Reading the stories of these courageous men and women not only helps us discover the principles that we will use to guide our own lives but also teaches us about our black heritage and about America itself. It is crucial for us to know the heroes and heroines of our history and to realize that the price we paid in our struggle for equality in America was dear. But we must also understand that we have gotten as far as we have partly because America's democratic system and ideals made it possible.

We are still struggling with racism and prejudice. But the great men and women in this series are a tribute to the spirit of our democratic ideals and the system in which they have flourished. And that makes their stories special and worth knowing. ❧

GEORGE
WASHINGTON
CARVER

1

A
COMMAND
PERFORMANCE

ALL RIGHT, MR. Carver. We will give you 10 minutes."

With those words, Representative Joseph W. Fordney, the Republican from Michigan who chaired the powerful House Ways and Means Committee, recognized the tall, middle-aged black man seated at a table across from the committee members. Fordney and the other members of this congressional panel had called for a hearing on January 21, 1921, to consider whether to recommend that the federal government put a tariff on imported peanuts. The man who was now about to speak had come to the nation's capital to argue in favor of the proposed tax, which was intended to protect the American peanut industry from foreign competition.

The witness's name was George Washington Carver, and although he was highly regarded in agricultural circles, the congressmen probably did not know what to make of him at first. He was wearing an old, wrinkled suit with a flower in the lapel. He spoke in an oddly high-pitched voice, telling the committee that he was a scientist engaged in agricultural research in Tuskegee, Alabama. Then, like a magician upon a stage, he began to take an odd

Carver's laboratory work at Tuskegee Institute in the first two decades of the 20th century contributed greatly to his growing reputation as a creative chemist. By 1921, when he appeared before the House Ways and Means Committee to discuss the many uses of the peanut, he was on the verge of becoming a nationally known scientist, the so-called Wizard of Tuskegee.

variety of foodstuffs out of a box and place them on the table in front of him.

"I am especially interested in southern crops and their possibilities," the 56-year-old Carver announced, "and the peanut comes in, I think, for one of the most remarkable crops that we are all acquainted with."

Spreading the various products on the table took Carver several minutes, and the committee members watched him with amusement. At one point, Chairman Fordney, in a reference to Prohibition—the national ban on liquor that was then in effect—jokingly told the scientist, "If you have anything to drink, don't put it under the table."

Carver said he was not yet ready to show them anything to drink. "They [the drinks] will come later," he said, "if my 10 minutes are extended."

Most of the committee members promptly burst into laughter. But one of the congressmen, Representative John N. Garner of Texas, feared that this congressional hearing was not being taken seriously enough. "Let us have order," he said. "This man knows a great deal about this business."

What Carver knew had come from 25 years of hard work at the Tuskegee Institute, one of the nation's leading schools for blacks. In his laboratory and in the fields of the institute's agricultural experiment station, he had conducted wide-ranging research on peanuts, sweet potatoes, cotton, and numerous other crops. Little by little, his work had brought him increasing recognition.

By early 1918, when World War I was well under way, Carver had become such a well-known agriculturalist that the United States Department of Agriculture had begun consulting him for ways to overcome the wartime food shortage. Shortly after the war ended, his experiments with peanuts drew the attention of southern peanut growers and processors, who saw him as a good spokesman for their

Carver began raising peanuts at Tuskegee's experiment station around 1903. He ultimately claimed to have developed more than 300 products—including foods, beverages, dyes, and cosmetics—that were derived from the legume.

industry. In fact, it was their sponsorship that had brought him to Washington, D.C., on this chilly winter day to convince the congressional committee of the peanut's value and of the need for the government to support the American peanut industry.

Now, while the congressmen looked on with increasing interest, Carver proceeded to identify and describe, one by one, the products he had laid on the table—all of them made solely from peanuts or using peanuts as a key ingredient. "Here is a breakfast food," he said, picking up one of the products. "I am very sorry that you cannot taste this, so I will taste it for you." He did so, and the congressmen laughed again.

The genial scientist from Tuskegee did not win over all of the politicians, however. Representative John Q. Tilson of Connecticut could not resist making a racist jibe. As Carver argued that the peanut

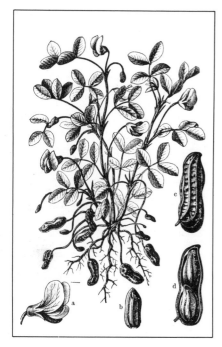

One of the many products Carver made from peanuts was a milk substitute. "It is without doubt the most wonderful product that I have yet been able to work out," he said, "and I see within it, unlimited possibilities."

and sweet potato could provide "a perfectly balanced ration," Tilson echoed a stereotyped notion of blacks by cracking, "Do you want a watermelon to go along with that?"

Carver deflected the tasteless joke gracefully. "Of course," he said, "if you want a dessert, [the watermelon] comes in very well, but you know we can get along pretty well without dessert. The recent war has taught us that."

After Carver's allotted 10 minutes came and went, Representative Garner, who repeatedly supported Carver during his testimony, asked that the scientist's time be extended. Minutes later, when it was clear to the committee that Carver still had much to talk about, Chairman Fordney declared, "Go ahead, brother. Your time is unlimited."

The products made from peanuts certainly seemed unlimited. Carver showed the committee samples of candies, peanut milk, several breakfast foods, mock oysters, instant coffee, Worcestershire sauce, cosmetics, and other products. When he presented some fruit punches, he reassured the committee that none of them contained an ingredient that would violate Prohibition.

Carver wound up testifying for nearly an hour. He demonstrated the products with a flair for showmanship that brought repeated laughter from the committee members. They craned their necks to see what he would show them next and seemed genuinely impressed both by Carver's presentation and by the sheer variety of the items he unveiled.

Carver capped his testimony by saying that the peanut had about twice as many uses as the ones he had just indicated. To that, Representative Allen T. Treadway of Massachusetts responded, "Well, come again and bring the rest."

A hearty round of applause echoed through the hearing room as Carver started to pack up his wares.

Chairman Fordney agreed with his fellow officials that the scientist's presentation had been effective. "We want to compliment you, sir," he told Carver, "on the way you have handled your subject."

As it turned out, Carver's appearance before the House committee, which contributed to the imposition of a tariff on imported peanuts, charmed not only the congressmen. The publicity that came from his witty testimony marked the beginning of his rise to the status of a national folk hero. Indeed, his humor, his politeness, his apparent humility, his ready ability to engage an audience's interest—all of the qualities he displayed in Washington, D.C., that day—would, in the years ahead, capture America's fancy and win him nationwide fame.

An image of Carver ultimately emerged in which he was depicted as the savior of southern agriculture, a brilliant "creative chemist" who found hundreds of new uses for the peanut, the sweet potato, and other crops. He was showered with honors, he became the subject of several biographies (and one biographical movie), and for many years, he was one of the very few blacks to be mentioned in textbooks. All told, he became the first black man of learning to emerge as a folk hero to the entire nation.

Such mythmaking in effect clouded Carver's actual accomplishments. Although he was proclaimed a great creative scientist, his real strengths were as a teacher, a scientific popularizer, a pioneer in agricultural education who sought to raise the living standards of poor farmers, and a devoted friend who deeply touched the lives of the many people who came into contact with him. That he rose to such heights of national prominence had less to do with the reality of Carver's life and career than it did with America's need to put forth a symbol of black achievement—especially one with such humble beginnings. ❧

American peanut farmers were producing close to 40 million bushels annually by 1920, prompting members of the industry to form the United Peanut Association of America, an organization whose general aim was to lobby for a tariff on imported peanuts. By inviting Carver to speak at its first convention, held that September in Montgomery, Alabama, the group set the stage for his appearance before the House Ways and Means Committee four months later.

OBSCURE BEGINNINGS

GEORGE WASHINGTON CARVER was born into slavery on a farm near the village of Diamond, Missouri, during the waning months of the Civil War. His mother, Mary, belonged to Moses Carver, a frontiersman and homesteader who had settled in the southwestern corner of the state about 25 years earlier with his wife, Susan. Independent, proud, and thriving on their 240 acres, the Carvers were to be the only real parents George would ever know.

Though Moses Carver opposed slavery in principle, hiring labor for his Newton County farm proved difficult; so, in 1855, he bought Mary from one of his neighbors. She was then 13 years old, and over the next decade she bore at least four children, including twin girls who apparently died as infants. Two sons survived: Jim, born in 1859, and George, born, as he would recall, around 1864 or 1865.

The identity of George's father is not precisely known, but he was probably a slave on a nearby farm—a man who died around the time George was born. "I am told," the scientist wrote in 1922, "that my father was killed while hauling wood with an ox

Carver spent his early years near Diamond, Missouri, a western frontier village much like the one shown here. He was raised on a farm that boasted more than 200 acres of grains and grasses, an orchard, and a vegetable garden.

*Moses Carver, George's foster fa-
ther, was a German immigrant
who strongly opposed slavery.
Nevertheless, in the mid-19th
century he purchased a slave—
George's mother, Mary—because
he needed help on his farm.*

team. In some way he fell from the load, under the wagon, both wheels passing over him."

George never got to know his mother, either. They were separated shortly after his birth. Their parting was a traumatic event that reflected the turbulent times in which it occurred.

Missouri, a slave state that nevertheless remained part of the Union during the Civil War, was the scene of extraordinary tensions both before and after the outbreak of war in 1861. Governor Claiborne Fox Jackson was a proslavery man who favored secession, and a majority of the Missouri legislature agreed with his views. However, considerable Union sentiment had entered the state during the preceding three decades with the arrival of new settlers, and secession from the Union was rejected by a state convention elected to consider the issue.

Jackson's subsequent attempts to claim Missouri for the Confederacy were thwarted by Union forces, and he and several members of the legislature were forced to flee the capital of Jefferson City. They eventually ended up in Neosho, only eight miles from Diamond and the Carver farm. After enacting an order of secession there, they were driven out of the state entirely and remained in exile throughout the war.

As such events suggest, the Missouri populace was deeply divided in its loyalties during the Civil War. In the border regions especially, guerrilla warfare erupted with a vengeance, pitting Confederate-sympathizing "bushwhackers"—including William Quantrill and Frank and Jesse James—against Unionist "jayhawkers." Ambush, theft, murder, swift and bloody raids on farms and settlements—these were the forms that the fighting took.

Union sympathizers like Moses Carver were prime targets for the roving rebel bands, and bushwhackers raided his farm at least three times between 1863 and

1865. On one occasion, they suspended the farmer from a tree by his thumbs, burned his feet with hot coals, and demanded to know where he had hidden his money. Despite the torture, he refused to tell them, and they left. They were more successful on a later raid, causing him thereafter to bury his money in various places around the farm.

Near the end of the war, the bushwhackers came again. Running from the sound of their horses, Moses Carver managed to rush the five-year-old Jim to safety, but Mary and the infant George were not so lucky. The raiders rode away with the slave mother and her baby, carrying them into Arkansas, a Confederate state that lay some 20 miles to the south.

A kindly man who had come to love Mary and her sons, Moses was determined to reclaim the abducted mother and child. To do so, he approached a neighbor named John Bentley, a Union scout who was knowledgeable about the guerrilla bands and their movements. Bentley agreed to go in search of the kidnapped pair, and within a few days he returned with George. He had been unable to find Mary, however, and what became of her would never be known. For returning the baby, Moses rewarded Bentley with one of the prized possessions of the Carver farm: a racehorse.

Meanwhile, the long and bloody Civil War was drawing to a close. General Robert E. Lee, com-

The bill of sale for George's mother, Mary. She arrived on Moses Carver's farm in 1855, when she was 13 years old.

mander of the Confederate forces, finally surrendered to his Union counterpart, General Ulysses S. Grant, at Appomattox, Virginia, on April 9, 1865. Over the next month and a half, the Confederate armies acceded one by one to their defeat. The momentous task of putting a traumatized nation back together lay ahead.

The end of the war introduced a new reality to American life: emancipation of the slaves. In Missouri, they were freed under the provisions of a new state constitution. As orphans of the war, Mary's two children were fortunate that the Carvers were innately decent people. Having no children themselves, the white couple raised George and Jim as their own.

Clearly, the loss of his natural parents and the circumstances of his early childhood affected George Washington Carver deeply. As he told one of his biographers later in his life, "There are so many things that naturally I erased from my mind. There are some things that an orphan child does not want to remember. . . ." Even so, his memories of his foster parents were always fond ones. The Carvers, he recalled, did their best to give him and his brother a good home.

Jim, being the stronger and healthier of the two boys, grew up helping Moses with the harder tasks of the farm: caring for livestock, planting, and harvesting. In George's case, recurring respiratory ailments, which left him frail and sickly for much of his childhood, limited his duties to helping Susan around the house with such tasks as mending clothes, cooking, tending the family garden, and doing laundry.

Growing up near woods and wildlife gave George an appreciation of nature at a very early age. When he was not helping Susan Carver with the housework, he explored the woods and marveled at the rocks and the trees, the birds and the animals. "I wanted to know every strange stone, flower, insect, bird, or beast," he recalled years later. "No one would tell me." His main source of knowledge at the time, a *Webster's Elementary Spelling Book*, did not provide answers to the questions he was asking.

George indulged his fascination with nature by starting a collection of rocks, plants, insects, frogs, and reptiles. Susan Carver was not happy when George brought these discoveries into the house. After a time, she had him empty his pockets at the door whenever he returned from one of his visits to the woods.

Before long, Susan and Moses Carver recognized that George's curiosity and eagerness to learn made him special. From his work with Susan in the garden, it became clear that he had a particular gift for nurturing plants. He even began a little garden of his own in the woods. There he transplanted and cultivated plants of various sorts, carefully observing the conditions that enabled them to grow and be healthy. He soon became known around Diamond as the "plant doctor," and neighbors called on him frequently to nurse their sickly flowers and plants back to health.

Closely tied to George's love of nature was a deeply mystical religious sense. He came to see the wonders of nature—not to mention his own special talents—as evidence that God was everywhere. As an adult, he was always quick to credit "the Creator" for whatever he was able to accomplish in the laboratory.

Exactly how much religious training George received in the Carver home is not exactly known. Moses Carver was reputedly a freethinker who distrusted organized religion and stayed home from church on Sundays. Nevertheless, George and Jim apparently attended the services at Diamond's non-denominational church, hearing sermons by a num-

A sickly child, Carver was often excused from performing farming chores during his youth. "I literally lived in the woods," he said. "I wanted to know every strange stone, flower, insect, bird, or beast."

The young Carver (left) and his brother, Jim. According to George, they "grew up together, sharing each other's sorrows."

ber of preachers of various Protestant faiths. By the time George was 10 or so, he had become a Christian.

An integral part of George's religious beliefs was a faith in divine visions. He claimed to have had his first such experience while still a child. Longing for a pocketknife, he saw an image of one in a dream. The next day, he ran to the spot in Moses Carver's field that had appeared in his dream, and sure enough, the knife was there, protruding from a half-eaten watermelon.

Being such a bright child, George yearned for more formal schooling than he was receiving at home, and his foster parents, though barely educated themselves, tried to provide it for him. The color of his skin, however, made this difficult. Even though the new state constitution, adopted, in 1865, mandated public education for blacks, they were often denied admission by the local schools.

In 1876, the Carvers found a private tutor for George. But it was not long before he was asking more questions than his teacher could answer. His spirits must have brightened when, in 1877, Moses and Susan decided he was old enough to attend the school for blacks at Neosho, the county seat.

With his enthusiasm for obtaining an education no doubt mingled with the pain of leaving the Carver farm for the first time since he had been abducted, the 12 year old set out for Neosho, making the 8-mile trip on foot. George arrived in town too late to find lodging, so he chose to sleep in a barn. As it turned out, the barn belonged to a black couple, Andrew and Mariah Watkins.

Like the Carvers, the Watkins did not have children of their own. When they discovered the youngster, they were happy to give him a place to stay as long as he helped with the household chores. This lucky set of circumstances was made even better because the Watkins home was near the school. In addition, Neosho was close enough to Diamond to allow George to visit the Carvers on weekends.

Though obviously fond of George, Mariah Watkins was a firm believer in discipline and hard work, and she kept him busy. He even had to come home during recess to study and do laundry. A deeply religious woman who read regularly from the Bible, she introduced George to the African Methodist Episcopal church, which was fast becoming the leading denomination of black Christians throughout the South. Mariah Watkins's influence no doubt did much to confirm George's faith.

George's stay in the Watkins household lasted only about a year. The teacher at the Neosho school was a black man named Stephen Frost, and the range of his knowledge and his preparation for teaching unfortunately fell far short of George's hopes and expectations. George found once again that he knew more than his teacher did. If he was to obtain the education he desired, he would have to look elsewhere.

So, in the late 1870s, George Carver became a wanderer. He trained his sights on the state of Kansas, which lay to the northwest. A family traveling to the town of Fort Scott agreed to let him accompany them, and thus began a new phase in his life. ❧

3

MIDWESTERN WANDERINGS

THE MOVE TO Fort Scott, Kansas, in 1878 took George Carver nearly 100 miles away from his birthplace. Never before had he ventured so far on his own. When Moses and Susan Carver learned of his decision, he later recalled, they were "indignant," fearing for his delicate health. Yet he was determined to broaden his horizons beyond the little corner of Missouri he already knew so well.

After arriving in Fort Scott, the young Carver quickly discovered the value of the domestic skills he had honed in the households of Susan Carver and Mariah Watkins. In exchange for cooking and doing housework, he found room and board at the home of a blacksmith, Felix Payne. Carver earned spending money by working at a grocery and taking in laundry from guests at the local hotel. He also furthered his educational quest by entering school.

But again it was not long before Carver felt compelled to move elsewhere. This time, however, the circumstances that made him decide to leave were far more terrible than dissatisfaction with the quality of the education he was receiving. Rather, his stay in Fort Scott brought him face-to-face with a grisly lesson in race relations that haunted him for the rest of his life.

On March 29, 1879, a black man accused of raping a 12-year-old white girl was taken into custody and imprisoned at the county jail in Fort Scott. That night a mob of white men stormed the jail and hauled

Carver's quest for an education manifested itself in many ways, including a desire to learn about music, voice, and painting in addition to arithmetic, grammar, and science. He took his first art lessons while in Kansas, and thereafter he painted whenever his schedule allowed.

the prisoner outside. Tying a rope around his neck, they dragged him through the streets, strung him up from a lamppost, and brought the public lynching to a savage climax by setting fire to the body. A huge crowd—of which the 14-year-old George Carver was a member—witnessed the brutal vigilante action.

This kind of scene, though more typical of the South than of the Midwest, became all too familiar to blacks over the next few decades. Whenever and wherever these lynchings occurred, the message was the same. White extremists were telling blacks that whites made the rules and that established racial boundaries should never be crossed. Carver's own reaction to what he saw in Fort Scott was to get out of town as quickly as possible.

Fortunately for Carver, the next several years in Kansas brought him happier memories. He continued his education at Olathe, near Kansas City, where he lived with a black couple, Ben and Lucy Seymour. He then stayed briefly in nearby Paola before traveling 150 miles westward during the summer of 1880 to rejoin the Seymours at their new home in Minneapolis, Kansas. Attending the mostly white high school there, he made many friends who encouraged him in his long quest for knowledge. He supported himself by opening a laundry, and in addition to nurturing his proven botanical talents, he developed an interest—and skill—in both painting and music.

There was one unhappy note that marred these years. In 1883, Carver saw his brother, Jim, for the last time. That summer, George traveled by train to Missouri to visit Jim and their foster parents. Shortly after returning to Kansas, George received the news that Jim had died of smallpox. It was thus ironic that George, who had always been known as the frail one, would outlive by many years his more robust and active brother.

Although Carver declared years later that he had "finished [his] high school work" in Minneapolis, it is not clear whether he actually received a diploma. In any case, by 1884 he was out of school and on the move again. This time he landed in Kansas City, where he worked for several months as a typist and stenographer in the telegraph office.

Carver had hardly quenched his thirst for knowledge, however. In 1885, he applied by mail to Highland College, a small Presbyterian school in Highland, Kansas. The college accepted him, but when he arrived for registration, he met with severe disappointment. Seeing that he was black, the college officials refused to admit him.

The degree of bitterness and frustration Carver felt at this setback can only be guessed, but it *is* clear that he chose at this point to put off his schooling,

During Reconstruction and later, black schools were underfunded and lacked a sufficient number of qualified teachers. Carver, who grew up in regions inhabited mostly by whites, attended predominantly white schools, which received much better funding than the nation's black institutions did.

at least temporarily. He remained in Highland for a while, doing domestic work for a white family, the Beelers, who owned a fruit farm outside of town. Then, in 1886, he decided to try his hand at something completely new: homesteading.

It may be that in making this decision Carver saw himself following in his foster father's footsteps. Moses Carver had built a good life for himself and his wife—and subsequently for Jim and George—by clearing and farming a tract of land in frontier Missouri. George Carver may well have thought that by doing something similar he could also prosper. Certainly, given his skill with plants, tilling the soil must have seemed like a logical thing to do.

Carver learned from the Beeler family about new settlements on the plains of west-central Kansas. One of the Beelers' sons had gone to that area some years before and had opened a store in Ness County. His store then became the center of a community named after him. Beeler, Kansas, sounded to Carver like a good place to make a new beginning.

The land in Ness County was subject to the terms of the Homestead Act of 1862, which Congress had passed as a way of encouraging settlement in the country's vast stretches of western territory. Under the law's provisions, anyone could pay a small registration fee and file a claim to 160 acres of public land. After five years of living on and cultivating the tract, the homesteader could then gain permanent title to it.

Despite the cheapness and availability of land, supporting oneself by homesteading could be hard and costly—working the land required labor and equipment. Accordingly, many settlers ended up selling their claims before obtaining final title. Claims that switched hands in this way were called "relinquishments," and it was such a relinquishment that Carver purchased shortly after his arrival in Ness County during the summer of 1886.

In 1886, Carver moved to Ness County, Kansas, and built a sod house, much like the one shown here, with bricks made of thick earth cut from the prairie. He remained a homesteader for roughly two years before moving to Iowa and enrolling in college.

Carver's tract was located south of the town of Beeler. His first task was to build a house, which took him several months. During this period, he found work—and lodging—by helping another settler, George Steeley. Like most of the residents of Ness County, Steeley was white. Yet it did not seem to matter to him that Carver was black, and in the months ahead Carver found acceptance within the entire community as he shared in the common struggle of life on the prairie.

Due to the lack of timber, the house Carver built for himself was like that of many of his neighbors—made from sod bricks. He cut the bricks himself from the firm, grassy earth and constructed a tiny, thick-walled, single-room dwelling. It had a door, one window, and a roof made of sod and tar paper. He furnished it with a bed, a few chairs, a small table, and a stove. Nearby, he planted 17 acres with corn and other vegetables and tried—without success—to find water, resigning himself eventually to hauling water from Steeley's adjoining land. In addition to doing what was needed to survive, he kept up his scientific interests by collecting local rock and mineral specimens and starting a makeshift conservatory of native plants.

Not content to keep to himself, Carver also took part in community life. He joined the local literary society, played the accordion at community dances, and took his first art lessons from Clara Duncan, a local black woman who had previously taught at the college level. His white neighbors soon recognized him as one of the most gifted and knowledgeable residents of Ness County, and years later, after he had left the area and had become famous, he still corresponded with a number of people he had befriended during his stay in Beeler. In a 1935 letter to the editor of the Ness County newspaper, he wrote: "I want to say . . . to the good people of Ness County that I owe much to them for what little I have been able to accomplish, as I do not recall a single instance in which I was not given an opportunity to develop the best that was within me."

In September 1890, Carver entered Simpson College, a small Methodist school in Indianola, Iowa, where he was the only black on campus. His classmates were quick to accept him, however. "They made me believe I was a real human being," he said.

For all Carver's attachment to the people of Ness County, his ultimate destiny was not in making a life as a Kansas "sodbuster." He borrowed $300 in 1888 to secure final title to his land but chose not to stay on it much longer. The region's fierce weather—with its winter blizzards and summer droughts—made life especially hard, and it is more than likely that he found farming an inadequate way of satisfying his intellectual curiosity, not to mention his basic subsistence needs. So, probably in 1889, he left Ness County and once more became a wanderer, this time heading east. He held on to the deed to the land until 1891, when trouble with his loan payments forced him to turn it over to his creditor.

By 1890, Carver's wanderings had taken him as far as Winterset, Iowa. There he found work as a hotel cook and again opened a laundry. His religious faith took him to several local churches, and at one of them, he met a well-to-do couple, Dr. and Mrs. John Milholland. His friendship with them was to be one of the most significant of his life.

The Milhollands, who frequently invited Carver to their home, were impressed by the breadth of his knowledge (all the more remarkable when one considered his erratic education) and his artistic and musical talents. They were sure that this young man, by then about 25 years old, was destined for better things. And so they helped bring his life into sharper focus by urging him once more to pursue a higher education.

Carver may well have balked at the idea at first, remembering his unjust rejection by Highland College. But the Milhollands knew of a school, Simpson College in nearby Indianola, that admitted students without regard to race. With his friends' encouragement, he applied and was accepted.

In September 1890, Carver arrived on campus. His wanderings were nearly over. ❧

"For quite one month I lived on prayer beef suet and corn meal," Carver said of his early days at Simpson College. *"Modesty prevented me telling my condition to strangers."*

4

A
COLLEGE
MAN

SIMPSON COLLEGE WAS a small school operated by the Methodist church, and Carver found its atmosphere warm and hospitable, even though he ended up spending only a year there. No other blacks were on campus at the time, but the acceptance he received from his teachers and fellow students was gratifying. "The people are very kind to me here," he wrote in a letter to the Milhollands, "and the students are wonderfully good. . . . I have the name unjustly of having one of the broadest minds in school."

To pay his way, Carver turned to a tried-and-true means of support. He opened a laundry, working out of a little shack in which he also lived. His furnishings were so meager that some of his fellow students took up a collection to supply him with three chairs and a table, which, as he informed the Milhollands, they left for him anonymously while he was in class.

Carver's ambitions at Simpson were not focused on science, and, in fact, he did not take any science courses while he was there. Interested mainly in painting, he enrolled in an art class taught by a young woman named Etta Budd. As it happened, she was

Carver attending an art class at Simpson College, where he was the only male student in the fine arts department. He went to the school chiefly so he could pursue his interest in painting.

J. L. Budd, a professor of horticulture, was one of Carver's favorite teachers at Iowa State. Carver studied art with Budd's daughter, Etta, who taught at Simpson College.

the daughter of a horticulture professor at the Iowa State College of Agricultural and Mechanical Arts, and it was not long before she noted Carver's botanical interests. Flowers were often the subjects of his paintings, and he sometimes showed her plants that he was growing. Although Etta Budd was impressed by his gifts as a painter, she feared that he could never support himself that way. Carver obviously had similar fears, for he took to heart her suggestion that he transfer to Iowa State and pursue a scientific career.

The thought of leaving Simpson and giving up his artistic aspirations made for a difficult—and probably painful—decision. In the end, however, Carver reasoned that he could better serve the needs of humanity, especially those of poor black farmers, by becoming an agriculturist. As his letters of this period show, he felt a strong religious sense that he was meant for some special mission. "I realize that God has a great work for me to do," he wrote at one point. Scientific agriculture had obvious practical value, and given his talents with plants, it became increasingly clear to him that this was the direction he should take.

Located in Ames, just north of the state capital of Des Moines, Iowa State was an excellent choice for studying agriculture. Chartered in 1858, with the land granted by the state government, and centered in one of the country's major farming regions, it was among the first schools to give serious attention to research and education in this field. Carver could scarcely have received better training at any other institution.

Yet he had problems adjusting to the school. In August 1891, shortly after his arrival, he penned a homesick letter to the Milhollands, complaining that he did not like Iowa State as much as Simpson because "the helpful means for a Christian growth is not so good." Unlike the people at Simpson, not everyone at Iowa State was concerned with making him feel welcome. Some people shouted racial slurs at him during his first day there. He was not allowed to live in a dormitory, as the white students did. Instead, the faculty converted an old office into sleeping quarters for him. Nor was he allowed to eat in the students' dining hall. He had to take his meals in the basement with the kitchen employees.

When one of Carver's white friends in Indianola, Mrs. W. A. Liston, heard about his problems, she immediately went to Ames to cheer him up. She strolled around the campus grounds with him and joined him for dinner in the basement. Although the dining arrangements apparently did not change as a result of her visit, he felt better about the place after she spent the day with him.

In fact, Carver's sense of belonging increased steadily over the next five years as he made many new friends and shared in a broad variety of campus activities. Participating in groups ranging from the Welsh Eclectic Society (a campus debating club) to the German Club and the Art Club, he threw himself wholeheartedly into college life. He organized an Agricultural Society, arranged prayer meetings with other devout students, became the first trainer and masseur for the Iowa State football team, and was active in the Iowa State chapter of the Young Men's Christian Association, serving as its missionary chairman and, in 1894, as a delegate to the National Students' Summer School at Lake Geneva, Wisconsin. He also joined the National Guard Student Battalion (enrollment in the organization was compulsory for all male students), where he eventually achieved the highest student rank, that of captain.

Despite his busy schedule of activities, not to mention the various odd jobs he had to perform in order to scrape by, Carver did not neglect his studies.

Carver at Iowa State, in his National Guard Student Battalion uniform. The school's military division was one of many campus activities in which he participated.

A political cartoon of James Wilson, another of Carver's professors at Iowa State, who later became U.S. secretary of agriculture and was known as being sympathetic to needy farmers. Like Carver, he was a devout Christian, and the two men regularly attended group prayer meetings in Wilson's office at the college.

On a 4-point scale, his average in even his weakest subjects, history and mathematics, never fell below 3.0. His best subjects, not surprisingly, were botany and horticulture, in which his grades ranged from 3.9 to 4.0. He received his training under a first-rate faculty, which included two future U.S. secretaries of agriculture, James Wilson and Henry C. Wallace.

Carver became highly regarded by his teachers for his talents in grafting plants (uniting parts of two plants so that they grow as one) and cross-fertilizing them (transferring the germinating cells from one plant to another). His undergraduate thesis, entitled "Plants as Modified by Man," dealt with his experiments in crossbreeding certain plants to produce hybrid varieties (offsprings of a cross between two different species or subspecies) that were hardier and more attractive than nature's originals. His work in this area inspired Professor Wilson to observe, "In cross-fertilization . . . and the propagation of plants, Carver is by all means the ablest student we have."

Carver's gifts impressed not only his teachers; in one notable case, they impressed a faculty child. According to one version of the story, Carver was examining a plant on the college grounds one day when he encountered an unusually bright six-year-old boy who asked him various questions about what he was doing. Intrigued by the child's curiosity, which reminded him of the thirst for knowledge that had possessed him during his own childhood, Carver asked the boy his name and learned that he was Henry A. Wallace, son of Professor Wallace. After that, the boy often accompanied Carver on his regular walks in the woods.

This friendship between the black student and the professor's child was significant in light of what the boy later accomplished. As an adult, Henry A. Wallace became, like his father, a scientist, an Iowa State professor, and a secretary of agriculture; he then

Henry C. Wallace, an Iowa State professor who also became U.S. secretary of agriculture. His son, who later became U.S. secretary of agriculture as well as vice-president, befriended Carver in 1894 and called him the "kindliest, most patient teacher I ever knew."

went on to serve as vice-president from 1941 to 1945 under Franklin Roosevelt and to run as the Progressive party candidate for president in 1948. Wallace was to credit Carver with first sparking his interest in plant life. Recalling the nature walks he took with Carver as a child, he said that Carver "could cause a little boy to see the things which he saw in a grass flower."

Carver's abilities with plants were not the only talents to bring him recognition during his Iowa State years. Painting remained his first love, and in 1892 he was encouraged to enter some of his works in a state art exhibition in Cedar Rapids. He hesitated at the idea because he lacked a good suit of clothes and

Pencil drawings by Carver (above and on opposite page).

the money to make the trip. Some of his fellow students then "kidnapped" him and rushed him off to a clothing store for a new suit. After he was fitted and the suit was paid for, they presented him with a ticket to Cedar Rapids.

It was a successful trip. One of the paintings Carver exhibited, *Yucca and Cactus* (a subject taken from the time he lived in Ness County), was chosen to represent Iowa at the 1893 World's Columbian Exposition at Chicago—a spectacular fair celebrating the 400th anniversary of Christopher Columbus's discovery of America.

Carver received his Bachelor of Agriculture degree in 1894. His teachers felt that he showed great promise and wanted him to continue his education. They also wanted to put his skills to use in Iowa State's classrooms, this time on the other side of the teacher's desk. Carver thus enrolled in the program for the Master of Agriculture degree and was appointed to the faculty as an assistant in biology, which enabled him to teach freshman courses.

As a graduate student, Carver was just as impressive as he had been as an undergraduate. Performing his work under the guidance of L. H. Pammel, a noted expert on plant diseases and fungi, he showed remarkable skill at finding specimens of fungus—a type of plant that lacks chlorophyll and reproduces asexually. He contributed hundreds of them to Iowa State's collections, and Professor Pammel remembered him as "the best collector I have ever had in the department or have ever known."

Carver also collaborated with Pammel on several scholarly articles and proved a popular teacher with his own students. In fact, he might well have stayed at Iowa State as a faculty member—which was what his teachers wanted him to do—if it had not been for his ever-growing feeling that he should do something more to help other blacks.

Two black schools courted Carver with job offers before he had even completed the requirements for his master's degree. The first was Alcorn Agricultural and Mechanical College in Mississippi. Even though the salary proposed by Alcorn was no larger than what Iowa State was already paying him as an assistant in biology, Carver gave serious consideration to the school's offer. He hesitated, however, mainly because he wanted to finish work on his degree. Then, in late March 1896, a letter with another offer arrived from Alabama. It was signed by a man already becoming well known across the country as a black leader, Booker T. Washington.

Washington had been appointed principal of Tuskegee Normal and Industrial Institute in Tuskegee, Alabama, when the school was founded in 1881. From its beginnings, the institute's emphasis was on practical vocational training designed to help blacks gain an economic foothold in society. Agriculture was supposed to play a key role in Tuskegee's program, but for 15 years Washington had been unable to secure funds for a separate agriculture department. Finally, in 1896, the money for such a department arrived by way of the John F. Slater Fund for Negro Education, a philanthropic organization established by a wealthy Connecticut textile manufacturer.

In keeping with his general policy of hiring blacks for faculty positions, Washington wanted to place a qualified black at the head of the new agricultural school. The Slater Fund trustees doubted that he would be able to find such a person. Accordingly, when Washington heard about Carver—who was then the only black in America to have received advanced training in scientific agriculture—he sought the graduate student out at once.

Carver did not jump at the offer. It took the exchange of several letters with Washington before he agreed to take the position. He explained his hes-

Booker T. Washington became the leading black spokesman in the late 19th century, a time when most blacks in the South were rural farmers being victimized by racial discrimination and exploited by a savage sharecropping system. Instead of protesting the obvious oppression, Washington called on blacks to rise in the world through a program of self-help.

itation by citing the offer from Alcorn and his desire to finish his master's degree.

Still, Carver was quick to compliment Washington on the work being done at Tuskegee and to stress his own commitment to the cause of black education. "It has always been the one great ideal of my life," he wrote, "to be of the greatest good to the greatest number of 'my people' possible and to this end I have been preparing myself for these many years." He believed, he said, that the sort of education Tuskegee provided "is the key to unlock the golden door of freedom to our people."

Washington, for his part, seemed determined to bring Carver to the institute and offered him a yearly salary of $1,000 plus board. "If we cannot secure you," he told Carver, "we shall be forced perhaps to put in a white man. . . . We will be willing to do anything in reason that will enable you to decide in favor of coming to Tuskegee."

Eventually, after Washington assured Carver that he need not come to Tuskegee until he had acquired his master's degree, the scientist agreed to join the staff. In his acceptance letter to Washington—dated May 16, 1896—he wrote: "I am looking forward to a very busy, very pleasant and profitable time at your college and shall be glad to cooperate with you in doing all I can through Christ who strengtheneth me to better the condition of our people. . . . Providence permitting I will be there in Nov."

After spending the summer finishing his degree requirements, Carver decided to skip the Iowa State graduation ceremonies and set out in October for Alabama. There he would find a world unlike any he had yet encountered. ❧

SOUTHWARD
TO
TUSKEGEE

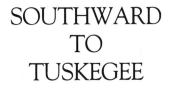

CARVER'S JOURNEY FROM Ames, Iowa, to Tuskegee, Alabama, in the fall of 1896 covered nearly 1,000 miles. But the significance of the move involved much more than the vast distance he traveled. The 31-year-old agriculturist had never before lived in the Deep South or among large numbers of blacks. Now he was in the very heart of a region where blacks were numerous (outnumbering whites in many areas) and where a whole array of peculiar laws and customs were enforced by whites to keep blacks "in their place."

Life for blacks in the South was hard—and getting harder—at the time of Carver's arrival at Tuskegee. In fact, the turn of the century has been called the lowest point in the history of American race relations. The turbulent events that began with the Reconstruction period immediately following the Civil War and continued through the rest of the 19th century had brought about this sorry state of affairs.

With the South in a shambles after the war, the North had to decide how to remodel the devastated and impoverished southern society. Among the many problems to be dealt with was the fate of the former

Carver first arrived at Tuskegee Institute in 1896 and remained there for nearly 50 years. "This line of education," he said of the school's policy of promoting skilled labor, "is the key to unlock the golden door of freedom to our people."

The students at Tuskegee, the nation's leading black industrial school, learned a variety of vocational skills, including building carriages (above) and making shoes (on opposite page). "No race can prosper," the institute's principal, Booker T. Washington, said, "till it learns that there is as much dignity in tilling a field as in writing a poem. . . . The opportunity to earn a dollar in a factory just now is worth infinitely more than the opportunity to spend a dollar in an opera house."

slaves. Not surprisingly, most southern whites were far from ready to accept blacks as equals. Left to their own devices, whites granted few privileges to blacks and sought to keep them at the lowest social level—as slaves in almost every way but name.

Things began to improve for blacks around 1868. The Radical Republicans—members of the Republican party who had always been the staunchest supporters of emancipation—were in control of Congress, and under them Reconstruction entered a new phase. The Radicals' programs included efforts to ensure that the freed slaves got their civil rights. Measures were adopted enabling blacks to vote, hold office, own land, obtain schooling, and use public facilities. The local whites resisted these efforts, and often this resistance took the form of terrorism. White supremacist groups such as the Ku Klux Klan sprang up, using violence and intimidation to deny blacks their rights.

Eventually, the North grew weary of what was called "the Southern problem," and the power of the Radical Republicans waned and finally collapsed. Conservative whites in the South recaptured control of their state governments and congressional seats. Starting in the mid-1870s and continuing through the 1890s, whatever rights blacks had gained during Radical Reconstruction were steadily eroded. Segregation laws that separated the races—and denied blacks equal opportunities for education and the use of public facilities—were put in place and then upheld by the U.S. Supreme Court.

In an 1883 decision, the high court in effect dismantled the Civil Rights Act of 1875, which had outlawed discrimination in such facilities as restaurants and stores. Then, in 1896—the same year Carver went to Tuskegee—the *Plessy v. Ferguson* decision put the court's stamp of approval on the "separate but equal" doctrine. The court said in this decision that separate facilities for blacks were legal so long as they were equal to white facilities. In actual practice, though, the rule was separate but *unequal*.

Southern states also adopted laws to deny blacks their political rights. To keep blacks from voting, such measures as poll taxes and tests of reading ability were enacted. These laws capitalized on the widespread poverty and illiteracy of the black population. As a side effect, they eliminated many poor white voters as well.

Economic oppression was perhaps the heaviest burden that southern blacks had to bear. The vast majority of the South's 5 million blacks were farmers, and though by 1880 a fifth of them possessed their own land, a much larger number was still working on land belonging to a relatively small group of white landowners. They were no longer slaves but tenant farmers.

The form of tenant farming that became a way of life for most blacks was sharecropping. This system (which, again, trapped many poor whites) developed out of necessity. At first, it seemed to benefit both the landowners who had no cash to pay for farm labor and the farm workers who could not buy or rent land. With sharecropping, the landowner could obtain labor by providing each worker with a cabin, supplies, and a small part of the acreage to farm. In return for farming the land, the sharecropper could keep a portion—usually half—of the money from the crops he raised.

Sharecropping proved an inefficient way of farming, however, and it was worsened by a host of interrelated problems that plagued southern agriculture. These included an overwhelming dependence on a single cash crop—cotton—that depleted the soil with each growing season, fluctuating farm prices, poor agricultural methods, and a credit system that kept farmers perpetually in debt. In short, southern

Under Booker T. Washington's guidance, Tuskegee Institute became the seat of what was known as the "Tuskegee machine": an influential political group, headed by Washington himself, that sought economic advancement for black Americans by having them accommodate themselves to racial segregation.

farming was in terrible shape, and blacks were the hardest hit victims.

As if dire poverty and the legal forms of discrimination were not bad enough, blacks also had to face the growing severity of white prejudice. By the 1890s, the South was full of white extremists who believed that, free of slavery, blacks were quickly degenerating into beasts who posed a particular threat to white women. These whites openly preached violence as a way of handling what they called "the race problem." Lynchings, often involving an accusation of interracial rape, became commonplace. (Though it took place in the Midwest, the incident Carver had witnessed in Fort Scott, Kansas, in 1879 was typical of the kind of mob action that occurred in the South.)

The whites who favored the use of violence against blacks were not just those from the lowest classes. Some of them, like "Pitchfork Ben" Tillman of South Carolina, were among the region's major political leaders. As these extremists gained power, the quality of black life further deteriorated.

Such was the South to which Carver came. In the midst of it all, the Tuskegee Institute was a leading haven for blacks, a shelter against the storm. This was largely because of Booker T. Washington.

By the mid-1890s, Washington was well on his way to becoming the most powerful black leader in America. Born a slave in 1856, he had so distinguished himself as a teacher at Virginia's Hampton Normal and Agricultural Institute (from which he had earlier graduated) that he was chosen, at only 25 years of age, to head the black normal school at Tuskegee, which had just been established by an act of the Alabama legislature. Modeling the institute after Hampton, Washington skillfully courted northern white financial support, sought to appease the southern white establishment, and worked tirelessly to build up the school and its programs.

In 1881, Tuskegee held its first classes in a church. Washington then moved the institute to a newly purchased 100-acre farm that became the school's permanent site. Over the next few decades, with the aid of student labor and materials produced in the institute's own brickyard, one building after another arose as a campus was carved from the farmland.

Although Tuskegee was originally conceived as a training facility for elementary school teachers, it soon added industrial courses in trades such as carpentry and blacksmithing. When Carver arrived in 1896, the school's enrollment was edging toward

Carver (front row, center) with the agricultural faculty at Tuskegee Institute shortly after his arrival in 1896. Throughout his long tenure at the school, he said little about black rights. "I believe in the providence of God working in the hearts of men," he maintained, "and that the so-called, Negro problem will be satisfactorily solved in His own good time, and in His own way."

Editor and author W. E. B. Du Bois was a vocal critic of Booker T. Washington's accommodationist policies. Instead of working within the framework of racial segregation, as Washington suggested, Du Bois called for the formation of an educated, "talented tenth" of black leaders to fight for unequivocal black rights.

1,000, and the campus boasted some 40 buildings. Carver was joining a flood of new faculty whose ranks swelled from 30 to 109 between 1891 and 1901.

In Washington's view, the kind of practical vocational training that Tuskegee offered was the solution to the seemingly insurmountable problems of blacks in the South—and many people of both races agreed with him. In 1895, while Carver was still pursuing his graduate studies at Iowa State, Washington had captured the national spotlight with a speech he gave before an audience of blacks and whites at the Atlanta Cotton States and International Exposition. The approach to race relations Washington outlined in his speech, the so-called Atlanta Compromise, called for blacks to put aside their efforts for political and social equality and to strive instead for economic and educational self-improvement. At the same time, he appealed to whites to give blacks a chance to advance themselves in the economic arena.

White leaders were hopeful that bringing industry to the South could lift the region out of its dismal poverty, and Washington played to those hopes. In his speech, he identified blacks as a work force that "without strikes and labour wars, tilled your fields, cleared your forests, and brought forth treasures from the bowels of the earth. . . ." They were ready and willing, he said, to prove themselves as loyal, law-abiding participants in the building of a revitalized South.

Washington raised his hand high above his head as he reached the climax of his speech. "In all things that are purely social we can be as separate as the fingers," he proclaimed, "yet one as the hand in all things essential to mutual progress." Speaking these words, he dramatically opened and closed his upraised fingers to illustrate his point. The applause that greeted his conciliatory message was long and loud.

Washington believed that social and political rights would follow for blacks only *after* they had proven their economic usefulness. That he was willing, for the moment, to make concessions to the southern system did much to strengthen his leadership position. Many whites felt less threatened by a black man who seemed to accept the separation of the races, and partly as a result of this view, Washington's power and influence rose steadily from the 1890s onward.

Washington eventually created a "Tuskegee machine" that he used to spread his doctrines, advance the careers of those who thought as he did, and thwart those who disagreed with him. Before his death in 1915, Washington's racial vision and power-brokering methods would come under fire from other black leaders, most notably the editor and scholar W. E. B. Du Bois. But earlier, at the turn of the century, Washington came to be seen by much of the country—black and white, North and South—as *the* spokesman of his race.

Washington and Carver were very much in agreement in their views on race relations and black advancement. In one of his letters to Washington at the time he was considering the Tuskegee offer, Carver cited a recent speech by the principal and declared, "I said amen to all you said; furthermore you have the correct solution to the 'race problem.' " As one who had struggled patiently for an education and had been rewarded for it, Carver seemed a living embodiment of Washington's philosophy of black self-improvement.

With such agreements in outlook, the two men had high hopes for a good working relationship when Carver arrived at Tuskegee. But as they were both to discover, the task of creating a new department at a struggling black institution would have more than its share of strains. ❧

Blacks would make social gains, according to Booker T. Washington, only after they had made economic gains. "Whatever other sins the South may be called upon to bear," he said, "when it comes to business pure and simple it is in the South that the Negro is given a man's chance in the commercial world."

6

SATISFACTIONS AND FRUSTRATIONS

THE WORK LOAD that Booker T. Washington placed on Carver following his arrival at Tuskegee in 1896 was heavy. Carver's main responsibilities were to administer the agriculture department, direct the agricultural experiment station, teach a full schedule of classes, assume responsibility for Tuskegee's agricultural extension efforts in the rural South, and manage the institute's two farms. In addition, he was expected to serve on various committees (including the institute's executive council, an advisory panel to the principal), act as the school's temporary veterinarian, supervise the beautification of the campus grounds, and even oversee the maintenance of the school's sanitary facilities.

The burden of these responsibilities taxed Carver's abilities severely. Over the next 20 years, his talents proved decidedly stronger in some areas than in others. The duties at which he most excelled were his teaching, his work with the experiment station, and his efforts to extend the benefits of Tuskegee's programs to poor farmers in outlying areas.

In the classroom, Carver showed a natural ability to captivate and inspire his students—many of whom

---

"Everyone here recognizes that your great fort[e] is in teaching and lecturing," Booker T. Washington told Carver after he arrived at Tuskegee. "There are few people anywhere who have greater ability to inspire and instruct as a teacher and as a lecturer than is true of yourself."

had not even finished elementary school. To teach them was a challenge, and Carver met it admirably. Genuinely concerned with reaching his students, he was most aided by his great love and reverence for the subjects he taught. "Whether his course was labeled botany, chemistry, or agriculture," wrote Linda McMurry, author of a 1981 Carver biography, "what he taught was an appreciation of the miracles and beauties of nature."

An ecologist before the word became fashionable, Carver taught that everything in nature was interrelated. To demonstrate this, he had his classes study a single plant in depth and showed them how a whole variety of natural processes—chemical and biological—came into play to produce and nurture it. To Carver, understanding how these different processes interacted was the essence of learning.

Always stressing the concrete over the abstract, Carver illustrated his points with plant and mineral specimens he collected during his regular hikes in the woods and fields. He encouraged his students to make similar discoveries. For example, he had his botany classes compete with each other in collecting specimens. Such methods reflected Carver's belief that the student should participate as much as possible in the educational process. He felt that the teacher should be more than a predigester of facts; the best teacher, in Carver's view, was one who enabled students to discover things for themselves.

Though Carver worked his classes hard, he was a popular teacher. The scope of his knowledge became so well known on campus that some of his students even tried to fool him once. On this occasion, a group of boys carefully assembled a fake specimen from parts of different insects and then challenged the professor to identify the strange bug they claimed to have found. But Carver was not fooled. The insect, he declared, was "a humbug."

Carver enjoyed joking with his students, sometimes indulging in physical horseplay. One of his favorite forms of play was to administer mock whippings, and he liked to "threaten" his favorites with beatings if they did not behave. His affection for his "children" (as he liked to call them) also went beyond fun and games. He loaned money to the needier ones from time to time, and when possible, he tried to help students find jobs or further their education after they left Tuskegee. He also exchanged letters with a large number of his former students, often following their progress over the course of many years.

Carver never married, although he came close in 1905, when he apparently considered taking Sarah Hunt, the sister-in-law of a Tuskegee official, as his bride. The courtship dissolved, however, for reasons Carver was hesitant to discuss. He would say only that he and the woman discovered that they had different goals in life.

Carver (top row, fourth from left) with fellow faculty members of the Tuskegee Institute in 1897, shortly after he joined the school's staff. The only teacher there with a degree from a white college, he was the institute's highest-paid professor.

Carver's chief responsibility at Tuskegee was establishing and overseeing the institute's agriculture program. "For recreation," he said, "I go out and hoe, pull weeds and set plants myself."

Carver surmounted his loneliness with a deep religious conviction that came to play an important role in his relations with students. In 1907, at the request of several students, he organized a Bible class that met in the library on Sunday evenings. At these meetings, he linked his Christian beliefs with his work as a scientist. He talked about the way "the Creator" was revealed in the wonders of nature. He believed that science and religion in no way contradicted one another. "We get closer to God," he wrote years later, "as we get more intimately and understandingly acquainted with the things he has created." Carver's Bible class, which he taught up until his death, became a mainstay of Tuskegee campus life.

If Carver's teaching and relations with his students were marked by an ability to inspire, his direction of Tuskegee's agricultural experiment station was marked by an ability to do valuable work with very limited resources. The 10-acre station was established at the institute in 1896, shortly after Carver's appointment to the faculty. Its operation was financed by a meager annual allotment from the state of $1,500.

By contrast, the experiment station at the all-white Alabama Polytechnic Institute in nearby Auburn received $15,000 annually in federal funds as well as money from other sources. And whereas a staff of several scientists with different areas of specialization carried out the research at Auburn, Carver was expected to do virtually all the work of the Tuskegee station himself. The lack of support for Carver's station was typical of how black institutions were treated at the time. Considering such limitations as well as the multitude of demands on his time and talents, Carver's work at the experiment station was admirable indeed.

The basic purpose of Carver's station was the same as that of other agricultural research stations: to conduct experiments with different kinds of crops, soil fertilizers, and farming methods and to report on this research. Yet the general aim of Tuskegee's programs—addressing the needs of an impoverished and oppressed people—when coupled with the limited funding, gave Carver's station a special emphasis. It tended to deal with agricultural methods that were within reach of the poorest of farmers. "Even though

Students at work in the fields of Tuskegee's experiment station, where Carver tested varieties of crops and fertilizers.

his experiments were aimed at all levels of farming," Linda McMurry noted, "Carver spent significantly more time on projects that required hard work and the wise use of natural resources rather than expensive implements and fertilizers."

Much of Carver's research involved finding ways of building up the southern soils that were worn out from so much cotton planting. This led to experiments with crop rotation, organic fertilizers, and various types of new crops that returned nutrients to the soil, such as velvet beans, black-eyed peas, sweet potatoes, peanuts, alfalfa, and soybeans.

Though it was important to demonstrate the soil-building properties of such crops, Carver realized that farmers needed other reasons to grow them. Thus, his research emphasized ways that these plants could be used to enrich a family's diet and to feed livestock. Carver's overriding concern was to help poor farmers improve the quality of their life and become more self-sufficient. He encouraged them to depend less on purchased goods and more on products that they could produce themselves.

Carver wanted southern farmers to grow crops other than cotton, but Booker T. Washington, a die-hard pragmatist who recognized that cotton would continue to be the principal cash crop in the region for some time to come, insisted that Carver test it as well. Carver was reluctant at first but finally went ahead when the principal allowed him to use nine additional acres for the purpose. In 1905, he planted several varieties of cotton, including a hybrid variety that he produced himself through crossbreeding.

Carver's hybrid brought good results for a few farmers who planted it. Unfortunately, it never gained widespread use. Carver's cotton experiments did gain some international publicity, however, as officials in both Germany and Italy sought his advice on the suitability of various types of cotton for certain kinds of soil.

Experiments with different types of crops represented one direction of Carver's research; experiments with methods of cultivation represented another. Carver was especially interested in testing organic fertilizers of both plant and animal origin, such as composts and manure, which were readily available to any farmer, especially those who could not afford the chemical varieties. This interest typified his general scientific outlook as well as his concern for poor farmers. He firmly believed, he said, that "nature produces no waste" and that uses could be found for even the "lowliest" of substances. His later experiments with the "humble peanut"—the plant that became the key to his national fame—reflected this same point of view.

U.S. secretary of agriculture James Wilson, one of Carver's professors at Iowa State, proved a valuable friend to Tuskegee's agriculture program during his 16-year tenure. "Call on me freely," he wrote to Carver, "for any help you need in the line of seeds or anything of that kind and I will lean your way heavily."

Carver's friendship with James Wilson, his former professor at Iowa State, brought some benefits to the Tuskegee experiment station. After Wilson became secretary of agriculture under President William McKinley in 1897, Carver often sought the aid of Wilson's agency, the U.S. Department of Agriculture (USDA). Because Carver's facility did not receive a share of the federal funds allotted to Alabama, the USDA might well have ignored the experiment station, but Wilson tried to help Carver whenever he could.

When Carver wanted to set up a weather station in 1899, for example, the USDA donated the necessary equipment. Furthermore, a number of Carver's experiments were carried out in collaboration with the USDA. Over the next several years, he received agency support for a variety of projects, ranging from attempts to cultivate silk to more conventional experiments with such crops as sugar beets, black-eyed peas, and peanuts. This support came mainly in the form of materials—seeds, fertilizers, and equipment. The Alabama legislature controlled the distribution of money from the U.S. government, so Wilson was unable to boost Carver's meager funding.

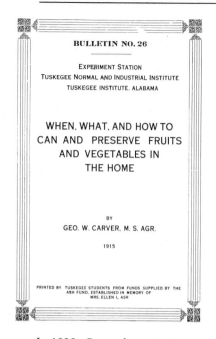

BULLETIN NO. 26

EXPERIMENT STATION
TUSKEGEE NORMAL AND INDUSTRIAL INSTITUTE
TUSKEGEE INSTITUTE, ALABAMA

WHEN, WHAT, AND HOW TO
CAN AND PRESERVE FRUITS
AND VEGETABLES IN
THE HOME

BY
GEO. W. CARVER, M. S. AGR.

1915

PRINTED BY TUSKEGEE STUDENTS FROM FUNDS SUPPLIED BY THE
ASH FUND, ESTABLISHED IN MEMORY OF
MRS. ELLEN L. ASH

In 1898, Carver began issuing periodicals (above and on opposite page) that publicized his efforts at Tuskegee's experiment station. He announced in the very first bulletin, "Every effort will be put forth to carry out the two-fold object of the Station, viz.: that of thoroughly equipping the student along the lines of practical and scientific agriculture; also the solving of many vexing problems that are too complex for the average farmer to work out for himself."

An important part of Carver's experiment station work was the publication of bulletins that reported the results of his research. The bulletins produced by other experiment stations were usually directed to other agricultural researchers, not to laymen. Carver, however, in keeping with his aim to reach what he called "the man farthest down," wrote most of his bulletins in very simple language. Usually focusing on a single plant or agricultural problem, many of his bulletins included practical advice, including cultivation techniques and recipes, as well as scientific information that a teacher might use. The titles of some of his bulletins—such as *How to Build Up Worn Out Soils, Successful Yields of Small Grain, Saving the Sweet Potato Crop, How to Make Cotton Growing Pay,* and *The Pickling and Curing of Meat in Hot Weather*— illustrate Carver's concern for practical application of his research. Because of their readability and their practical focus, Carver's bulletins were greatly in demand and widely distributed.

Neither Carver's research nor the information he included in his bulletins constituted anything close to a scientific breakthrough. Indeed, other experiment stations were performing similar kinds of research, and the agricultural advice Carver dispensed was hardly original. What made his work special was his concern for the needs of small farmers and his effectiveness in translating the accepted principles of scientific agriculture into understandable language.

In addition to his agricultural research and the bulletins that resulted from it, Carver sought to reach poor farmers even more directly. Under his guidance, the school broadened its agricultural extension programs aimed at raising the farmers' standard of living and improving their methods of farming.

Helping blacks outside its walls had been a major concern of the Tuskegee Institute from its beginnings. Soon after becoming principal, Washington made frequent trips to the surrounding countryside. Even as one who knew more than a little about the problems of black life, he was shocked by the extreme poverty of the sharecroppers. He saw teenagers with no clothes to wear and families living in the single room of a ramshackle cabin, subsisting on a diet of pork fat and cornbread. On such trips, Washington talked to the farmers about ways to improve their conditions. Gradually, he developed more formal means of reaching them through the school's facilities.

In 1892, Washington invited about 75 farmers, mechanics, schoolteachers, and ministers to visit Tuskegee and discuss their needs. To his surprise, about 400 people showed up. After the success of this first "Farmers' Conference," he started holding such meetings on an annual basis.

Carver took over this program after his arrival and improved on it. He used the Tuskegee experiment station to demonstrate methods of increasing crop yields to the visiting farmers, and in an act of even more immediate value, he procured free garden seed from the USDA for distribution at the conference. Later, he supplemented these allotments with seed produced at the experiment station.

Carver soon saw that yearly meetings were not enough to meet the dire needs of the farmers. Following the model of a program that had been successful at Iowa State, he set up monthly meetings of what was called the Farmers' Institute. These meetings, which began in November 1897, provided specific advice about crop rotation, the use of fertilizers, and ways of restoring depleted soils. In addition, the farmers brought in samples of their crops and had Carver analyze their successes and failures.

When the farmers' wives began to join their husbands at the meetings, cooking demonstrations by Tuskegee's senior girls became a regular feature. In

BULLETIN NO. 31   JUNE 1925

How to Grow the Peanut and 105 Ways of Preparing it for Human Consumption

Seventh Edition
January 1940

By
GEORGE W. CARVER, M. S. in Agr.
Director

EXPERIMENTAL STATION
TUSKEGEE INSTITUTE
Tuskegee Institute, Alabama

Carver oversaw the beautification of Tuskegee's grounds in addition to fulfilling his responsibilities as a teacher and administrator. He also managed the school's sanitary facilities and served for a time as the institute's veterinarian.

1898, the Farmers' Institute participants held their first fair at Tuskegee, displaying what they had grown in their gardens and prepared in their kitchens. From one-day gatherings attended by a few hundred people, these annual affairs grew over the next few years into events lasting several days and drawing thousands.

In 1904, Carver launched "A Short Course in Agriculture" at Tuskegee. Scheduled during the winter months, when farmers were least busy, the short course was a school for farmers that at first lasted for six weeks but was later cut to two. Carver and other members of the agricultural faculty instructed the attendees in a wide range of practical procedures, from the use of machinery to judging livestock, from organic fertilization to ways of making dairy products. Barely 20 farmers took advantage of the course during its first two years, but word about it spread steadily. By 1912, attendance at the course reached more than 1,500.

Carver was aware early on that extension programs requiring participants to gather at a central location like the Tuskegee campus would reach only the better-informed farmers. Thus, in his early years at Tuskegee, Carver assumed Washington's practice of traveling around the countryside and talking to farmers where they lived. Carver gained an even broader view of the needs and conditions of southern blacks as the Tuskegee extension programs became the model for similar programs at black schools

throughout the South. He soon found himself in de-
mand as a speaker at such conferences.

In 1902, Carver journeyed to Ramer, Alabama,
to visit a farmers' exhibition at a black school outside
the town. He was accompanied by a white woman
photographer named Frances B. Johnston, a north-
erner who was traveling through the South to observe
black schools. Nelson E. Henry, one of the teachers
at the school, met them at the Ramer train station
after dark.

Apparently, the presence of a white woman
among black men aroused the anger of Ramer's white
populace. A crowd gathered at the station "to see
what would happen," as Carver described the scene
in a letter to Washington. He climbed into a buggy
with Johnston and Henry and headed for the home
of a black family, where the photographer was to
spend the night.

Henry soon decided, however, that it would be
better for the photographer to stay in town, so he
and Johnston returned to Ramer. There, Carver
wrote, Henry "was met by parties and after a few
words was shot at three times. Of course, he ran and
got out of the way and Miss Johnston came to the
house where I was. I got out at once and succeeded
in getting her to the next station where she took the
train the next morning. . . . I had to walk nearly all
night . . . to stay out of [the whites'] reach."

Carver went back to Ramer in daylight to find
that "everything was in a state of turbulency and a
mob had been formed to locate Mr. Henry and deal
with him." After Carver returned to Tuskegee, the
institute launched an investigation that took the mat-
ter before the governor. Despite reassurances from
the more moderate townspeople of Ramer, Henry and
the other teacher at the school resigned their posi-
tions out of fear of further incident, and the school
itself was moved farther away from the town. Carver,

in summing up the episode, called it "the most frightful experience of my life."

Nevertheless, this racial incident did not stop Carver from seeking to bring practical information to other farmers. In 1904, Washington hit on the idea of outfitting a wagon with various kinds of demonstration materials to create what he called a "moveable school" that could be taken out to farmers on a regular basis. The idea excited Carver. He drew a rough sketch of how the wagon might be outfitted and proposed a series of demonstration lectures. Funds for building and equipping the wagon were soon obtained from Morris K. Jesup, a New York banker, and from the Slater Fund. Tuskegee students built what became known as the Jesup Wagon, and a member of Carver's agriculture faculty became its first operator.

By 1906, the wagon's success had attracted the attention of Seaman Knapp, a special agent for the USDA. At Washington's suggestion, Knapp agreed to put the Jesup Wagon under USDA supervision. Operation of the wagon then fell to Thomas Campbell, a former student of Carver's, who became the USDA's first black demonstration agent.

Although Carver's teaching duties, experiment station research, and extension work gave him much to be proud of, his first 20 years at Tuskegee were a time of considerable frustration as well as satisfaction. The enormous demands that were being made of him were part of the reason. But certain aspects of his personality also played a role.

In contrast to his warm relations with his students, Carver never quite got along with other members of the Tuskegee faculty and staff. To a large degree, this was his own fault. Arriving at the institute filled with high hopes, he was also brimming with a certain arrogance. Because Washington had practically begged him to come and because he held

Carver and his students examine a cow skeleton at the Tuskegee museum, which the scientist helped establish.

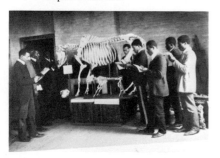

an advanced degree from a white college, Carver felt that he was unique and deserved special treatment.

Within a month of his arrival, Carver was complaining about his accommodations, claiming that he needed an extra room for his scientific collections. The request for two rooms did not go over well at a school where a bachelor teacher was usually required to share a single room with another teacher. And Carver did not make things any better when he confided that he expected to leave Tuskegee "as soon as I can trust my work to others, and engage in my brush work."

Such attitudes made Carver's colleagues resentful; other factors did so as well. His $1,000 annual salary was more than twice what many of the teachers were being paid. His midwestern background made him an outsider in the eyes of the southerners who dominated the Tuskegee staff. Even the fact that his skin was darker than that of the other faculty members made him suspect. In early 20th-century America, feelings of prejudice against dark-skinned blacks by light-skinned blacks were common. The result of all this

The Jesup Wagon, a movable school devised in 1904 by Booker T. Washington, was designed and outfitted by Carver. When the wagon began touring the Alabama countryside two years later, it contained many of Carver's laboratory products, thus helping to spread his reputation as an agriculturist and a chemist.

was that Carver made few friends, apart from his students, within the campus community.

Carver's adjustment problems at Tuskegee can partly be traced to the special circumstances of his earlier life. Except for his childhood relationship with his brother, Jim, and his stays in the Watkins and Seymour households, he had lived and associated mostly with whites: Moses and Susan Carver, the Ness County homesteaders, the Millhollands, and the faculty and students of Simpson College and Iowa State. He had, of course, known white bigotry in various forms—the Fort Scott lynching, the Highland College rejection, the difficulties of the first few weeks in Ames—but these negative experiences were clearly outweighed by positive ones.

The white people Carver knew best had nothing but praise and encouragement for him. So it is not surprising that throughout his life, he felt more comfortable among whites than among blacks. And it is also not surprising that this made it hard for him to fit in at an all-black institution such as Tuskegee.

The biggest adjustments Carver to had to make, however, were to the demands of Booker T. Washington. For years, the Tuskegee principal had poured his boundless energy into building up the school, and he wanted the same commitment and discipline from his teachers and staff. When they failed to live up to his expectations, he was hard on them.

Washington was supremely concerned with practical matters. He had little patience for dreamers or dabblers, and Carver was both. Given a choice, Carver might have preferred to teach a few classes, conduct research at the experiment station, and, whenever he felt so inclined, take up his paintbrushes or go wandering in the woods. But Washington expected him to be a full-time administrator with the ability to pull a new department together and run it efficiently. Carver proved less than competent in this capacity, which required strong organizational skills.

Tensions mounted as Washington came to feel that Carver was mismanaging Tuskegee's various agricultural operations and improperly supervising the people under him.

The institute's poultry yard, in particular, turned into a problem that would not go away. Under Carver's administration, the yard proved disastrously unproductive, and to Washington this was intolerable. Not only were such operations expected to produce money, but they were also expected to enhance Tuskegee's image.

Carver became defensive when confronted with these problems. He had grown accustomed to receiving praise in his pre-Tuskegee days, so he was easily hurt by any kind of criticism. When Washington faulted him, he always countered by reminding the principal of his heavy work load and his inadequate resources and personnel. He felt that Washington gave him too little support and relied too much on other people's opinions of what he was doing.

One of those people was John H. Washington, Booker's half brother, who served as the school's superintendent of industries and helped run things when the principal's ever-increasing activities drew him away from the campus. John Washington was no supporter of Carver, and Carver resented taking orders from him. As early as 1898, such frictions caused Carver to hint that he would resign if his working conditions were not improved.

Booker T. Washington recognized Carver's many talents, especially his abilities as a teacher. But the scientist's complaints irritated him. He urged Carver to complain less, swallow his pride, and do as he was told. Yet the problems continued. Carver's ego was repeatedly wounded, and Washington's patience was repeatedly tested.

Matters worsened in 1902, when a young man named George R. Bridgeforth joined the agricultural faculty. A bitter feud erupted between him and

Booker T. Washington, in attempting to supervise all aspects of Tuskegee's operations, made it hard for staff members to fulfill their duties. Carver's tenure at the institute was made even more difficult by the principal's half brother, John (shown here), who was the school's superintendent of industries and a frequent critic of Carver's efforts as an administrator. "Many times," the scientist complained in 1902, "no attention is paid to my wishes and things passed over my head which work contrariwise to my efforts to carry out the schools wishes."

Carver's difficulties with Booker T. Washington and Tuskegee's executive council continued through 1904, when he wrote to the principal, "Kindly accept my resignation to take effect." Although Carver offered to leave the school and investigated other job possibilities many times, he never did resign.

Carver almost immediately. Brash and outspoken, Bridgeforth was soon convinced that he could do a better job of running the agriculture department than Carver could. He aired his cutting judgments in letters to both Washington and Carver himself.

Carver was outraged. As if Washington's criticisms were not bad enough, he was now being subjected to criticism by a subordinate. Forced to mediate their disputes, Washington often took Bridgeforth's side.

The troubled poultry yard became the main focus of the conflict. In 1904, a special committee investigated the operation and found it "in very bad condition." The man Carver had put in charge of the yard claimed that, on Carver's instructions, he had filed false reports about the loss of chickens and the number of eggs being produced each day. Carver denied having given such orders, but Washington's confidence in him, already shaky, was undermined still further.

Spotting an opportunity to rise in the department at Carver's expense, Bridgeforth, along with several other faculty members, proposed a reorganization of the department that would relieve Carver of many of his duties, including his status as director of agriculture. A new committee was appointed to investigate Bridgeforth's recommendations. It concluded that the department's functions should be divided between Carver and Bridgeforth. Carver would become director of the experiment station and agricultural instruction, while Bridgeforth would become director of agricultural industries. This proposal was an attempted compromise that would assign Carver and Bridgeforth the duties to which each seemed best suited.

Carver's pride was bruised, however. He scoffed at the reorganization plan, rejecting the new title proposed for him as "too far a drop downward." He asked Washington to accept his resignation but backed off from this position a few days later. Instead of resigning, he demanded (among other things) that he remain in charge of the poultry yard. Washington agreed to let Carver keep his title and gave him a second chance to prove himself with the poultry operation. It was a short-lived victory.

The feuding between Carver and Bridgeforth continued for another decade. Carver threatened to resign several times, and he did, in fact, seek out jobs elsewhere—none of which ever materialized. Amazingly, despite continued problems and criticisms, he retained control of the poultry yard until 1913.

Bridgeforth also made gains, however, and Carver reluctantly gave in to two reshufflings of the department that chipped away at his responsibilities. In 1908, the department was reorganized in exactly the way that Carver had rejected in 1904: Bridgeforth was made director of agricultural industries, and Carver became director of agricultural instruction and the experiment station. In 1910, Carver got another title change: He was made director of the department of research and experiment station, a position that reduced his teaching load to whatever classes he wanted to teach and separated him from Bridgeforth's jurisdiction. Nevertheless, the infighting dragged on for several more years, and Carver was never really satisfied with the changes that were made.

Problems of this sort made Carver feel he was not properly appreciated at Tuskegee. The feuding caused him to withdraw gradually from teaching and to focus his energies on research. It also led him to seek recognition outside of the institute.

As the success of his extension work put him in increasing demand as a speaker, Carver came to relish this public role more and more in the coming years. By 1915, he was moving in a direction that would soon bring him fame at the national level. ❧

7

THE ROAD
TO FAME

THROUGHOUT HIS FIRST 20 years at Tuskegee, Carver supplemented his experiment station work with research he performed indoors, in the laboratory. Late in this period, he began to concentrate more and more on lab research while cutting back on other activities. His work in the laboratory ultimately became a cornerstone of the nationwide fame he achieved.

Ironically, a laboratory was not part of the facilities Carver was given when he first came to the institute. Compelled to devise one on his own, he rummaged through the campus trash piles for whatever he could use. Old bottles and jars were his first pieces of lab equipment, and his writing desk served as a table for his experiments. He often referred to his laboratory as "God's little workshop," and every day he made a point of praying before stepping inside.

Carver's "lab," if one could call it that, remained primitive for several years. Not until the departmental reorganization of 1910 was Carver promised a fully equipped facility. Even then, equipment was slow in coming, and several more years passed before his laboratory was truly adequate.

Carver (second from right) in his Tuskegee laboratory, where his investigations paved the way for his rise as the first nationally known black scientist. He said of his efforts, "I am trying to get our people to see that their color does not hold them back as much as they think."

Nevertheless, Carver made effective use of this crude apparatus during his early years at Tuskegee. He analyzed soil samples to determine their richness and the sort of fertilizers that might be needed to increase each soil's productivity. Searching for ways to improve the diets of southern farmers, he investigated various crops and plants for their nutritional properties, especially protein content. This led to numerous recipes using black-eyed peas, sweet potatoes, and peanuts, which he published in his bulletins. Intrigued by the clays he encountered in the Alabama countryside, he began to experiment with ways of producing paints and wood stains from their pigments.

Like his research in the experiment station fields, Carver's lab work was undertaken with the poor farmer in mind. Even though he became involved in an effort to manufacture his paints as early as 1902—a plan that for some reason collapsed—he was not concerned at first with commercial applications. His focus instead was on products and processes that sharecroppers, rural schoolteachers, and other people of limited means could duplicate cheaply and easily for themselves.

It was in the later years of Booker T. Washington's administration at Tuskegee that Carver began to think increasingly of how the results of his research might be put on the market. He was responding in part to Washington's desire for anything that might generate good publicity for the institute. He was also trying to counter the criticisms of those such as George Bridgeforth and John Washington, who scoffed at his abilities. And, too, he felt that devising new products from crops such as sweet potatoes and peanuts was simply an extension of one of his earlier aims—that of encouraging alternatives to cotton planting.

Thus, as his teaching and other responsibilities declined, Carver turned his attentions to what was called "creative chemistry." In fact, during the 1910 reorganization of the agriculture department, the title "consulting chemist" was proposed for Carver, and he was ready to assume the role. Dreamer that he was, Carver had visions of creating a whole variety of products that would be instrumental in revitalizing the South.

The dream proved elusive. In 1911, Carver became involved in a second commercial scheme to manufacture products derived from local clays, and again, for reasons now hazy, the enterprise failed to get off the ground. At about the same time, some successful experiments with ways of preserving pork built up his hopes that meat companies might adopt his methods. But apparently none did.

Despite such disappointments, Carver did not stop dreaming. He remained optimistic that one day a commercial breakthrough would result from his endeavors in the lab. Eventually, one of his dreams did come true—the dream of gaining recognition outside the walls of Tuskegee. His extension work and the growing number of speaking engagements that resulted from it made him a celebrity in regional agricultural circles. Although his products were never commercially adopted, several of them (notably his paints and wood stains) were used locally, bringing him praise and favorable publicity in state newspapers. Then, in 1915, the first in a series of events occurred that edged Carver closer to the national spotlight.

In the fall of that year, Washington was on a speaking tour of eastern cities when he became seriously ill. He was hospitalized in New York in early November and then taken back to Tuskegee a few days later. All the while, his condition steadily worsened. He died on November 15.

Washington's death was a heavy blow to Carver. For months, he was deeply depressed and declined to teach class. He had greatly admired Washington in

A persuasive public speaker, Booker T. Washington made Tuskegee the best-supported black school in the nation during his 34-year reign as principal, which ended with his death in 1915. Carver then took over Washington's role as chief fund-raiser for the institute.

"I am anxious to have as many students as possible come in direct contact with you," Robert Russa Moton, Booker T. Washington's successor at Tuskegee, told Carver. "I know of no other persons who can give the inspiration, saying nothing about the technical instruction that you can give."

spite of their frequent arguments, and he probably felt guilty at having bickered with him so much. In a letter to one of the principal's aides, Carver wrote, "I am sure Mr. Washington never knew how much I loved him, and the cause for which he gave his life."

The death of Washington brought a new principal to the school, Robert Russa Moton. Like Washington, he came to Tuskegee from Virginia's Hampton Institute. But unlike his predecessor, Moton enjoyed completely genial relations with Carver. Moton respected the scientist and sought to keep him happy. Under Moton's administration, Carver was gradually released from his teaching responsibilities during the regular term; within a few years, he was teaching only in the summer session, when refresher courses for schoolteachers were held. This, of course, allowed him to spend more time in the laboratory.

Another development that probably pleased Carver was the departure of his old rival George Bridgeforth. Apparently unhappy with Moton's leadership, Bridgeforth left Tuskegee in 1918 to become a county agricultural agent. Thus, Washington's death, while it grieved Carver deeply, ultimately brought about changes that worked in the scientist's favor.

In fact, Moton and other Tuskegee administrators found Carver a useful "replacement" for Washington. With Washington gone, the institute needed a star to attract both publicity and contributions. Carver increasingly fit the bill, and so the school began to feature him and his work prominently in its various publications. This became another important stepping-stone in Carver's path to renown.

Carver enjoyed a double stroke of good fortune in the fall of 1916, when two prestigious organizations honored him. First, he was asked to join the advisory board of the National Agricultural Society. Shortly afterward, he was elected a fellow of England's Royal Society for the Encouragement of the Arts. The second honor was especially significant in Carver's career. For an American black to be recognized by a British society was deemed remarkable, and the newspapers took due note.

A year later, Carver's work attracted attention of a different sort. In April 1917, the United States entered World War I, which had been devastating the European countries for nearly three years. The resulting food shortages—due to the disruption of trade, the diversion of crops to feed the troops, and wartime mobilization, which saw able farmers and workers leave their businesses to join the military—sparked the U.S. government's interest in ways of saving and preserving foods and other goods. Several products and processes with which Carver had been experimenting drew notice, especially a method for making bread by using sweet potatoes as a partial substitute for wheat.

The USDA brought Carver to Washington, D.C., in January 1918 to discuss the bread-making process, and plans were made for large-scale experiments utilizing a device that could dry 10,000 bushels of sweet potatoes and help convert the tuberous roots into flour. Although this drier was not installed at Tuskegee, as Carver hoped it might be, the scientist was often consulted while the USDA experiments proceeded. The full potential of the project was never realized, however; the war ended late in 1918, and with wheat no longer scarce, interest in sweet-potato flour faded.

The government was not the only party attracted by Carver's work during this period. Around the beginning of the war, a representative of the renowned inventor Thomas Edison approached Carver with a job offer that reportedly included an enormous salary. Carver was always vague about the details of the offer, although some sources put the salary figure as high as $200,000, an exorbitant amount for the early 20th century.

Carver said years later that he refused the offer because he preferred to stay in the South rather than move to New Jersey, where the Edison lab was located. The South, he proclaimed, had greater agricultural possibilities, and it was there, he felt, that he could do his greatest service. How much truth there is in the story of the Edison offer is not exactly known, but in the years ahead it would become a popular part of the Carver legend.

Although Carver's research encompassed several southern crops, it was one plant in particular—the peanut—that clinched his rise to national fame. In 1919, he developed a process for making "peanut milk" and enthusiastically touted its flavor, nutritional value, and capacity for use in cooking and baking. When representatives of the peanut industry heard about it, they were impressed with Carver's claims that the product possessed "unlimited possibilities." It turned out, however, that a method for making peanut milk had already been patented in 1917 by an Englishman.

Discovering this fact ended yet another of Carver's hopes for a commercial breakthrough. But it did not disillusion the peanut growers and processors. They liked Carver's personality and recognized his value as a spokesman for their industry. Accordingly, the scientist benefited from their sponsorship.

In 1920, the United Peanut Association of America asked Carver to address its convention, which met in Montgomery, the Alabama state capital. Even as a guest speaker, Carver was forced to observe southern racial customs. To reach the upstairs meeting room, he had to take the freight elevator instead of the regular passenger elevator, which was reserved for whites only.

During World War I, inventor Thomas Edison reportedly offered Carver a six-figure salary to work at the Edison Laboratory in New Jersey. Carver declined the offer, opting to remain at Tuskegee and help serve "his people"—a heroic act of self-sacrifice that did much to boost the Carver legend.

Once Carver reached the podium, however, he managed to dazzle the skeptical white audience, much as he had dazzled his students at Tuskegee. His talk, "The Possibilities of the Peanut," in which he demonstrated the variety of uses for the crop, was heartily received. An editorial in the *Peanut Promoter* noted how Carver overcame the audience's doubts and "verily won his way into the hearts of the peanut men."

A few months later, Carver dazzled a different group with a similar demonstration. In January 1921, he made what became a widely celebrated appearance before the House Ways and Means Committee. For Carver, it was but a short step from the meeting in Montgomery to the congressional hearing room in Washington, D.C. The United Peanut Association arranged for his appearance in the nation's capital as

Carver saw his reputation rise in the South through appearances at county fairs and demonstrations, where he displayed a range of products that could be grown by the average farmer. He is shown here at an exhibit around 1916.

"The average farmer," Carver said, "goes on trying to raise cotton in the same old extensive way, which means nothing but failure, more or less, for him." As an alternative to cotton, he promoted such crops as the peanut and the sweet potato, which, unlike cotton, do not rob the soil of its nutrients.

part of its lobbying effort on behalf of a proposed peanut tariff. Fearing competition from abroad, the American peanut industry wanted Congress to tax peanuts being imported from other countries. Carver, they felt, would be an effective proponent of their interests, and they were right. Shortly after his appearance, the tariff was enacted.

Carver's testimony before the congressional committee brought him far more publicity and recognition from the newspapers than he had previously received. As stories about Carver began to spread, the Tuskegee professor was credited with almost single-handedly creating the peanut industry. According to these stories, the peanut was an unimportant crop until Carver found new and diverse uses for it, making it a major part of southern agriculture and helping to free the South from its dependency on cotton.

The truth was far different. Peanut growing and processing already constituted a well-established industry when its representatives sought out Carver. Most of the uses for the peanut that Carver demonstrated so compellingly in his lectures were not developed by him—and he did not claim that they were. In fact, as early as 1896, the USDA had issued a comprehensive bulletin explaining the value and potential of the plant.

Carver's own work with the peanut did not begin until 1903, and it took several more years before he started to engage actively in creative chemistry, searching for new products that might be made from familiar crops. His own bulletin, *How to Grow the Peanut and 105 Ways of Preparing It for Human Consumption*, drew heavily on the earlier work of other agriculturists and did not appear until 1916. Nevertheless, because Carver was so effective in talking about the peanut, it was easy for the public to assume that he was personally responsible for all the many uses he demonstrated. And what he demonstrated seemed marvelous.

So, at nearly 60 years of age, Carver finally saw his name become a household word. Newspapers and magazines began to hail his genius in countless human interest stories. A wide variety of groups started to seek him as a lecturer and as a spokesman for their particular interests.

In large part, Carver's achievements were blown out of proportion so that white consciences could be soothed. The white-controlled press manipulated Carver's public image to show that blacks in America could accomplish great things within the framework of segregation laws and widespread bigotry. Carver, in effect, became a token of black achievement.

Carver himself was guilty of pandering to the whites who turned him into a folk hero. Perhaps too concerned with gaining their favor, he seemed to accept all too readily the gross injustices of racial segregation. Yet he never endorsed segregation, and if he appeared to tolerate it, he did so with the hope for a better future. A sincere optimist who frequently expressed a sense of solidarity with his fellow blacks, he held to a vision that a truly just and color-blind America would one day come.

Ironically, the fame Carver attained was for work that today appears rather insignificant. His earlier efforts in agricultural education were far worthier achievements than his dabblings in creative chemistry, but they were not the stuff of which fame was made. The American public wanted to be amazed, and creative chemistry was to be the way Carver amazed them. ◗

"To those who have as yet not learned the secret of true happiness," Carver said, "which is the joy of coming into the closest relationship with the Maker and Preserver of all things: begin now to study the little things in your own door yard, going from the known to the nearest related unknown for indeed each new truth brings one nearer to God."

8

THE
FOLK HERO

BY THE 1920s, Carver was free of most of the duties at Tuskegee that had so burdened him during Booker T. Washington's administration. He continued to teach in the summer school, hold Sunday night Bible classes, and conduct experiments in his laboratory. His work in the fields of the experiment station, however, had begun to decrease steadily after 1915, mainly because of his advancing age and a schedule that kept him away from the campus much of the time. He also issued fewer bulletins.

Finally, in 1925, Carver discontinued his outdoor research altogether. A new building was put up on the spot where he had once investigated crops and cultivation techniques. He still issued an occasional bulletin under the imprint of the Tuskegee experiment station. But these reports were few and far between.

Carver's research in the 1920s focused almost entirely on creative chemistry. He renewed his efforts to find commercial markets and producers for his products—products he hoped would transform the South. As his fame grew following his appearance in

"The primary idea in all of my work was to help the farmer and fill the poor man's empty dinner pail," said Carver, shown here in 1940. "My idea is to help the 'man farthest down', This is why I have made every process just as simple as I could to put it within his reach."

Throughout his life, Carver maintained that "the master analyst needs no book; he is at liberty to take apart and put together substances, compatible or non compatible to suit his own particular taste or fancy." Nevertheless, his reliance on divine revelation instead of scientific methods often put him at odds with the scientific community.

Washington, D.C., several companies, some as large and well known as Ralston-Purina, expressed interest in his discoveries and fed his dreams.

Because Carver cared little for the day-to-day details of transacting business, he found a young man named Ernest Thompson, whom he had known for several years, to help him in these endeavors. An heir of a well-to-do white family from the town of Tuskegee, Thompson became Carver's business manager. It was his job to seek out potential investors and manufacturers and to help secure patents.

Early in 1923, Thompson arranged for an exhibit of Carver's products at the Cecil Hotel in Atlanta, Georgia. He hoped to attract commercial interest and financial backing for Carver, and in this he succeeded. By March, several prominent southern businessmen, including a former Georgia governor, were planning the formation of a company that would sell Carver's formulas and processes to other firms, which would then manufacture them. The firm, incorporated later that year, was called the Carver Products Company.

In its four years of existence, however, the company accomplished little beyond obtaining patents for three of Carver's processes: two for paints and one for cosmetics. These were the only patents ever secured in Carver's name, and none was ever commercially developed. Thompson, as it turned out, was no more adept at business matters than Carver, and the other officers of Carver Products were unable to give much time to the company. Finding investors to take on its projects proved to be a tough—and finally insurmountable—problem, and the company died a quiet death.

Only one Carver product was ever commercially manufactured and marketed during this period, and it was not very successful. The product, an emulsion of creosote and peanuts called Penol, had been developed by Carver in 1922 as a medication. Creosote, a liquid distilled from wood tar, was widely used at the time to treat tuberculosis and chronic bronchitis. Carver believed that the peanut content in his formula added nutritional value to the medication and prevented the irritation and nausea that creosote could cause when ingested.

In 1926, Thompson joined with several Tuskegee businessmen to found the Carver Penol Company and manufacture the product. The sales were disappointing, however, and in 1932 Thompson sold the rights for the manufacture and distribution of Penol to a Virginia company. They did not have much success with it either.

One of the reasons why Carver never successfully marketed a product was that he was a restless researcher who often shifted directions when a new idea hit him. Throughout the 1920s and 1930s, his research projects were at least remarkable for their diversity: making paper from peanut shells, creating a synthetic marble from wood shavings, using cotton in a number of road-paving processes, and developing an artificial rubber from sweet potatoes. Yet his long-time dreams for a commercial breakthrough never came true.

Although the stories that circulated about Carver often credited him with creative miracles, few of his products and processes ever got beyond his laboratory or exhibit tables. Manufacturers found it cheaper and easier to use other materials and methods for making the kinds of goods to which he devoted his research. Most likely, he would have enjoyed greater commercial success if he had focused more systematically on fewer projects, working out their problems to the fullest extent.

It was sometimes reported that Carver's work was utilized by companies without his receiving proper credit, and Carver himself said that he was uninterested in who manufactured his products after he had developed the formulas. However, Carver was secretive about his work and left almost no records aside from his three patents. As a result, it is hard to say what his uncredited contributions may have been.

Nevertheless, Carver's fame blossomed despite his lack of commercial success. The press, anxious to publicize a few black heroes, continued to exaggerate his accomplishments, and Carver usually let such reports stand without trying to correct them. After so many years of feeling undervalued at the Tuskegee Institute, he cherished the widespread attention he was receiving and apparently was reluctant to say anything that might detract from his image.

Clearly, Americans found Carver a very appealing figure. In fact, his personality and public image were probably as important to his becoming a national celebrity as was his purported wizardry. In time, a particular perception of Carver arose—that of an aging, unassuming, and eccentric genius selflessly devoted to his work, his people, and his adopted region.

The public liked many things about Carver. His theatrical flair, his sense of humor and sincerity, and his ability to explain his subject in simple but vivid terms were keys to his success with lecture audiences. His deep religious faith was also important. In his speeches and interviews, he almost always referred to the Bible and divine guidance. His accomplishments, he was fond of saying, were not his doing but were the work of God. As he told a reporter for the *Atlanta Journal* who questioned him about the permanency of the clay paints he had developed: "Why should they not be permanent? God made the clay in the hills; they have been there for countless generations, changeless. All I do is prepare what God has made, for uses to which man can put it. It is God's work— not mine."

Such words made Carver appear profoundly humble, and this image was supported by his lack of concern for outward appearances. Although he received many gifts of clothing, he preferred to wear old, threadbare suits, usually highlighted by a flower in the lapel. He could certainly afford better, but he was indifferent to money. Throughout his first two decades at the institute, he never received a salary increase; only in 1919 did Robert Moton give him an unsolicited raise. Stories were often told of how he left his paychecks in his desk for months until he was reminded that they had not been cashed.

Carver's fame and public image received an added boost when word spread about the Edison job offer. Although the offer had been made around 1917, it was not well publicized until Carver gained prominence in the 1920s. Then it became one of the familiar anecdotes used to characterize the scientist. That his talents were recognized by Edison bolstered the idea of Carver's genius; that he turned down the offer was taken as evidence of his devotion to a higher mission.

Carver's renown depended to a huge extent on the various groups that gave him recognition. In 1923, two organizations with quite different aims honored him. During the March exhibit of Carver's

Carver attending an agricultural exhibition around 1920, one of the many trips he made to promote his work at Tuskegee. He complained at times, "I am away from the school so much that it is impossible to conduct a scientific experiment of value."

Carver's genial demeanor at public appearances was a key ingredient in his rise as a folk hero. "I always look forward to introductions about me," he once said with characteristic humility and humor, "as good opportunities to learn a lot about myself that I never knew before."

products at the Cecil Hotel, the Atlanta chapter of the United Daughters of the Confederacy (UDC), a conservative southern women's group, sent Carver a letter of "interest and appreciation" for the work he was doing. Scarcely three months later, the National Association for the Advancement of Colored People (NAACP) awarded him the Spingarn Medal, perhaps the most prestigious national honor given to blacks. Recognition by these disparate groups was a sign of Carver's rising symbolic importance among people of both races.

The UDC endorsement was one way southern whites could tell the rest of the country that their system of racial segregation was not so bad if someone like Carver could succeed under it. In fact, the organization's response to Carver was typical of how many whites would come to feel about him in the years ahead. That Carver seemed so humble, devout, and uncritical of southern racial practices made it easy to hold him up as "a credit to his race"—living proof that blacks who worked hard could earn a share of the American dream.

The NAACP award, on the other hand, was recognition by a group with a much different view of race relations. Founded in 1908 by W. E. B. Du Bois and others as an alternative to Booker T. Washington's brand of leadership, the NAACP actively sought to change the way blacks were treated rather than to accommodate the white establishment, as Washington had so often done. Although Carver's perspective on racial matters remained closer to Washington's vision than to that of the NAACP, he had nevertheless become a visible example of black achievement, and that was what the NAACP wished to honor. The implication of the Spingarn Medal was that blacks were just as capable as whites and thus deserved equal rights and treatment.

Carver rarely spoke out directly on race relations, and it was probably this that made it possible for two such different organizations to honor him. Advocating a clear position might well have put off one or the other group; in making few public statements on the issue, Carver became an all-purpose symbol. On the rare occasions when he did address racial questions, he expressed the belief that all people were part of God's family and that social equality for blacks would come in due time. A firm believer in the Golden Rule, he envisioned a world in which everyone would realize, he said, that "each individual, no matter what his color or creed, has his particular task to do in life." A persistent optimist, Carver felt that the power of love would ultimately conquer racial hatred and injustice.

Rather than address racial issues directly, Carver most often sought to get his message across by personal example. In his speeches, he usually confined himself to talking about his research, his views on nature, and his vision of a vital and productive South that made full use of its underdeveloped resources. He thus sought to open closed white minds by proving that blacks could think innovatively about matters of concern to all people.

Two organizations in particular gave Carver a public forum: the Young Men's Christian Association (YMCA) and the Commission on Interracial Cooperation (CIC), based in Atlanta. After World War I, amid heightened racial tensions, these two groups began to work together to promote a dialogue between blacks and whites. The CIC, a moderate body that had the blessing of the Tuskegee Institute, was seeking black speakers to address white audiences, and Carver's rising renown, eloquence, and proven success with white listeners made him a natural choice.

In 1923, the CIC leadership arranged for Carver to address white college students attending a YMCA summer regional conference at Blue Ridge, North Carolina. As he spoke to the group about the wondrous resources of nature and how they might be utilized for the good of humanity, he noticed among the crowd a young man who seemed especially attentive. After the speech, they met. The young man's name was Jimmie Hardwick, and when he told Carver that he wanted to talk to him further, Carver declared, "Of course! I'd like you for one of my boys."

Hardwick was not sure what Carver meant by the remark, but two days later he found out. A lifelong bachelor, Carver explained that when he formed friendships with young people who were receptive to his message, he thought of them as his adopted children. "In my work," he told Hardwick, "I meet many young people who are seeking truth. God has given me some knowledge. When they will let me, I try to pass it on to my boys." Hardwick, a Virginian descended from slave owners, was moved. "I'd like to be one of your boys, Professor Carver, if you will have me," he said.

There were to be many like Jimmie Hardwick over the years. Everywhere Carver spoke—at colleges, at meetings of religious organizations, at other YMCA conferences—he found new "children" for his "family," and just as he had done with his former Tuskegee students, he often initiated correspondences that lasted for years. The hundreds of letters exchanged between Carver and his "children" were usually filled with emotion and mutual affection. Carver was enor-

Carver knitting in his Tuskegee home. His artwork and handicrafts were, he insisted, "my soul's expression of its yearnings and questions in its desire to understand the work of the Great Creator."

Carver with his "brush work," which he said "will be of great honor to our people showing to what we may attain, along, science, History literature and art." More than 70 of his works are now on display at the George Washington Carver Museum in Tuskegee, Alabama.

mously fond of young people, and they in turn often idolized him and saw him as a true friend and mentor.

In many cases, it is clear that Carver's personal example did indeed change minds that had previously held to prejudiced notions of black inferiority. "You have shown me the one race, the human race," one of his boys wrote. "Color of skin or form of hair mean nothing to me now."

One of the more dramatic instances of Carver's ability to promote interracial goodwill occurred in 1924, when he returned to the Blue Ridge conference. As a racial protest, the white delegations from Florida and Louisiana had planned to walk out during Carver's lecture. The Tuskegee professor so captivated the gathering, however, that the walkout never materialized.

When Carver was finished, the leader of the Florida group stood up and apologized to him for what he and the others had planned to do. And during the next few days, Carver was besieged by dozens of students who wanted to meet him. Many invited him to speak at their own campuses, and many more joined his "family."

Following Carver's example, a number of young people he came to know played their own roles in the cause of better race relations. Jimmie Hardwick, for one, remained active in the YMCA and helped arrange some of Carver's later tours. Another young man, Howard Kester, combined his Christian beliefs with socialist convictions and worked actively to promote racial justice. With his life frequently threatened by white supremacists, Kester investigated lynchings and helped to organize sharecroppers of both races into a union. Like Hardwick, he remained a close friend of Carver's until the professor's death.

Late in 1924, one of Carver's speaking appearances had repercussions that he did not anticipate. In November, he made his first trip to New York City, where he addressed a meeting of the Women's Board of Domestic Missions of the Reformed Church in America. Before a crowd of 500 at the Marble Collegiate Church, he talked on a theme dear to him: the relationship between his scientific work and his religious faith. He told the audience that he relied on divine inspiration in his research. "No books ever go into my laboratory," he declared. "I never have to grope for methods. The method is revealed at the moment I am inspired to create something new."

The audience applauded heartily, but two days later a different reaction to his speech appeared in a *New York Times* editorial. Entitled "Men of Science Never Talk That Way," the editorial said that Carver's words showed a deplorable disregard for the accepted methods of science. The editorial argued that Carver, by "scorning" books and attributing his success to inspiration, was inviting ridicule on "an admirable institution [Tuskegee] and the race for which it has done and is still doing so much."

Deeply hurt, Carver penned a reply to the *Times*, asserting that his message had been misinterpreted. "Inspiration is never at variance with information," he wrote. "In fact, the more information one has, the greater will be the inspiration." He summarized his academic credentials and included a lengthy list of the scientists whose books he had studied. Carver argued that books were primarily of use to the scientist who was not already "a master of analytical work." He declared that a "master analyst"—a category in which he apparently included himself—needed no book but was "at liberty to take apart and put together substances to suit his particular taste or fancy."

Carver closed his reply with an example of what he meant by inspiration. He described how, during his visit to New York, he had been struck by the exotic edible roots being sold in the city's vegetable markets:

Carver's 1925 exhibit at the Southern Exposition in New York, which was aimed at luring northern investors to the South. The Alabama exhibit was called "the drawing card of the exposition, by far the most original exhibit of all" by one of the show's organizers.

> Just as soon as I saw these luscious roots, I marveled at the wonderful possibilities for their expansion. Dozens of things came to me while standing there looking at them. I would follow the same or similar lines I have pursued in developing products from the white potato. I know of no one who has worked with these roots in this way. I know of no book from which I can get this information, yet I will have no trouble in doing it.
>
> If this is not inspiration and information from a source greater than myself, or greater than anyone has wrought up to the present time, kindly tell me what it is.

The *Times* did not print Carver's letter. Yet many of Carver's friends came to his defense. They circulated copies of his reply, and a number of other newspapers picked it up. In fact, so many people came forward to reassure and defend him that he finally decided the controversy was, in the end, a good thing.

The *Times*, though, had a point. To the extent that Carver relied on divine inspiration in his work, his methods were unorthodox and unscientific. It is doubtful that very many other scientists, even religious scientists, would wholeheartedly endorse such an approach. Yet among religious groups, Carver's statements were endearing and enhanced his image all the more.

For the rest of the 1920s and well into the 1930s, Carver's fame continued to build. He remained a

Science and religion were absolutely inseparable to Carver. "Nature in its varied forms," he said, "are the little windows through which God permits me to commune with Him, and to see much of His glory, majesty, and power by simply lifting the curtain and looking in."

popular speaker with student audiences, touring white colleges throughout the South and elsewhere. In addition, he continued to appear at farmer's conferences, black schools, and state fairs, as well as gatherings of civic clubs, NAACP chapters, and other groups. In 1928, Simpson College (his first alma mater) gave him an honorary doctor of science degree—another award in what was to become, by the time of his death, a long string of honors. (The honorary doctorate was especially pleasing because many people had been mistakenly calling him "Dr. Carver" for years.)

The peanut industry, which had been so instrumental in Carver's rise to prominence, continued to use him as a publicist and to give him publicity in return. Its trade publications, most notably *The Peanut Journal*, carried dozens of his articles and also printed numerous pieces about him. Such exposure fixed Carver in the public mind as the Peanut Man even though his actual research with this plant decreased after 1924.

Even though Carver's own experimental work rarely involved peanuts anymore, his peanut expertise was still in demand. The Tom Huston Company of Columbus, Georgia, a peanut processor well known for its product Tom's Peanuts, consulted Carver on a regular basis about a variety of technical problems and even offered him a job on its research staff in 1929. Though he declined the offer, he continued to aid the company—without pay—for several more years. In fact, a year after making the job offer, the firm asked him to tackle one of the thorniest problems it had ever faced.

In the spring of 1930, the company had asked several farmers in Alabama, Georgia, and Florida to experiment with two varieties of Virginia peanuts, hoping to determine whether such types could be grown successfully in the lower South. When a sizable portion of the experimental crops failed, company officials suspected plant disease. They consulted scientists at several agricultural stations in the three states, most of whom said disease was not a key factor in the crop failure.

Skeptical of what the scientists were saying, the company turned to Carver, who conducted his own investigation and identified fungal infections as a major source of the problem. Although Carver had studied such plant diseases as a graduate student and had collected and identified many fungus specimens over the years, he was certainly not a specialist in this field of research. Nevertheless, when the USDA was finally brought in to investigate on its own, Carver's findings proved to be remarkably accurate. The talents that had impressed his Iowa State professors so many years before were undiminished.

Paul R. Miller, the scientist who conducted the USDA investigation, became friendly with Carver and encouraged him to send whatever fungus specimens he discovered to other USDA researchers. Carver did so, and his findings turned up several new species as well as varieties that had not been previously seen in the United States. In 1935, the USDA recognized Carver's work by appointing him a collaborator in its Mycology and Plant Disease Survey.

This episode shows one direction Carver's career might have taken if he had chosen in 1896 to remain at Iowa State rather than join the Tuskegee faculty. He might well have obtained a Ph.D. in botany (something he had always wanted to do but that his Tuskegee work load had not permitted) and done significant research on plant diseases. Such a specialized career would likely not have made him a public figure, however. As things turned out, he became a well-known scientist even though his scientific skills were applied to projects that bore no real fruit. ❧

9

BEYOND THE LEGEND

❧

Iₙ THE EARLY 1930s, Carver achieved an even higher degree of fame. The awards were as plentiful as ever, the requests for speaking appearances unceasing, and the press attention nearly always favorable. Then, in 1932, James Saxon Childers published an article in *American Magazine*, and it had an enormous impact on the Carver legend.

Entitled "A Boy Who Was Traded for a Horse," the story helped spread the myth that Carver had all but created the peanut industry, and it played up his image as a kindly, humble eccentric, shuffling along the Alabama backroads in a patch-covered coat. There had been many articles about Carver before, but this one was probably the most widely read. After it was published, Carver's mailbox was flooded with letters—a response that was repeated five years later when *Reader's Digest* reprinted the article.

In 1933, another article added a new dimension to the Carver legend, bringing to light an area of his work not widely publicized before. The Associated Press, a news agency whose stories were carried by hundreds of newspapers, produced an article sug-

Carver studies a bronze bust of himself that was unveiled at a 1937 ceremony commemorating his 40-year association with Tuskegee.

gesting that Carver had developed a new therapy for treating people crippled by polio. This story not only buttressed Carver's fame; it brought a stream of polio victims to Tuskegee seeking Carver's help.

Peanut oil massages were the basis of Carver's therapy, for he believed that the nutritive properties of the oil could restore withered tissues. He reached this conclusion in the 1920s, he said, when some women using one of his cosmetic products complained that the lotion made their faces look fat. Apparently, the peanut oil contained in the product caused the skin to expand as it was absorbed.

This led Carver to try massages with peanut oil on a frail, anemic Tuskegee boy. When the boy gained 30 pounds over the course of a month, Carver was sure he was on the brink of a major breakthrough. He believed that the oil's nutrients had entered the bloodstream through absorption into the skin and, almost miraculously, had given the boy improved health.

Carver later tried his peanut oil massages on two polio patients. Again, the results were impressive, and after the Associated Press story broke, Carver was besieged with requests for help. A number of people wrote to him, and many others got into their cars and drove to see him at Tuskegee.

In 1934, Carver started devoting his weekends to treating selected patients with his massage therapy. From this work came dozens of testimonials to the success of his treatments, and a number of doctors tried out his procedures. Carver saw the results he achieved as one more example of how God worked through him. "Truly," he wrote to a friend, "God is speaking through these peanut oils I am working with. Marvelous, some come to me on crutches, canes, etc. and in time go away walking."

Despite Carver's conviction that the peanut oils were the key to his patients' recovery, it is much more likely that the other features of his therapy—

Carver's recommendation of peanut oil massages as therapy for polio aroused a great deal of public interest in the 1930s. He is shown here in 1937 sorting out the many requests for help that he received in the mail.

expert massage and a regimen of exercise and hot salt baths—were the real remedies. Carver had been a skillful masseur ever since his days as a trainer for the Iowa State football team. What he did with his hands was probably far more effective than the type of oil he used. Though at least one prominent doctor thought the peanut oil might have special value, the medical profession as a whole remained skeptical.

At the same time that his massage therapy was sending him in a new direction, Carver was returning to some of his older concerns. In the early 1930s, with the country in the midst of the Great Depression, he resumed many of the goals of his earliest research and teaching. He became less concerned with the commercial potential of creative chemistry; instead, he began to reemphasize the importance of diet, nutrition, and economical ways to feed one's family.

Carver's commercial failures of the previous years may have been one of the reasons why he chose to refocus his work, but the hard times besetting the country were obviously the key factor. The dire state of the economy discouraged new commercial ventures, and with so many people out of work and going hungry, he again saw the need to encourage self-sufficiency and ways of making the best use of available resources. He thus wrote articles and pamphlets on possible solutions to the hunger problem, contributed dozens of recipes to various publications, and issued bulletins on natural fertilizers and raising livestock.

In 1935, a philanthropic grant enabled the institute to hire an assistant for Carver, whose age and declining health were draining his energies. Austin Curtis, a young man with a chemistry degree from Cornell University, got the job. Carver came to think of Curtis as a son, and the younger man liked to call himself Baby Carver. He helped the professor with his research and took on some projects of his own. After so many years of working alone, Carver finally had an assistant at just the point when his laboratory work was drawing to a close.

While his "real work" declined, Carver's value as a symbol continued to rise. The most significant new group to adopt him during the 1930s was the so-called chemurgic movement. Through its journal and national council, it sought to promote research "in Chemistry and related Sciences" that would aid agriculture—precisely the kind of work Carver had been doing for decades.

In 1937, Carver addressed three different chemurgic conferences. At the meeting in Dearborn, Michigan, he met the movement's best-known sponsor: the auto manufacturer Henry Ford. Carver and the industrial giant immediately became good friends. Between the time of their first meeting and Carver's death, they visited each other on several occasions and exchanged letters. Recognition by prominent whites meant much to Carver, and he was especially proud to know Ford. In one letter, Carver told him, "I consider you the greatest man I have ever met."

Also in 1937, Carver was honored at a Tuskegee celebration marking his 40 years of service to the

Carver samples some of his peanut products with car manufacturer Henry Ford. They formed their close—and well-publicized—friendship in 1937, when the scientist attended a conference in Michigan that was sponsored by the automobile magnate.

institute. The ceremonies included the unveiling of a bronze bust of Carver and a speech by H. E. Barnard, director of the Farm Chemurgic Council. In his address, Barnard praised Carver's early research for anticipating much of what was currently being done in the field. The celebration was highly publicized in national magazines and in newspapers throughout the country. Additional recognition came that same year when the National Technical Association and the Mark Twain Society both made Carver an honorary member.

By then, Carver had begun appearing on a number of nationally broadcast radio programs, including "It Can Be Done" and "We the People." The Smithsonian Institution produced a series of broadcasts that

Henry Ford (right) and his son Edsel flank Carver at a facsimile of the scientist's birthplace in Greenfield Village, a set of historic buildings in Dearborn, Michigan. The automobile manufacturer erected the cabin as well as a nutrition laboratory to honor Carver. "In my opinion," Ford said, "Professor Carver has taken Thomas Edison's place as the world's greatest living scientist."

chronicled his life story; other radio programs detailed his life as well. The cumulative effect of these profiles enhanced his reputation even further.

Carver's fame was heightened in 1938 when his life received the "Hollywood treatment." His career was depicted in a short film called *The Story of Dr. Carver*, produced by Pete Smith for the Metro-Goldwyn-Mayer studio and directed by Fred Zinnemann, later to become a top Hollywood filmmaker. An actor played Carver in his younger days, and the scientist portrayed himself as an older man.

The awards and recognition continued to snowball. Several significant honors came in 1939. Carver was awarded an honorary membership in the American Inventors Society; received a Roosevelt Medal, given in memory of President Theodore Roosevelt; and became the first black to address a forum sponsored by the *New York Herald-Tribune*.

Despite his revered status, Carver was not immune from the humiliations and absurdities of American racial practices. His lecture tours in the segregated South posed travel and accommodation problems. Jim Crow laws, which called for separate facilities for blacks and whites, prompted friends such as Jimmie Hardwick to drive Carver to speaking engagements so that he would not have to suffer the ignominy of segregation on public transportation.

In 1939—almost 10 years after Carver was denied a place in a sleeping car on a train trip to Dallas, Texas, because he was black, thereby creating a storm of protest in black newspapers—a visit to New York aroused another controversy. Arriving at the New Yorker Hotel, where they had reservations, Carver and Austin Curtis were told that no rooms were available. While the 74-year-old Carver waited in a foyer, reporters were called in, and after more than 6 hours, the hotel finally assigned the scientist and his assistant to rooms. Although the hotel management insisted that no racial snub was intended, the incident brought a flood of editorials in papers throughout the country decrying the treatment Carver had received.

Carver faced this matter while he was in poor health. He had been hospitalized in 1938 with what his doctors diagnosed as pernicious anemia, a serious disease caused by a deficiency of certain stomach and liver secretions; in earlier years, it was usually considered fatal. Carver's doctors began injecting him with a liver extract containing vitamin B_{12}, a new way of treating the ailment. Though many people, including the scientist himself, feared that he would die, he became well enough by 1939 to return to the laboratory and take on a few speaking engagements.

Carver and Austin Curtis continued to work on several projects, but Carver's days as a researcher and creative chemist were largely over. By the late 1930s, the USDA, under Secretary Henry A. Wallace (the same Henry A. Wallace who as a little boy had taken nature walks with Carver in Ames, Iowa), was pouring considerable money into agricultural research. The agency set up regional laboratories designed to find new uses for surplus crops, and Carver, with his failing health and meagerly funded lab, could hardly match their work.

Carver welcomes President Franklin D. Roosevelt to Tuskegee in 1939. Four years later, on July 14, 1943, Carver joined U.S. presidents George Washington and Abraham Lincoln as the only Americans to have their birthplace designated as a national monument.

Carver's last major undertaking was not a research project but an effort to preserve his legacy and to establish a means by which others could carry on his work. During his final years, he turned his attention to setting up the George Washington Carver Museum and Foundation in Tuskegee. Curtis proved an enormous asset in this effort, drawing up plans and soliciting contributions. In 1938, the institute designated an old laundry building for conversion into a museum and laboratory.

As work on the facility began, Carver, who had lived on campus during his entire career at Tuskegee, moved from a dormitory to a guest house adjoining the proposed museum so that he could more easily supervise the work in progress. A year later, 2,000 people attended the opening of the partially completed museum. And two years after that, another big crowd flowed into the building for the opening of its art rooms, which displayed Carver's paintings and handicrafts.

Because contributions were modest, the professor himself ended up giving his life savings—$60,000 by the time of his death—to the establishment of the Carver Foundation. In addition to the museum, the foundation set up research fellowships for students to follow in Carver's footsteps. Aware that he was nearing the end of his life, Carver saw the museum and foundation as a way of emphasizing and preserving the inspirational qualities of his career.

For similar reasons, Carver also cooperated fully with a writer named Rackham Holt, who was preparing a biography of him for publication by Doubleday, Doran and Company. The elderly scientist agreed to numerous interviews with Holt, and upon reading a draft of her manuscript in 1940, he was delighted with the flattering portrait she had drawn. He called it "the most fascinating piece of writing I have read."

Accordingly, Carver became concerned when publication delays arose. In 1942, he wrote to Holt: "I was hoping so much that this book could be finished before it had to close with something sordid. . . ." He was referring to the possibility that he might die before the book's release.

Sadly, the "sordid" thing Carver feared came to pass before Holt's biography appeared. Late in 1942, Carver made one last trip to Dearborn, Michigan, where Henry Ford had just completed building a nutritional lab in Carver's honor and had put up a replica of Carver's childhood home in Ford's outdoor museum, Greenfield Village. The trip must have drained the last of Carver's resources, for he was noticeably frail when he returned to Tuskegee in November. Still, he insisted on going about his daily activities until he suffered a painful fall in December while entering the Carver Museum.

Carver died a few weeks later, on the evening of January 5, 1943, at the age of 77. He was buried on the campus of Tuskegee, near the grave of Booker T. Washington.

The flow of honors had continued unabated in the last year of Carver's life: a Thomas A. Edison fellowship, membership in the Laureate Chapter of the Kappa Delta Pi education society, an honorary doctorate from Selma University. There was more to come after his death. His Missouri birthplace was declared a national monument in 1943, the same year that a steamship was named after him; a postage stamp in his honor was issued in 1947, and a Polaris submarine was named after him in 1956. He was elected to the Agricultural Hall of Fame in 1969 and to the Hall of Fame for Great Americans in New York in 1973. The two colleges he had attended—Simpson and Iowa State—both dedicated science buildings to him, and Rackham Holt's biography, published in 1943 and revised in 1962, fixed the popular image of Carver—saintly, selfless, brilliant—in the public mind for following generations, serving as the standard account of his life and work.

In recent years, historians have demonstrated that Carver was much more complicated than the folk hero who had found such public favor. It is true that he could be kind, generous, and dedicated to serving others. Literally hundreds of people—his students, the young men and women he "adopted" on his lecture tours, and scores of others, both influential and ordinary—were profoundly affected by his personal qualities and admired him deeply; he returned their love and admiration with the same intensity. Yet, as many of his colleagues at Tuskegee would no doubt have testified, he could also be arrogant, secretive, egocentric, and difficult to work with. Although there were many sides to his character, only the positive ones were publicized when America at large discovered him. Thus, his life became enshrouded in myth.

One unfortunate result of the Carver mythmaking was the extent to which it distorted his scientific accomplishments. Carver lived in an era in which invention and innovation were highly prized, an age in which men like Edison and Ford could become national heroes. To fit the growing legend, Carver's modest accomplishments in the laboratory were overrated by the press, and the truly significant features of his work and vision—his praiseworthy efforts to help the poorest of his farmers, his deep love and appreciation of the beauty and unity of nature—were lost in the hoopla.

A Carver commemorative stamp issued by the U.S. post office in 1947.

Relishing the publicity, Carver, at least for a time, also seemed to lose sight of his original aims. Late in his life, he admitted to some of his friends that his many years of pursuing the elusive goal of a commercial breakthrough were misguided and self-deceiving.

Nevertheless, Carver remained an inspirational role model for many blacks, and he has frequently been cited by black organizations and newspapers as one who strove against the odds to be something other than what whites expected blacks to be. Among whites, there can be no doubt that he opened the hearts and minds of many with whom he came in contact, and some of them—such as the social activist Howard Kester—drew inspiration from his example and worked actively against injustice. And, too, because Carver was one of the world's best-known black Americans, his well-publicized encounters with racism, such as the sleeping-car incident of 1930 and the New Yorker Hotel incident of 1939, reminded the country of the deficiencies in its system that were yet to be resolved.

Carver's legacy is, to be sure, a mixed one, and when scholars began to reexamine his life and demolish the myths about his scientific contributions that surrounded his later career, there were some who

The George Washington Carver Museum in Tuskegee, Alabama, was opened to the public in 1941 and still stands as a testament to Carver's life and vision.

suggested that he deserved to be forgotten. Others, taking a more balanced view, emphasized his earlier work at Tuskegee, the impact of his friendships, and the relevance of his particular vision of nature: He always saw the natural world as a unified whole in which each part was related to all the other parts—a view that would find favor among modern-day ecologists and environmentalists.

Out of Carver's love and respect for nature came his emphasis on utilizing resources that were both readily available and easily renewable. In his own lifetime, such ideas were steamrollered by the prevailing notion that bigger is better. Indeed, the developers of modern technology have often sent it forward at a headlong pace, pursuing short-term goals at the costly expense of long-term effects. A depleted and polluted environment has been one result of this shortsightedness.

Carver was himself partly seduced by the spell cast by the notion that bigger is better, as his failed efforts at commercializing his research demonstrate. Yet he returned to many of his earlier concerns when the depression hit, and among his chief aims in establishing the Carver Museum and Foundation was the preservation of his original vision, which he feared was being misunderstood. That became evident when a reporter at the 1941 opening of the museum's art rooms asked him how he had been able to accomplish so many different things.

"Would it surprise you," Carver answered, "if I say that I have not been doing many DIFFERENT things? All these years, I have been doing one thing." He then recited several lines from a poem by Alfred, Lord Tennyson that, in effect, summed up Carver's own life:

> Little flower—but if I could understand
> What you are, root and all, and all in all,
> I should know what God and man is. ❦

CHRONOLOGY

————— ❦ —————

c. 1864	Born George Washington Carver in Diamond, Missouri
1877	Begins his formal education in Neosho, Missouri
1884	Attends high school in Minneapolis, Kansas
1885	Denied admission to Highland College in Kansas
1886	Becomes a homesteader in Ness County, Kansas
1890	Enrolls at Simpson College in Iowa
1891	Transfers to Iowa State College of Agricultural and Mechanical Arts
1894	Receives a Bachelor of Agriculture degree; becomes a member of the Iowa State College faculty
1896	Receives a Master of Agriculture degree; becomes director of agriculture and director of the agricultural experiment station at Tuskegee Institute in Alabama
1898	Begins issuing bulletins on his experiment station work
1916	Named to the advisory board of the National Agricultural Society; elected a fellow of England's Royal Society for the Encouragement of the Arts
1918	Engaged as a consultant in agricultural research by the U.S. Department of Agriculture
1919	Develops peanut milk
1921	Appears before the House Ways and Means Committee
1923	Awarded the Spingarn Medal; Carver Products Company is formed
1926	Carver Penol Company is formed
1928	Receives honorary Doctor of Science degree from Simpson College
1933	Peanut oil massages become widely publicized
1935	Named collaborator to the U.S. Department of Agriculture's Mycology and Plant Disease Survey
1938	Appears in *The Story of Dr. Carver*
1939	George Washington Carver Museum and Foundation at Tuskegee is opened to the public
1943	Dies on January 5 at Tuskegee, Alabama

FURTHER READING

———————— ❧ ————————

Elliot, Lawrence. *George Washington Carver: The Man Who Overcame.* Englewood Cliffs, NJ: Prentice-Hall, 1966.

Harlan, Louis R. *Booker T. Washington: The Making of a Black Leader, 1856–1901.* NY: Oxford University Press, 1972.

———. *Booker T. Washington: The Wizard of Tuskegee, 1901–1915.* NY: Oxford University Press, 1983.

Holt, Rackham. *George Washington Carver: An American Biography.* rev. ed. Garden City, NY: Doubleday, 1962.

Kremer, Gary R. *George Washington Carver: In His Own Words.* Columbia: University of Missouri Press, 1986.

Mackintosh, Barry. "George Washington Carver: The Making of a Myth." *Journal of Southern History* 42, no. 4 (November 1976).

McMurry, Linda O. *George Washington Carver: Scientist and Symbol.* NY: Oxford University Press, 1981.

Manber, David. *Wizard of Tuskegee.* NY: Crowell-Collier, 1967.

Washington, Booker T. *Up from Slavery.* Garden City, NY: Doubleday, 1933.

Williamson, Joel. *A Range for Order: Black-White Relations in the American South Since Emancipation.* NY: Oxford University Press, 1986.

Woodward, C. Vann. *Origins of the New South, 1877–1913.* Baton Rouge: Louisiana State University Press, 1951.

INDEX

———— •❀• ————

PICTURE CREDITS

GENE ADAIR holds a master's degree in fine arts from Columbia University. He worked as both a teacher and a journalist before joining Oxford University Press in New York. He is currently the marketing manager of the University of Georgia Press.

NATHAN IRVIN HUGGINS is W.E.B. Du Bois Professor of History and Director of the W.E.B. Du Bois Institute for Afro-American Research at Harvard University. He previously taught at Columbia University. Professor Huggins is the author of numerous books, including *Black Odyssey: The Afro-American Ordeal in Slavery, The Harlem Renaissance,* and *Slave and Citizen: The Life of Frederick Douglass.*